The New Middle Ages

Series editor

Bonnie Wheeler
English & Medieval Studies
Southern Methodist University
Dallas, Texas, USA

The New Middle Ages is a series dedicated to pluridisciplinary studies of medieval cultures, with particular emphasis on recuperating women's history and on feminist and gender analyses. This peer-reviewed series includes both scholarly monographs and essay collections.

More information about this series at
http://www.springer.com/series/14239

Christopher Vaccaro · Yvette Kisor
Editors

Tolkien and Alterity

palgrave
macmillan

Editors
Christopher Vaccaro
College of Arts and Sciences
University of Vermont
Burlington
VT, USA

Yvette Kisor
Ramapo College of New Jersey
Mahwah
NJ, USA

The New Middle Ages
ISBN 978-3-319-86985-8 ISBN 978-3-319-61018-4 (eBook)
DOI 10.1007/978-3-319-61018-4

Cover illustration: Karl Denham/Alamy Stock Photo

Printed on acid-free paper

This Palgrave Macmillan imprint is published by Springer Nature
The registered company is Springer International Publishing AG
The registered company address is: Gewerbestrasse 11, 6330 Cham, Switzerland

Dedication and Acknowledgements

This collection is dedicated to Prof. Jane Chance, Andrew W. Mellon Distinguished Professor Emerita of English (Rice University) for her indefatigable dedication to the field of Tolkien Studies and her inspiration to many scholars who followed in her path. Professor Chance has published on Tolkien since 1980; she founded Tolkien at Kalamazoo (IMC) in 2001 and has continued to work tirelessly in the field. She has fought hard to break the glass ceilings within the Academy, ensuring that the work of women scholars and of Tolkien scholars be taken seriously.

Jane Chance has inspired each of the contributors in this collection. She is to them a professor, mentor, colleague, and friend. Each worked very hard to deliver an exceptional essay to us by our many deadlines and for that we are grateful. We wish to thank Palgrave (Springer) Publishing and Bonnie Wheeler, editor of the New Middle Ages series, specifically for accepting our proposal for an important thematic collection.

We must acknowledge as well the many family members, friends, colleagues, departments, students, teachers, and librarians who assisted, advised, and supported us in the process of producing this collection.

Contents

Editors and Contributors

About the Editors

Christopher Vaccaro is Senior Lecturer at the University of Vermont, where he has taught courses on Tolkien and early medieval British literature since 1999. He is the editor of *The Body in Tolkien's Legendarium* (McFarland 2013). He has published "'And One White Tree': The Cosmological Cross and the Arbor Vitae in *The Lord of the Rings* and *The Silmarillion*" (Mallorn 42, August 2004), contributed entries for *The J.R.R. Tolkien Encyclopedia* (Routledge 2006), and has his essay 'Morning Stars of a Setting World': Alain de Lille's *De Planctu Naturæ* and Tolkien's Legendarium as Neo-Platonic Mythopoeia forthcoming in *Mythlore* (fall 2017). His interests include Beowulf, Old English language and literature, and queer theory.

Yvette Kisor is Professor of English at Ramapo College where she teaches courses in medieval literature, British literature before the eighteenth century, the history of the English language, Tolkien, and even Harry Potter. Her publications on medieval literature can be found in *Anglo-Saxon England*, *The Chaucer Review*, and *ANQ*, as well as numerous edited collections; her publications on Tolkien appear in *Mythlore* and *Tolkien Studies* as well as *The J. R. R. Tolkien Encyclopedia: Scholarship and Critical Assessment* (Routledge 2006) and *MLA Approaches to Teaching: J. R. R. Tolkien's* The Lord of the Rings *and Other Works* (MLA 2015), among others. Her most recent book, co-authored with Michael D. C. Drout et al, *Beowulf Unlocked: New Evidence from Lexomic Analysis* was published by Palgrave Macmillan in 2016.

Contributors

Amy Amendt-Raduege teaches English at Whatcom Community College, where she leads classes in British literature, folklore, superheroes, Shakespeare, and, of course, Tolkien. She has published extensively on Tolkien's work.

Melissa Ruth Arul is a researcher of Tolkien literature. Besides Tolkien, her interest includes fairy tales, folklore, and fantasy. She completed her Masters in English Literature from the University of Malaya, Malaysia. Completing her dissertation, *A Critical Study of the Self and the Other in Selected Texts of J. R. R. Tolkien* led to her presenting a paper, "Elvish Identity—A Journey" at the "Festival in the Shire" in Wales in 2010. Her paper "The Yoke of Pride and Shame: An Essay on Joseph Conrad's Lord Jim and J. R. R. Tolkien's Túrin Turambar" has been published for *Tolkien and the Classics*, edited by Gruppo italiano di Studi Tolkieniani in 2015. She currently teaches English literature at the IGCSE level at Sri Kuala Lumpur, a private school since 2012. Melissa finds teaching and interacting with rambunctious students an enriching and passionate experience. During her spare time, she enjoys drinking good beer, socializing, and reading manga.

Deidre Dawson has written reviews for the *Journal of Tolkien Research* and *Tolkien Studies* and is the author of essays in the *MLA's Approaches to Teaching Tolkien's* The Lord of the Rings *and Other Works*. She is also a scholar of the eighteenth century and has published a monograph on Voltaire's correspondence and several co-edited volumes on the French and Scottish Enlightenments. Deidre has held tenured positions as Associate Professor of French at Georgetown University and as Professor of Language and Culture at Michigan State University.

Verlyn Flieger is Professor Emerita at the University of Maryland, where she taught courses in Tolkien from 1977 to 2012. She now teaches online courses for Signum University in Tolkien, Arthurian literature and comparative mythology. Her books on Tolkien include *Splintered Light*, *A Question of Time*, *Interrupted Music*, and *Green Suns* *and Faërie*, and editions of Tolkien's essay *On Fairy-Stories*, and his short story *Smith of Wootton Major*. With Carl Hostetter, she edited *Tolkien's Legendarium: Essays on The History of Middle-earth*. With David Bratman and Michael D. C. Drout, she edits *Tolkien Studies*. She has also published two fantasy novels, *Pig Tale* and *The Inn At Corbies' Caww*; an Arthurian novella, *Avilion*; and short stories, "Green Hill Country" in *Seekers of Dreams*, a collection of fantasy stories; and "Igraine at Tintagel" in *Amazing Graces*, an anthology of women's fiction.

John Holmes has taught Tolkien, medieval literature and more at Franciscan University of Steubenville since 1985. He has published about a dozen essays on various aspects of Tolkien's fiction and, more recently, Tolkien's poetry. He is currently editing a collection of essays on Tolkien and *Beowulf*. He lives in Steubenville, Ohio, with his wife and 75% of their four sons, all of whom share his interest in Tolkien somewhat, though in truth they all prefer Harry Potter.

Kristine Larsen is Professor of Astronomy at Central Connecticut State University, where her research and teaching focus on the rich interplay between science and society. She is the author of *Stephen Hawking: A Biography* and *Cosmology 101*, and co-editor of *The Mythical Dimensions of* Doctor Who and *The Mythical Dimensions of Neil Gaiman*. Her work on the science of Middle-earth and Tolkien and gender has appeared in *Tolkien Studies, Mallorn, Amon Hen, Silver Leaves,* and *Lembas*, as well as in myriad chapters in edited volumes.

Robin Anne Reid is a Professor in the Department of Literature and Languages at Texas A&M University–Commerce. Her teaching areas are creative writing, critical theory, and marginalized literature. She was the co-director of two N. E. H Tolkien Institutes for School Teachers on Teaching Tolkien (2004, 2009) with Dr. Judy Ann Ford, History, A&M–Commerce. Her most recent Tolkien publications are an essay on female bodies and femininities in *The Lord of the Rings* in *The Body in Tolkien's Legendarium*, edited by Christopher Vaccaro, and a bibliographic essay on the history of scholarship on female characters in Tolkien's work in *Perilous and Fair: Women in the Works and Life of J. R. R. Tolkien*, edited by Janet Brennan Croft and Leslie A. Donovan. She is working on creating the Tolkien Corpus Project, an interdisciplinary digital humanities project in collaboration with Dr. Christian Hempelmann, Computational Linguistics, A&M–Commerce.

Valerie Rohy is Professor of English at the University of Vermont. She is the author of *Impossible Women: Lesbian Figures and American Literature* (Cornell, 2000), *Anachronism and Its Others: Sexuality, Race, Temporality* (SUNY, 2009), and *Lost Causes: Narrative, Etiology, and Queer Theory* (Oxford, 2014). She has also co-edited *American Local Color Writing, 1880–1920* (Penguin, 1998). She published an essay on *The Lord of the Rings* and sexuality in *Modern Fiction Studies* in 2004.

Stephen Yandell is Associate Professor of English at Xavier University where he teaches a range of courses on medieval literature, including "Tolkien and his Medieval Sources." His earliest Tolkien research, "'A Pattern Which Our Nature Cries Out For': The Medieval Tradition of the Ordered Four in the Fiction of J. R. R. Tolkien," appeared in the 1992 *Proceedings of the J. R. R. Tolkien Centenary Conference, Keble College, Oxford*, and more recent work is included in *The J. R. R. Tolkien Encyclopedia*. His research interests include medieval prophecy (he is co-editor of *Prophet Margins: The Medieval Vatic Impulse and Social Stability*), Middle Welsh literature (his translation of *Math, Son of Mathonwy* appears in *Medieval Literature for Children*), and medievalism (with chapters appearing in *The Disney Middle Ages* and *Mass Market Medieval*). His work also extends to Tolkien's Inklings colleagues, most notably C. S. Lewis, with research included in *C. S. Lewis: Life, Works, and Legacy* and *C. S. Lewis, Views from Wake Forest*. Yandell recently stepped down from serving as Director of Xavier's Center for Teaching Excellence to become Director of the University Scholars program.

CHAPTER 1

Introduction

Christopher Vaccaro and Yvette Kisor

> The fact or state of being other or different; diversity, difference, otherness; an instance of this[1]

Thus *The Oxford English Dictionary* (a project in which Tolkien participated) defines "alterity." The concept appears fairly straightforward: alterity is that which is Other, different.[2] *The Oxford English Dictionary* also tells us that the term, though present in English since the late fifteenth century, has only been in common use since the mid-twentieth century, especially "in critical and cultural theory." Much of critical and cultural theory of the last fifty or so years is concerned with defining, explaining, and dealing with "the Other." The concept is both simple and complex—the idea that the Self is defined in relation to that which it is not seems both self-evident and demanding of deeper explanation. How we as both individual and cultural entities define the Other, how we encounter the Other, and how we deal with the Other are an

C. Vaccaro (✉)
University of Vermont, Burlington, USA

Y. Kisor
Ramapo College, Mahwah, NJ, USA

C. Vaccaro and Y. Kisor (eds.), *Tolkien and Alterity*, The New Middle Ages, DOI 10.1007/978-3-319-61018-4_1

important theme in Tolkien's works as we will see and very much a concern of a modern political praxis as well as a scholarly activism based on modern critical and cultural theory.

In psychology, the concept goes back to identity formation, the developmental process by which we gain a concept of a Self that is recognized as separate from an Other. Carl Jung, Sigmund Freud, and Jacques Lacan all weigh in on this important issue. Jung's "shadow" archetype identifies those personal and primal traits that often remain hidden from public view. These characteristics are frequently displaced onto an Other, who then becomes the repository of all that we dislike in ourselves. Jung believed that these traits needed to be confronted and recognized in the Self, a process necessary for the integration of the psyche.[3] Sigmund Freud's exploration of the intersection between aesthetics and psychoanalysis led him to revisit the concept of the "uncanny" (*unheimlich*), the fear and rejection of what is unknown in the Self that drives an individual back to what is familiar.[4] In literary terms, it has come to mean also the recognition of these rejected and horrific traits in others, who become then simultaneously unknown and known. Anna Freud's clarification of her father's work on defense mechanisms provides specificity on the mechanism of "projection": an act of transferring qualities one wishes not to see in one's Self onto an Other.[5] For the psychoanalytic theorist Jacques Lacan, there is a key difference between the little other (lower-case *a* for French *autre*) and the big Other (upper-case *A* for French *Autre*): the little other "is not really other, but a reflection and projection of the ego," whereas "the big Other designates radical alterity, an other-ness which transcends the illusory otherness of the imaginary because it cannot be assimilated through identification"[6]; it is the Other that is truly Other. For Lacan, this Otherness is related to the mother in all "her strange, impenetrable alterity,"[7] and is also the Other sex, which, for both sexes, is the woman, for "Man here acts as the relay whereby the woman becomes this Other for herself as she is this Other for him."[8]

Julia Kristeva employs Lacan's concepts in her treatment on the "abject," a liminal and opposed identity in ambiguous relation to that of the subject. Suturing together a joyful pleasure (*jouisssance*) and abhorrence, the abject is for Kristeva "a 'something' that I do not recognize as a thing. A weight of meaninglessness, about which there is nothing insignificant, and which crushes me. On the edge of nonexistence and hallucination, of a reality that, if I acknowledge it, annihilates me."[9] The abject is not only radically and inaccessibly Other; it is a tantalizing and perpetual threat to the subject's existence.

The idea that a conception of the Other is a prerequisite for defining the Self runs throughout philosophy but is not as central as it might first appear; the Cartesian *cogito*, for example, locates knowledge of the Self in the recognition of the thinking subject alone. An emphasis on the Other is present in thinkers such as Hegel, Husserl, and Sartre,[10] but arguably it is Emmanuel Lévinas who makes alterity the central component of his philosophy. Lévinas' philosophy is based on an ethics of embracing the Other that acknowledges—insists on—the radical alterity of the Other. For Lévinas, the Other is unknowable and he defines his "ethics as first philosophy" in opposition to ontology, philosophy's traditional emphasis on the nature of being. In his conception, knowledge of the Self is rooted in the encounter with the Other and crucial to that relation is both the utter alterity of the Other and our desire for the Other. Our responsibility is to recognize the radical alterity of the Other and to seek the Other as neighbor. For Lévinas, language and the face-to-face encounter are key to establishing a relationship with the Other.[11]

But perhaps most familiar is the concept of the Other rooted in culture and tied to patriarchy and imperialism, the "Othering" that defines those one wishes to dominate according to their race, class, gender, sexuality, religion, geography, or what have you in order to justify treating some segment of humanity as less than some normative segment. This concept of the Other is intimately tied to issues of power and knowledge and is an abiding concern of postmodernism, feminism, and queer studies. "Othering" as a means of subordination goes back to Edward Said's *Orientalism*, Gayatri Spivak's "Can the Subaltern Speak?," Homi Bhabha's "The Other Question," Trihn T. Minh-ha's *Woman, Native, Other*, Mikhail Bakhtin's *Problems of Dostoevsky's Poetics*, and Simone de Beauvoir's *The Second Sex*, which addressed the issue in terms of oppression against women.[12]

In medieval studies (Tolkien's chosen field of study), the critical emphasis on alterity goes back to 1972 and Paul Zumthor's *Essai de poétique médiévale*, which asserted "l'éloignement du moyen âge, la distance irrécupérable qui nous en sépare," further defining that distance between the modern reader and the medieval text as "un abîme infranchissable."[13] In his 1974 review of Zumthor's book, Peter Haidu praises Zumthor for recognizing "the essential alterity of medieval literature … [and] plac[ing] this alterity at the very center of his critical project"[14];

he asserts that "[t]he alterity of medieval literature is clear, and no service to literary theory is rendered by disguising this alterity."[15] According to Haidu, this is not simply an alterity of language and history, for even with the philological training to read the strange and often difficult languages (to modern ears) and the historical knowledge to situate the texts in their contemporary milieu, "there remains a categorical epistemological gulf."[16] History and philology are not enough to allow us access to "the unknown customs of strange and distant peoples."[17] Haidu goes on to discuss "the radical disjunction between the consciousness of the modern reader and the consciousness either behind or within the text"[18] and states that when we encounter medieval literature, "we operate in the demesne of a cold, uncommunicative Other."[19]

In 1979, Hans Robert Jauss wrote in defense of the study of medieval literature on the basis of not only its "aesthetic pleasure" but also its "surprising otherness," affirming "the astounding or surprising otherness of the world opened up by the text."[20] This emphasis on the alterity of medieval literature is necessary, according to Jauss, because it has been obscured by the nineteenth-century project of an evolutionary model of history, which produced an illusion of continuity.[21] Instead, Jauss insists upon "a distant, historically absent past in all its surprising 'otherness,' … directed toward an *other*, understanding consciousness."[22] In his discussion of the alterity of medieval literature, Jauss emphasizes its orality, the lack of unity of author and work, and the communal and aural nature of its contemporary reception, and with Zunthor sees the printing press as "clos[ing] off medieval culture for us as 'the time before'."[23] He finds the alterity of medieval literature as well in its lack of emphasis on originality and "ownership" of its works, its fondness for repetition and "retelling,"[24] and in its synthesizing, systematizing tendencies, citing C.S. Lewis frequently as a precursor in conveying this understanding of medieval literature as Other.[25] For Jauss, "modernity means the recognition of a significance in medieval literature which is only to be obtained by a reflective passage through its alterity."[26]

For all the reasons that Jauss can cite Lewis, J.R.R. Tolkien's mythological project can likewise be invoked. The sense of the radical difference of the medieval is recreated in his Middle-earth through the "retelling" conceit he employs, the different cultures and created languages he introduces, and through the displaced and "queer" hobbits he provides as our entrée into this strange world. We meet many characters with attitudes toward difference that are disturbingly familiar to us; some embrace the Other, others reject it. The "Othering" for cultural dominance is played out in Middle-earth just as in our own world, and Tolkien's story allows us to understand where we should value such dynamics, whether of race, class, gender, sex, or geography. Most often, a rejection of difference defines those characters aligned with wickedness, domination, treachery, and depravity. Wise and benevolent characters see through the veils of culturally-constructed binaries and are the better for their expansive, even cosmopolitan awareness of their world's diversity.

One can find expressions of alterity even within Tolkien's own life. Growing up Catholic and an orphan, his life was inflected by a sense of difference from the other children around him. Being raised Catholic in a predominantly Protestant England, Tolkien experienced a distancing within his own family relations. Just prior to his father Arthur Tolkien's death in 1896, Tolkien and his younger brother were brought to a town outside of Birmingham, England. Tragically, Mabel Tolkien died when her oldest was only 12. Afterward, Tolkien was raised by a surrogate father figure, the priest, Father Francis Morgan. Later on, his own passionate engagement with issues surrounding Christianity would mark him as Other in a largely secular world.[27] As an adult, Tolkien was comfortable with his social status at both Leeds and Oxford, yet his field of study distinguished him from his colleagues. Starting off in the study of the Classics, Tolkien swiftly discovered his love of Northern European epic and eddas. His study and teaching of the Germanic languages set him further apart from those whose primary focus was literature.[28]

The current state of politics in the USA and around the world makes this study of alterity timely and crucial as country after country confronts issues of immigration, refugees, national identity, and borders. From the 2016 presidential elections in the USA to the Brexit referendum to the reactions to the attacks in Belgium, France, England, and Spain, various engagements with the Other have dominated the global struggle. Feminist and queer literary scholarship has made clear that even the academy must be (and has been) political.

At the forefront of the scholarly understanding of alterity in Tolkien's legendarium is Jane Chance. Difference in Tolkien's work is an abiding concern for Chance, explored in articles throughout her career, including "Power and Knowledge in Tolkien: The Problem of Difference in 'The Birthday Party'" (1992), "Tolkien and the Other: Race and Gender in Middle-earth" (2005), "Tolkien's Women (and Men): The Films and the Book" (2005), "Subversive Fantasist: Tolkien on Class Difference"

(2006), and "'In the Company of Orcs': Peter Jackson's Queer Tolkien" (2009).[29] Each of these exemplifies Chance's indefatigable examination of alterity in Tolkien's texts and anti-apartheid sentiments in his life. Her seminal work *Tolkien's Art: A Mythology for England* (1979) helped define the field of Tolkien scholarship; her *The Lord of the Rings*: The Mythology of Power (1992) offered a consideration of difference, of what is "queer," within Middle-earth communities.[30] In "Tolkien and the Other," Chance points to fantasy's subversive potential through which it can shape a reader's perceptions, arguing that a part of Tolkien's project was dedicated to the eradication of an "apartheid" or "apartness" predicated upon an ideology of prejudice and intolerance, noting that "what Tolkien has done, in his remaking of the Middle Ages, is to imbue his very modern fantasy with reality and its rediscovery—prejudice, discrimination, insensitivity toward those different from us, and selfishness."[31] Even the romance of Beren and Lúthien, according to Chance, exemplifies love's ability to connect and bridge the abyss between the races. In her latest investigation into the algebra of difference in the field, *Tolkien, Self and Other: "This Queer Creature,"* Chance has secured her position at the top of the field. The monograph examines Tolkien's life stages in relationship to his experiences of otherness and crafts compelling readings of his major and lesser-known works.[32]

Tolkien and Alterity brings together established and new scholars in the field. The emphasis is mainly literary and theoretical, addressing issues central to the subject such as gender, race, and sexuality alongside investigations into language and theology. A broad range of texts is covered from Tolkien's greatest to his lesser-known works as well as Peter Jackson's cinematic representations. *Tolkien and Alterity* also provides a useful and subject-defining emphasis on the state of the question, proposing pathways for further analysis.

The collection is organized into five sections: "The State of the Scholarship," "Women and the Feminine," "The Queer," "Language," and "Identities." Scholarship is the focus of Part 1. Yvette Kisor's "Queer Tolkien: A Bibliographical Essay on Tolkien and Alterity" provides an exhaustive catalog of essays in the field concerned in some way with queering the Self/Other binary (excluding race), as well as considering the future direction of the field. The intent is to have all in one place a convenient list of the material, which heretofore does not exist. Robin Anne Reid's "Race in Tolkien Studies: A Bibliographic Essay" analyzes the scholarship on the subject of race in Tolkien's legendarium and in Jackson's films. Through a more multidisciplinary approach, it vigorously examines the question of whether or not

Tolkien and his work perpetuate racist ideology or celebrate multi-cultural cooperation.

Part 2 "Women and the Feminine" addresses issues of female identity and feminine approaches to knowledge. Amy Amendt-Raduege provides a fresh perspective on a frequently under-appreciated female character. In "Revising Lobelia," Amendt-Reduege gives a compelling reading of Lobelia Sackville-Baggins as heroic matriarch, finding support both in Tolkien's inclusion of low-mimetic heroes alongside the more elevated and romantic ones and in his drawing from literatures and histories that contain multiple examples of valorous women. Kristine Larsen's "Medieval Organicism or Modern Feminist Science? Bombadil, Elves, and Mother Nature" deftly contrasts the traditional masculinist scientific approach in which nature is subjected to violent experimentation with Tolkien's more associative and passive approach whereby knowledge is gained at no expense to the natural world and with no requirement for its application. Larsen finds support in the "Athrabeth Finrod Ah Andreth" and in passages within *The Lord of the Rings.*

Part 3 "The Queer" brings attention to Tolkien's representation of normative and non-normative forms of reproduction and to experiences of marginalization and indeterminancy. Valerie Rohy's "Cinema, Sexuality, Mechanical Reproduction" brings to our attention the queer nature of Saruman's parthenogenic spawning of his Uruk-hai in Jackson's movies. Rohy argues that Saruman's sterile proliferation is the monstrous flip side to the sentimentalized queer love between Frodo and Sam. She recognizes at once an insistence on a heteronormative futurity in both the novel and the films and a tagging of the non-normative relations as waste of productivity and a product of waste. In "Saruman's Sodomitic Resonances: Alain de Lille's *De Planctu Naturae* and J.R.R. Tolkien's *The Lord of the Rings,"* Christopher Vaccaro compares the ethical framework of *The Lord of the Rings* to Alain de Lille's twelfth-century Chartrian Latin treatise. Vaccaro recognizes a number of commonalities between the excommunicated practitioners of vice in *De Planctu* and the character of Saruman. In light of this comparison, Saruman is seen as a signifier of a sodomitic (and potentially liberated) *eros* made alterior in the text. Stephen Yandell offers an additional queer reading in "Cruising Faery: Queer Desire in Giles, Niggle, and Smith." According to Yandell, Tolkien adopts imagery of the marginalized and indeterminate in order to distinguish between worldly and other-worldly identities and experiences. An unquenchable desire for

Faery and artistic creation becomes the identifying marker of Otherness in the three short stories.

Part 4 "Language" contains two striking essays. Deidre Dawson's "Language and Alterity in Tolkien and Lévinas" demonstrates how the construction of alterity in *The Lord of the Rings,* particularly through the use of dialogue, exemplifies the Lévinasian concept of language as an ethical engagement with the Other. And in "The Orcs and the Others: Familiarity as Estrangement in *The Lord of the Rings,*" Verlyn Flieger focuses on the English language jargon and slang of Tolkien's Orcs. Flieger examines how Tolkien uses familiar language as an alienating device. The jarring combination of familiar, if guttersnipe, language with the physical and social Otherness of the Orcs creates a disjunction between what they are and how they talk.

The last section of the collection is "Identities." Melissa Ruth Arul "Silmarils and Obsession: The Undoing of Fëanor" utilizes Julia Kristeva's theory of the abject to consider identity formation both in the individual, through the figure of Fëanor, and on the level of race, through the Calaquendi's self-definition over and against the Moriquendi. Fëanor is an illustration of a Self who was unsuccessful in removing the abject from within. For Fëanor, his fetish—the jewels known as the Silmarils—filled the space left behind by his mother Míriel. By applying Julia Kristeva's theory, she argues that the abjection of his kin and the kinslaying were caused by Fëanor's failure to integrate into the Symbolic order. John Holmes' "The Other as *Kolbítr*: Tolkien's Faramir and Éowyn as Alfred and Æthelflæd" uses the notion of the Kolbítr, the coal-biter from Icelandic saga, the non-masculine antihero who sits "biting the coals" of the hearth fire outside the masculine sphere of action, noting traces of this figure in Tolkien's heroes, and even in Tolkien himself. Invariably, however, the *kolbítr* ends up performing a surprising act of heroism. Holmes' essay focuses on the figures of Éowyn and Faramir, finding their analogs in the historical figures of Æthelflæd of Mercia and Alfred the Great, each an unlikely heroic figure called unexpectedly into heroic action.

The dedicatee of this volume, Jane Chance, in many ways pioneered the field of Tolkien and alterity, both through her own scholarship and the opportunities she provided to other scholars. This collection reveals the extent of her influence and demonstrates how the field can prove a fruitful one indeed.

Notes

1. "alterity, n.," OED Online, Oxford University Press, accessed July 5, 2016, http://www.oed.com/view/Entry/5788?redirectedFrom=alterity.
2. When referring to the concept of otherness as it relates specifically to alterity, we will from the start capitalize the term.
3. Jung called this process "Individuation." For more, see Carl Jung, "Conscious, Unconscious, and Individuation," in *The Archetypes and the Collective Unconscious*, 2nd edition, trans. R.F.C. Hull, vol. 9, pt. 1 of *Collected Works of C. G. Jung* (Princeton: Princeton University Press, 1981), 270–289.
4. In his 1919 essay *Das Unheimliche*, Freud responded to arguments by Ernst Jentsch and E.T.A. Hoffman. Sigmund Freud, "The Uncanny," in *The Uncanny*, trans. David McLintock (London: Penguin, 2003), 123–162. "Das Unheimliche," *Imago* 5.5-6 (1919): 297–324.
5. Anna Freud, *The Ego and the Mechanisms of Defense* (London: Karnac Books, 1992).
6. Dylan Evans, *An Introductory Dictionary of Lacanian Psychoanalysis* (London and New York: Routledge, 1996), 135–136.
7. Adrian Johnston, "Jacques Lacan," *Stanford Encyclopedia of Philosophy*, ed. Edward N. Zalta, accessed July 20, 2014, http://plato.stanford.edu/entries/lacan/.
8. Jacques Lacan, *Écrits* (Paris: Seuil, 1966), quoted in Evans, 136.
9. Julia Kristeva, *Powers of Horror: An Essay On Abjection*, trans. Leon S. Roudiez (New York: Columbia University Press), 1982. *Pouvoirs de l'horreur: Essai sur l'abjection* (Paris: Éditions de Seuil, 1980), 2.
10. See Georg Wilhelm Friedrich Hegel, *The Phenomenology of Spirit*, trans. A.V. Miller (Oxford: Oxford University Press, 1977). *Phänomenologie des Geistes* (Bamberg and Würzburg: Joseph Anton Goebhardt, 1807) and Jean-Paul Sartre, *Being and Nothingness: An Essay on Phenomenological Ontology*, trans. Hazel E. Barnes (New York: Philosophical Library, 1956). *L'Être et le néant: Essai d'ontologie phénoménologique* (Paris: Gallimard, 1943).
11. Emmanuel Lévinas, *Totalité et Infini: essai sur l'extériorité* (The Hague: Martinus Nijhoff, 1961), trans. Alphonso Lingis as *Totality and Infinity, An Essay on Exteriority* (Pittsburgh, PA: Duquesne University Press), 1969.
12. Edward W. Said, *Orientalism* (New York: Pantheon Books, 1978); Gayatri Chakravorty Spivak, "Can the Subaltern Speak?," in *Marxism and the Interpretation of Culture*, ed. Cary Nelson and Lawrence Grossberg (Urbana, IL: University of Illinois Press, 1988), 271–313; Homi K.

Bhabha, "The Other Question: Stereotype, Discrimination and the Discourse of Colonialism," in *The Location of Culture*, ed. Homi K. Bhabha (London and New York: Routledge, 1994), 66–92; Trihn T. Minh-ha, *Woman, Native, Other: Writing Postcoloniality and Feminism*, (Bloomington, IN: Indiana University Press, 2009); Mikhail Bakhtin, *Problems of Dostoevsky's Poetics*, trans. Caryl Emerson (Minneapolis: University of Minnesota, 1984); Simone de Beauvoir, *The Second Sex*, trans. H.M. Parshley (New York: Knopf, 1953), *Le Deuxième Sexe*, 2 vols. (Paris: Gallimard, 1949).

13. Paul Zumthor's *Essai de Poétique Medieval* (Paris: Éditions du Seuil, 1972), 19. Our English translation: "the remoteness of the Middle Ages, the unreclaimable distance that separates us" … "an impassable abyss."
14. Peter Haidu, "Making It (New) in the Middle Ages: Towards a Problematics of Alterity," *Diacritics* 4, no. 2 (Summer 1974): 2–11, at 4.
15. Ibid., 3.
16. Ibid.
17. Ibid.
18. Ibid.
19. Ibid.
20. Hans Robert Jauss, trans. by Timothy Bahti, "The Alterity and Modernity of Medieval Literature," *New Literary History* 10, no. 2 (Winter 1979): 181–229, at 182.
21. Ibid., 187, 203. It is also due, according to J.A. Burrow, to a reaction against the new critical emphasis on simply encountering poetry as poetry (492); see his "'Alterity' and Middle English Literature" *The Review of English Studies*, n.s., 50, no. 200 (Nov. 1999): 483-92. For a more cautious note, see Burrow's "The Alterity of Medieval Literature," *New Literary History* 10, no. 2 (Winter 1979): 385–390.
22. Jauss, "The Alterity and Modernity of Medieval Literature," 187.
23. Ibid., 188.
24. Ibid., 190–191.
25. Particularly Lewis' project in *The Discarded Image* (Cambridge University Press, 1964).
26. Jauss, 198. Speaking as to how theoretical frameworks seek to dismantle the "gulf": Glenn Burger offers considerations of how our binary perception of the past "as stable 'home' or absolute other" can be "destabilized" ("Queer Chaucer," *English Studies in Canada* 20 [1994]: 153–170). Carolyn Dinshaw calls for a return to a pleasurable and strategic connection to medieval texts and authors. See *Getting Medieval: Sexualities and Communities, Pre- and Postmodern* (Durham, NC: Duke University Press, 1999) and "Chaucer's Queer Touches / A Queer Touches Chaucer" *Exemplaria* 7.1 (Spring 1995): 75–92.

27. It should be noted that Christianity is hardly a monolithic ideology and has through its history possessed various features and relations to the social that could be labeled potentially alterior and non-normative, particularly around issues of sexuality and gender. See for example, Tison Pugh's *Chaucer's (Anti-) Eroticisms and the Queer Middle Ages* (Columbus: Ohio State University Press, 2014), where the author explores the queerness of decisions to remain chaste. In his commitment to a Church-sanctioned ethics, Tolkien would have likewise experienced a gulf between himself and others.
28. Jane Chance considers Tolkien's status as Other as well in her "Tolkien and the Other: Race and Gender in Middle-earth," in *Tolkien's Modern Middle Ages*, edited by Jane Chance and Alfred K. Siewers (New York: Palgrave Macmillan, 2005), 171–186.
29. These essays are discussed individually and at greater length in bibliographical essays in this volume by Robin Reid, "Race in Tolkien Studies: A Bibliographic Essay" and Yvette Kisor, "Queer Tolkien: A Bibliographical Essay on Tolkien and Alterity." In order of original publication: "Power and Knowledge in Tolkien: The Problem of Difference in 'The Birthday Party,'" in *Proceedings of the J.R.R. Tolkien Centenary Conference* (1992): 115–120; "Tolkien and the Other: Race and Gender in Middle-earth" (2005); "Tolkien's Women (and Men): The Films and the Book," *Mallorn* 43 (2005): 30–37; "Subversive Fantasist: Tolkien on Class Difference," in *Proceedings of the Conference on* The Lord of the Rings, *1954–2004: Scholarship in Honor of Richard E. Blackwelder*, edited by Wayne G. Hammond and Christina Scull (Milwaukee: Marquette University Press, 2006), 153–168; and "'In the Company of Orcs': Peter Jackson's Queer Tolkien," in *Queer Movie Medievalisms*, edited by Kathleen Coyne Kelly and Tison Pugh (London: Ashgate, 2009), 79–83.
30. *Tolkien's Art: A Mythology for England* (St. Martin's Press, 1979; rev. ed. Univ. Press of Kentucky 2001); *The Lord of the Rings: The Mythology of Power* (Macmillan/Twayne 1992; rev. ed. Univ. Press of Kentucky 2001).
31. "Tolkien and the Other: Race and Gender in Middle-Earth," 183.
32. Jane Chance, *Tolkien, Self and Other: "This Queer Creature,"* The New Middle Ages (New York: Palgrave 2016).

Bibliography

Bakhtin, Mikhail. *Problems of Dostoevsky's Poetics*. Translated by Caryl Emerson. Minneapolis: University of Minnesota, 1984.

de Beauvoir, Simone. *The Second Sex* Translated by H.M. Parshley. New York: Knopf, 1953. *Le Deuxième Sexe.* 2 vols. Paris: Gallimard, 1949.

Bhabha, Homi K. "The Other Question: Stereotype, Discrimination and the Discourse of Colonialism." In *The Location of Culture*, ed. Homi K. Bhabha, 66–92. London and New York: Routledge, 1994.

Burger, Glenn. "Queer Chaucer." *English Studies in Canada* 20 (1994): 153–170.

Burrow, J. A. "'Alterity' and Middle English Literature." *The Review of English Studies*, n.s., 50, no. 200 (Nov. 1999): 483–492.

———. "The Alterity of Medieval Literature." *New Literary History* 10, no. 2 (Winter 1979): 385–390.

Chance, Jane. "'In the Company of Orcs': Peter Jackson's Queer Tolkien." In *Queer Movie Medievalisms*, edited by Kathleen Coyne Kelly and Tison Pugh, 79–83. London: Ashgate, 2009.

———. "Power and Knowledge in Tolkien: The Problem of Difference in 'The Birthday Party.'" *Proceedings of the J.R.R. Tolkien Centenary Conference* (1992): 115–120.

———. "Subversive Fantasist: Tolkien on Class Difference." In *Proceedings of the Conference on* The Lord of the Rings*, 1954–2004: Scholarship in Honor of Richard E. Blackwelder*, edited by Wayne G. Hammond and Christina Scull, 153–168. Milwaukee: Marquette University Press, 2006.

———. *The Lord of the Rings: The Mythology of Power.* Macmillan/Twayne 1992; rev. ed. Univ. Press of Kentucky, 2001.

———. "Tolkien and the Other: Race and Gender in Middle-earth." In *Tolkien's Modern Middle Ages*, edited by Jane Chance and Alfred K. Siewers, 171–186. New York: Palgrave Macmillan, 2005.

———. *Tolkien's Art: A Mythology for England.* St. Martin's Press, 1979; rev. ed. Univ. Press of Kentucky, 2001.

———. Tolkien, Self and Other: *"This Queer Creature."* The New Middle Ages. New York: Palgrave, 2016.

———. "Tolkien's Women (and Men): The Films and the Book." *Mallorn* 43 (2005): 30–37.

Dinshaw, Carolyn. "Chaucer's Queer Touches / A Queer Touches Chaucer." *Exemplaria* 7.1 (Spring 1995): 75–92.

———. *Getting Medieval: Sexualities and Communities, Pre- and Postmodern.* Durham, NC: Duke University Press, 1999.

Evans, Dylan. *An Introductory Dictionary of Lacanian Psychoanalysis.* London and New York: Routledge, 1996.

Freud, Anna. *The Ego and the Mechanisms of Defense.* London: Karnac Books, 1992.

Freud, Sigmund. "The Uncanny." In *The Uncanny.* Translated by David McLintock. London: Penguin, 2003, 123-62. "Das Unheimliche." *Imago* 5.5-6 (1919): 297–324.

Haidu, Peter. "Making It (New) in the Middle Ages: Towards a Problematics of Alterity." *Diacritics* 4, no. 2 (Summer 1974): 2–11.

Hegel, Georg Wilhelm Friedrich. *The Phenomenology of Spirit*. Trans. A. V. Miller. Oxford: Oxford University Press, 1977. *Phänomenologie des Geistes*. Bamberg and Würzburg: Joseph Anton Goebhardt, 1807.

Jauss, Hans Robert. Trans. by Timothy Bahti. "The Alterity and Modernity of Medieval Literature." *New Literary History* 10, no. 2 (Winter 1979): 181–229.

Johnston, Adrian. "Jacques Lacan." *Stanford Encyclopedia of Philosophy*. Ed. Edward N. Zalta. 2014. Accessed July 20, 2014. http://plato.stanford.edu/entries/lacan/.

Jung, Carl. "Conscious, Unconscious, and Individuation." In *The Archetypes and the Collective Unconscious*, 2nd edition, trans. R.F.C. Hull, vol. 9, pt. 1 of *Collected Works of C. G. Jung*, 270–289. Princeton: Princeton University Press, 1981.

Kristeva, Julia. *Powers of Horror: An Essay On Abjection*. Trans. Leon S. Roudiez. New York: Columbia University Press, 1982. *Pouvoirs de l'horreur: Essai sur l'abjection*. Paris: Éditions de Seuil, 1980.

Lacan, Jacques. *Écrits*. Paris: Seuil, 1966.

Lewis, C.S. *The Discarded Image*. Cambridge: Cambridge University Press, 1964.

Lévinas, Emmanuel. *Totalité et Infini: essai sur l'extériorité*. The Hague: Martinus Nijhoff, 1961. Translated by Alphonso Lingis as *Totality and Infinity, An Essay on Exteriority*. Pittsburgh, PA: Duquesne University Press, 1969.

Minh-ha, Trihn T. *Woman, Native, Other: Writing Postcoloniality and Feminism*. Bloomington, IN: Indiana University Press, 2009.

OED Online. "alterity, n." Oxford University Press. Accessed July 05, 2016. http://www.oed.com/view/Entry/5788?redirectedFrom=alterity.

Pugh, Tison. *Chaucer's (Anti-) Eroticisms and the Queer Middle Ages*. Columbus: Ohio State University Press, 2014.

Said, Edward W. *Orientalism*. New York: Pantheon Books, 1978.

Sartre, Jean-Paul. *Being and Nothingness: An Essay on Phenomenological Ontology*. Translated by Hazel E. Barnes. New York: Philosophical Library, 1956. *L'Être et le néant: Essai d'ontologie phénoménologique*. Paris: Gallimard, 1943.

Spivak, Gayatri Chakravorty. "Can the Subaltern Speak?" In *Marxism and the Interpretation of Culture*, ed. Cary Nelson and Lawrence Grossberg, 271–313. Urbana, IL: University of Illinois Press, 1988.

Zumthor, Paul. *Essai de poétique médiévale*. Paris: Éditions du Seuil, 1972.

PART I

The State of the Scholarship

CHAPTER 2

Queer Tolkien: A Bibliographical Essay on Tolkien and Alterity

Yvette Kisor

The "queer" in Tolkien has been an ongoing concern in studies of his legendarium. Yet, what exactly is meant by this term? It is a term Tolkien uses often; in just the opening couple of pages of the first chapter of *The Lord of the Rings* those of Hobbiton refer to Buckland "where folks are so queer" and assert that the Brandybucks are "a queer breed," to cite just two instances (Tolkien uses some version of the term nine times in the opening chapter alone).[1] In Tolkien's usage, the adjective is clustered with others like "peculiar"[2] and not "natural"[3]; the relevant Oxford English Dictionary definition clearly indicated is "Strange, odd, peculiar, eccentric. Also: of questionable character; suspicious, dubious."[4] However, this meaning has been largely superseded, at least in the USA, by the meaning

I am grateful for the assistance of Bryan Potts in compiling and reviewing the essays discussed here and to Ramapo College of New Jersey for funding his research assistantship. An early version of this essay was presented at the 13th Annual Tolkien in Vermont Conference at the University of Vermont, Burlington, April 2016. I am grateful to Ramapo College of New Jersey for providing travel funding to attend the conference.

Y. Kisor (✉)
Ramapo College, Mahwah, NJ, USA

C. Vaccaro and Y. Kisor (eds.), *Tolkien and Alterity*, The New Middle Ages, DOI 10.1007/978-3-319-61018-4_2

first recorded by the Oxford English Dictionary in 1914, "Of a person: homosexual. Hence: of or relating to homosexuals or homosexuality,"[5] and since the term is often used to characterize Bilbo and/or Frodo, our bachelor hobbits, there has been a slippage between the two meanings in contemporary understanding, regardless of Tolkien's intentions.

What the two meanings have in common, of course, is *difference*; whether we mean odd or homosexual there is an understood departure from the perceived norm whether that difference is understood to be explicitly sexual or not. A related term, then, is "alterity," the subject of this volume, which the Oxford English Dictionary defines as "The fact or state of being other or different; diversity, difference, otherness; an instance of this."[6] This can accommodate much, but in the interests of space and time, and in order to maintain a clear focus, I am going to limit my discussion in this essay to queer Tolkien in a more limited sense. Thus, I will be excluding racial difference from my discussion, not because it is unimportant (cf. Helen Young's call to engage seriously with critical race theory in her 2015 review essay of Christopher Vaccaro's *The Body in Tolkien*),[7] but rather because the topic is of sufficient weight to merit its own separate consideration in this volume where it is carefully and thoroughly considered by Robin Anne Reid.[8] Similarly, I lay aside the question of women in Tolkien, again not because it is unimportant but because it is considered elsewhere; see, for example, the recent publication of *Perilous and Fair: Women in the Works and Life of J. R. R. Tolkien* edited by Janet Brennan Croft and Leslie A. Donovan, which features both classic and new essays on women in Tolkien, and especially the bibliographical essay on female characters it contains, again by Robin Anne Reid.[9]

I will limit this survey and discussion of scholarship instead to criticism that deals with what is "queer" in Tolkien in the more limited senses of both sexuality and identity, thus glancing at the two definitions I began with: queer sexuality, specifically homosexuality; identification of the Other, the different, as queer, as peculiar, as in some way suspicious. I will begin with the first of these.

One way of categorizing essays that deal with the possibility of queer sexuality in Tolkien is according to whether they find it there or not. Thus, we have critical treatments that insist that there is no homosexuality in *The Lord of the Rings*, that there is homosexuality in *The Lord of the Rings*, that there is homosociality, or that sexual ambiguity rules the day. Into the first group we might place essays by Daniel Timmons and potentially David M. Craig, in the second one by Valerie Rohy, in the third a piece by

Anna Smol, and in the final the assessment of Esther Saxey. On one end of the continuum then, Timmons and Craig, both published in 2001, are perhaps representative. In "Hobbit Sex and Sensuality in *The Lord of the Rings*," Daniel Timmons distinguishes between sex and sensuality, finding plenty of the latter, especially in Frodo's responses to Goldberry, Arwen, and Galadriel.[10] He finds the bond between Frodo and Sam to be a "spiritual" one, contrasted with the heteronormative bond Sam has with Rosie, and he sees no conflict between the two.[11] In a somewhat similar vein, in "'Queer Lodgings': Gender and Sexuality in *The Lord of the Rings*," David M. Craig notes the merging of religious spirituality with love in figures like Galadriel, and the pair of Aragorn and Arwen, but especially Frodo and Sam.[12] Again this love is a spiritual one, and while Craig acknowledges it as queer, he also sees it as refined beyond the plane of the sexual. Craig considers the history of male friendship especially in the context of WWI and Anglo-Catholicism and discusses the close personal relationships that develop in *The Lord of the Rings* as analogous. Both of these essays focus on the special nature of the friendship between Frodo and Sam, and that is typical of essays concerned with the possibility of homosexuality in *The Lord of the Rings.* Both Timmons and Craig acknowledge a deep, spiritual friendship between Frodo and Sam that is absent any overt homosexuality. While Craig sees the love between them as queer and Timmons does not, both see their love as spiritual, beyond (and above) the sexual.

At the other end of the spectrum from Timmons and Craig, we might place Valerie Rohy's "On Fairy Stories," part of the 2004 issue of *Modern Fiction Studies* dedicated to Tolkien.[13] In this queer reading of *The Lord of the Rings*, Rohy focuses on the frustrated, incomplete nature of all sexuality in the text, especially the homosexual relationship between Frodo and Sam. Her analysis builds on Lacan's notion of sexuality as always incomplete and the Ring as a Lacanian *point de capiton* (quilting point or anchoring point) of the narrative binding meaning and becoming a locus of desire. Just as the Ring is a desire that can never be fulfilled (only Sauron can possess it; those who desire it become possessed by it), it represents in its lack of completion sexuality itself. In this way, it is analogous to the courtly love relationship as Lacan understands it. The Ring thus becomes an externalization of an internal failure of sexuality and love. For Rohy, the reality of the queer love between Frodo and Sam is simultaneously its incompletion, its impossibility, as homosexuality becomes a "scapegoat for the failure of all sexual relations."[14]

In the same issue of *Modern Fiction Studies*, Anna Smol's "'Oh … oh … Frodo!': Readings of Male Intimacy in *The Lord of the Rings*" examines the relationship between Frodo and Sam in the context of British male friendship in WWI, noting the physical intimacy that emerges in the extreme circumstances of war.[15] In this, she takes a similar approach as Craig, as she acknowledges, but hers is a more in-depth consideration, and she sees Frodo and Sam as depicting the homosocial rather than the homosexual as Craig asserts (though he finds a spiritual rather than a physical relationship). She then turns to the contemporary reception of that relationship in film and fanfiction. She notes that the films downplay much of the physical intimacy of the books, but still maintain enough to create a discomfort that questions traditional Western masculinity. The survey of slash fanfiction she includes speaks to its variety, but establishes that most grows directly out of the homosocial relationships created by Tolkien. Whatever its roots in the experience of male intimacy in WWI, changing historical and cultural circumstances have created something that has grown beyond Tolkien's intentions.

Like Smol's piece, Esther Saxey's 2005 essay on "Homoeroticism" considers both novel and film depictions and finds persistent, but not definitive indications of homoeroticism in both the novel and film adaptation.[16] She reviews the textual evidence for homoeroticism, noting the "intense hierarchical homosocial relations"[17] of the novel and arguing that the exact natures of all relationships in the text "are ambiguous, and could easily be sexual."[18] She argues that, ironically, by emphasizing traditional romantic heterosexual relationships in the film, the male–male relationships become potentially more sexualized. As these five essays demonstrate, the subtext of Tolkien's novel, especially in regard to the novel's depiction of physical intimacy in the friendship of Frodo and Sam, is open to a range of interpretations, and the afterlife of the novel, particularly its film adaptation, brings out and interprets that subtext.

Other essays address the queer in Tolkien by investigating a broader definition of queerness focused on difference and ambiguity. David Halperin observes that the queer is "by definition whatever is at odds with the normal, the legitimate, the dominant … it describes a horizon of possibility whose precise extent and heterogenous scope cannot in principle be delimited in advance."[19] Annamarie Jagose asserts that "queer is less an identity than a *critique* of identity … it is more accurate to represent it as ceaselessly interrogating both the preconditions of identity and its effects."[20] Such an understanding of queer can be seen to inform a number of essays and unlike the essays considered above, they do not focus so strongly on the relationship between Frodo and Sam, but find queerness more broadly, and define that queerness in terms other than sexuality, or at least more broadly than sexuality.

In this regard, Jane Chance's work is seminal. She has interrogated this notion of queerness in a number of essays beginning with "'Queer' Hobbits: The Problem of Difference in the Shire."[21] This essay focuses on the politics of difference in the Shire, which associates queerness with "outside" and observes how Bilbo negotiates his negative identity as queer through his generosity and respect for the lower classes. As well as Bilbo, this chapter considers both Frodo and Gollum and sees the One Ring as symbolic of sameness; opposed to the Ring is respect for difference.[22] The Ring promises enhancement of the Self but ironically creates an erasure of the Self. The small drama of Self versus Other that plays out in the Shire is the lesson of the text writ small.

In her 2005 essay "Tolkien and the Other: Race and Gender in Middle-earth," Chance continues to explore the text's concern with difference.[23] Taking as a starting point *apartheid* "apartness," Chance traces Tolkien's attitudes toward difference through his scholarship ("Sigelwara Land," his edition and translation of the Old English *Exodus*, his essay on "overmod") and his own status as displaced orphan and religious minority, and later sidelined academically through his choice of field. Through negative examples, not only the domination of Sauron and Saruman, but the self-absorption of the Ents, as well as positive ones, primarily Frodo and his acceptance of Gollum, Chance explores Tolkien's abhorrence of prejudice born of difference. She also finds Tolkien's scholarship to provide a point of access to his fiction in her 2006 essay "Subversive Fantasist: Tolkien on Class Difference."[24] Here, Chance uses Tolkien's scholarship on Chaucer to interrogate class difference in his fiction, noting how he inverts aristocratic values in both. Class and regional differences established in the Shire become racial and national ones as Tolkien creates heroes who embody difference and cut across boundaries, observing that "what Tolkien decries is condemnation of any sort of alterity as queer and 'unnatural.'"[25]

In 2009, Chance turns to the film's portrayal of difference, focusing on the opposition between the hyper-masculine Orcs and the feminized pair of Frodo and Sam in her essay "'In the Company of Orcs': Peter Jackson's Queer Tolkien."[26] Her essay focuses on the particular scene in Jackson's film in which Frodo and Sam don Orc armor and temporarily join a company of Orcs moving through Mordor. Her examination of this scene and its novel counterpart finds that "Jackson's crucial scene in his film, 'In the Company of Orcs,' in echoing LaBute's film *In the Company of Men*, queers Tolkien by accentuating the hyper-masculinity and sadism of the Orcs and hypo-masculinity and gentleness of the disguised lovers Frodo and Sam. Underlying the feudal relationships of all the Hobbits, Tolkien's queerness tropes gender binaries throughout the epic."[27] Her 2016 book *Tolkien, Self and Other: "This Queer Creature"* continues her abiding concern with the queer in Tolkien.[28] This work is interested in the interplay between Tolkien's scholarly and creative work and how Tolkien's own sense of alterity finds expression in all his writing. Chance accounts for these resonances through an interrogation of Tolkien as queer, examining "his creation of a queer—nonnormative—mythology based on a privileging of the marginal."[29] This work draws on and expands many of the ideas present in the works discussed in this essay and that appear in the present volume.

Chance is not the only scholar concerned with the question of queer difference in *The Lord of the Rings*. In the same issue of *Modern Fiction Studies* that delivers the Rohy and Smol essays (the three make up the section titled "Queering *The Lord of the Rings*"), Jes Battis' "Gazing Upon Sauron: Hobbits, Elves, and the Queering of the Postcolonial Optic" explores the position of the Hobbits in the text as postcolonial subjects in a "matrix of cultural power."[30] Battis argues that the Hobbits are made queer through the gazes of others; this queering thus makes the male Hobbit the "most radical enunciation of the feminine"[31] within the text. The essay touches on gender binary deconstruction in Shelob and Galadriel and explores how the Hobbits are treated as colonial subjects by both the Eye of Sauron and the Mirror of Galadriel.

It is not always the Hobbits that become the locus of interest in explorations of queer difference in Tolkien's fiction. Lucia Opreanu looks at the figure of Gollum (a degraded hobbit) in her 2011 essay, while Jolanta N. Komornicka's 2013 essay focuses instead on the Orcs. In "The Inescapable Other—Identity Transitions and Mutations in the Construction of Tolkien's Gollum/Sméagol," Opreanu focuses on Gollum's sense of identity and relationship to Frodo, utilizing the concept of the *doppelgänger* as well as binary pairs in Tolkien (Gandalf/Saruman, Boromir/Faramir, Elves/Orcs, Shire/Mordor, etc.) as illustrating the Self/Other construction.[32] She observes the divided Self in Gollum in his use of language and his obsessive possessiveness and finds the text to demonstrate that identity is constructed through difference, and the Self finds its definition through its relation to the Other.[33] Komornicka, on the other hand, focuses on the Orcs in her consideration of the Other. In "The Ugly Elf: Orc Bodies, Perversion, and Redemption in *The Silmarillion* and *The Lord of the Rings*," Komornicka touches on the Orc as Other to all races of Middle-earth, associating the Orc with Jeffrey Cohen's Intimate Stranger, "a monsterized version of what a member of society can become."[34]

Difference and the relation with the Other are concerns as well for Benjamin Saxton. In his 2013 essay, "Tolkien and Bakhtin on Authorship, Literary Freedom, and Alterity," Saxton reads Tolkien in light of Bakhtin's notion of the author, noting how both partake in a collaborative view of authorship in which the author shares narrative duties with his characters and characters are subjects with agency rather than objects of authorial control.[35] He finds Bakhtin's concept of alterity demonstrated in character relationships in *The Lord of the Rings*, especially Self–Other relationships, noting the exemplification of Bakhtin's location of the Other in the Self; Frodo and Gollum are perhaps the most obvious example of this. Finally, he finds both authors share what he calls an "ethics of creativity" in their notions of authorship as shared and finds the mystery of free will and fate to be central to Tolkien's fiction. In interesting ways, Saxton's discussion of Tolkien's alterity, which Saxton sees as Bakhtinian, is strikingly similar to the ideas of French philosopher Emmanuel Lévinas, who sees the Self as defined in terms of the Other.

In Lévinas' conception, knowledge of the Self is rooted in the encounter with the Other, and crucial to that relation is both the utter alterity of the Other and our desire for the Other. Some of the most recent work on Tolkien and alterity utilizes Lévinas' ideas, such as Joseph Tadie's 2015 "'That the World Not Be Usurped': Emmanuel Levinas and J. R. R. Tolkien on Serving the Other as Release from Bondage."[36] Tadie focuses on the encounter between Bilbo and Gandalf in the opening chapters of *The Hobbit*, considering as well the Bilbo who appears in the Council of Elrond scene in *The Fellowship of the Ring* as a measure of Bilbo's ethical growth. In their initial encounter, Tadie sees in Bilbo the image of unreflective and indolent concupiscence and associates the initial figure he cuts with the dragon, and in Gandalf he perceives the ethically alert servant, finding their encounter to exemplify the positive change that can follow when "the voice of an-Other reaches the Self."[37]

Deidre Dawson's essay in this volume also finds a connection between Lévinas and Tolkien, and this philosopher provides a way of examining what many of the scholars whose work is discussed here are concerned with: How difference is imagined and how the queer functions in Tolkien's fiction, however figured.[38] In considering future directions for scholarship that focuses on alterity, the work of Lévinas has the potential to prove fruitful. What seems less likely to prove fruitful is a singular focus on the question of the homosexuality of characters in *The Lord of the Rings*. A move away from such a focus is already happening, as one can see from the chronology of such scholarship discussed here. Timmons' and Craig's essays were published in 2001, Rohy's and Smol's in 2004, and Saxey's in 2005. Little has appeared since. In a sense, the question is as settled as it can be. Did Tolkien write a homosexual relationship between any characters, specifically Frodo and Sam, in his novel? Clearly, no. Can readers find such relationship(s) in his novel? Clearly, yes.

For scholarship concerned with the sexual identity of characters in Tolkien's fiction, two areas provide possibilities for exploration. One is a broadening of interest in Tolkien's work beyond just *The Lord of the Rings*. As the foregoing survey of scholarship reveals, considerations of the queer in Tolkien are preoccupied with the characters of *The Lord of the Rings*. There is little consideration of even *The Hobbit*, let alone *The Silmarillion* or Tolkien's shorter works such as *Leaf by Niggle*, *Smith of Wootten Major*, etc. Stephen Yandell's essay in this volume goes some way to correct the imbalance, but many more areas are left to explore.[39] Strong, devoted male relationships are certainly in evidence in *The Silmarillion*, for example; one need only consider Beleg's devotion to Túrin and his tragic death at Túrin's hands (albeit accidental) or Finrod's commitment to Beren, also leading to his death. Fingon's rescue of Maedhros and the friendship between them could also be considered in this regard. A second avenue for scholarship concerned with the potential homosexuality of Tolkien's characters is a focus not on Tolkien's writing but on the adaptations of his work.

The adaptations most often a focus for scholarship are Peter Jackson's film adaptations of both *The Lord of the Rings* and *The Hobbit* and, increasingly, fanfiction. There has already been a fair amount of scholarly attention to Jackson's *The Lord of the Rings* trilogy which came out in 2001–2003, and three of the essays discussed here, Smol's, Saxey's, and Chance's "In the Company of Orcs," consider how Jackson's movies queer Tolkien's text, or expose the queerness already present. Valerie Rohy's essay in this volume does just this, focusing on Jackson's adaptation of the figure of Saruman.[40] However, Jackson's *The Hobbit* series was only released in 2012–2014, so scholarship is just beginning to appear in print. Some treatments which focus on the queerness of Jackson's adaptation have begun to appear in online venues, however. Thomas J. West, III's "The Exquisite Queerness of The Hobbit," for example, discusses several queer elements of the film, noting that its use of camp distinguishes it from Jackson's *The Lord of the Rings*.[41] West discusses fan interpretations of and creative responses to both Tolkien's text and Jackson's film as part of his discussion, and that inclusion points to another kind of adaptation that is increasingly becoming an area of scholarly attention.

Fan studies began as a version of reception studies but is becoming increasingly interested in the creative work produced by fans such as fanfiction and fan art. The Fan Studies Network, which was formed in 2012 and has held an annual conference since 2013, lists twelve journals devoted in some way to fan studies on their website.[42] This growing area of study intersects with a focus on queer Tolkien in promising ways. As Anna Smol notes in her essay reviewed here, slash fanfiction, which focuses on sexual relationships between characters of the same gender, is growing.[43] Smol discusses several examples and notes how such creations interrogate other aspects of difference such as social class, concluding that such works demonstrate how relationships such as Frodo's and Sam's "are to a large extent historically and culturally determined."[44] Though focused on race, Robin Anne Reid makes a similar call in her essay in this volume to expand scholarly focus to works written by fans that transform Tolkien's works.[45]

One question that arises is whether fans who create work responding to Tolkien's fiction are seeking to fill an absence perceived in Tolkien's text or responding to a latent queerness. The review of scholarship conducted here suggests that there would be little scholarly agreement on such a question; one imagines Timmons, for example, would claim the former while Rohy might assert the latter. However, the question posits perhaps a false dichotomy as well as a value judgment, implying that responding to a present but sublimated queerness in Tolkien's text would somehow be more legitimate than responding to an absence of the queer. In fact, a number of scholars have interrogated the gaps and silences of narrative as sites of meaning production. Allen Frantzen, for example, considers the gaps in the narrative of *Beowulf* to be "sites for reading and writing,"[46] focusing on the way readers of the poem create meaning in such spaces. Similarly, in James W. Earl's psychoanalytic approach to *Beowulf*, he considers such gaps and silences as places where readers "read [them] selves" in the narrative.[47] Earl focuses on the reader's desire and applies the psychoanalytic approach not to the poem itself, but rather to the readers' interactions with the poem, noting how the poem becomes "a screen for our projections" and aligning the silences in the narrative with "the silence of the analyst."[48] Akin to Earl's focus on how readers' desires interact with moments of narrative discontinuity, Gillian Overing too notes that it can be "difficult to separate text from reader, to disentangle the workings of desire within the reader from those operating within the narrative."[49] These scholars are writing about *Beowulf*,[50] but their concern with how the desire of the reader intersects with gaps and silences in narrative can be extended to the products fans create in response to texts like Tolkien's fiction. Tolkien wrote that his creation of Middle-earth would "leave scope for other minds and hands, wielding paint and music and drama,"[51] which would appear to give license to the creations of fans.[52] One imagines that slash fanfiction is not what Tolkien had in mind, but it is clearly in the minds of a good portion of his readers.

Other possible avenues for scholars interested in the queer in Tolkien utilize a broader concept of the queer than just the sexual, as the division of essays in this overview proposes. Already suggested are the possibilities offered by the work of Emmanuel Lévinas. Another might be suggested by the work of Tison Pugh, who brings queer theory together with genre criticism. In his *Queering Medieval Genres*, he looks at the propensity for the queer to subvert genre expectations.[53] He is utilizing a broader definition of the queer, advocating "a widened view of the implications of medieval queerness beyond the somewhat limited arena of sexual conduct."[54] He is focused on "medieval queerness" where the scholarship discussed here is on Tolkien, but given the presence of the medieval in Tolkien, the observations are perhaps more relevant than might at first appear. Pugh offers a definition of the queer taken from Richard Zeikowitz, a definition very much in line with what this essay suggests: "'Queer' can thus signify any nonnormative behavior, relationship, or identity occurring at a specific moment. It may also describe an alternative form of desire that threatens the stability of the dominant norm."[55]

Pugh is concerned with the propensity of the queer to destabilize narrative, observing that "through the introduction of the queer, previously marginalized agents radically reconfigure the parameters of subject and object inside and outside the narrative, both for the textual world created within the genre and for the audience of that genre."[56] Pugh is working with medieval genres, but the generic instability of much of Tolkien's work seems to invite such an approach. Pugh suggests as much, expressing his hope that "the hermeneutic of queering genres will likewise be of use to scholars of other historic periods."[57] The question of genre is already a topic of concern for scholars of Tolkien's work, as much of it defies easy categorization. To consider just *The Lord of the Rings*, it has been called an epic, a romance, and a novel, among other genres. It partakes of older genres at the same time it births a new one, high fantasy, while Tolkien himself called it a fairy-story. It also includes the fiction of being a translation of the Red Book of Westmarch, a translation of what are essentially the memoirs of Bilbo and Frodo. Pugh acknowledges "the great varieties of genres within a single piece of literature"[58] and notes that "a critical authorial strategy in queering genres (and thus obfuscating the promises of the genre contract) surfaces in the play between and among different genres."[59] Tolkien's work certainly demonstrates such generic play, and Pugh's approach offers interesting possibilities when applied to Tolkien. As Pugh observes, "Queering genres … allows us to see texts expand in directions unexpected and unexplored. As the conservative view of genre suggests, genres offer some constrictions, but, as the playfully queer view of genre highlights, they offer vast freedoms, subversions, and surprises as well."[60] Tolkien's work fits right in with this description.

As this survey of scholarship demonstrates, the idea of difference is central to Tolkien's work and the moral lesson of *The Lord of the Rings* concerns attitudes toward the queer. Jane Chance defines the "ethical drama of *The Lord of the Rings*" as the "tension between the 'normal' and the 'queer,'" posing the question as "How can individuals (and nations) so different from one another coexist in harmony?"[61] She finds the answer in that very difference, for "where the difference of one ends, the complementary difference of the other begins. The relationship is circular and yet based on both need and desire, necessity and obligation, the dance of Self and Other, until the music ends."[62] This focus on the relation with the Other, the response to difference, and the negotiation with the queer remain abiding concerns for Tolkien scholarship as it moves forward.

Notes

1. J. R. R. Tolkien, *The Fellowship of the Ring*, 2nd edition (Boston: Houghton Mifflin, 1987), I, i, 30.
2. Ibid., 29.
3. Ibid., 29, 30.

4. "queer, adj.1," OED Online, June 2016, Oxford University Press, accessed July 05, 2016, http://www.oed.com/view/Entry/156236?rskey=QOP7Ov&result=2, meaning 1.a.
5. Ibid., meaning 3.
6. "alterity, n.," OED Online, June 2016, Oxford University Press, accessed July 05, 2016, http://www.oed.com/view/Entry/5788?redirectedFrom=alterity.
7. Helen Young, review "*The Body in Tolkien's Legendarium* (2013). Edited by Christopher Vaccaro," *Journal of Tolkien Research*: 1.1 (2014), Article 5, http://scholar.valpo.edu/journaloftolkienresearch/vol1/iss1/5/.
8. See her essay in this volume, "Race in Tolkien Studies: A Bibliographical Essay."
9. Janet Brennan Croft and Leslie A. Donovan, eds., *Perilous and Fair: Women in the Works and Life of J. R. R. Tolkien* (Altadena, CA: Mythopoeic Press, 2015). Robin Reid's bibliographical essay is "The History of Scholarship on Female Characters in J. R. R. Tolkien's Legendarium: A Feminist Bibliographic Essay," 13–40.
10. Daniel Timmons, "Hobbit Sex and Sensuality in *The Lord of the Rings*," *Mythlore* 89 (2001): 70–79.
11. Ibid., 78.
12. David M. Craig, "'Queer Lodgings': Gender and Sexuality in *The Lord of the Rings*," *Mallorn* 38 (2001): 11–18.
13. Valerie Rohy, "On Fairy Stories," *Modern Fiction Studies* 50.4 (2004): 927–948.
14. Ibid., 944.
15. Anna Smol, "'Oh … oh … Frodo!': Readings of Male Intimacy in *The Lord of the Rings*," *Modern Fiction Studies* 50.4 (2004): 949–979.
16. Esther Saxey, "Homoeroticism," in *Reading* The Lord of the Rings*: New Writings on Tolkien's Classic*, edited by Robert Eaglestone (London: Continuum, 2005), 124–137.
17. Ibid., 129.
18. Ibid., 131.
19. David Halperin, *Saint Foucault: Towards a Gay Hagiography* (New York: Oxford University Press, 1995), 62.
20. Annamarie Jagose, *Queer Theory: An Introduction* (New York: New York University Press, 1996), 131–132, italics original.
21. Jane Chance, "'Queer' Hobbits: The Problem of Difference in the Shire," chap. 2 of *The Lord of the Rings: The Mythology of Power*, rev. ed. (Lexington: University Press of Kentucky, 2001), 26–37. The germ of this essay first appeared in 1995 under a slightly different title ("Power and Knowledge in Tolkien: The Problem of Difference in 'The Birthday Party'") as part of the *Proceedings of the J. R. R. Tolkien Centenary*

Conference; I consider here the version printed in the revised edition of *The Lord of the Rings: The Mythology of Power* (2001).

22. Ibid., 33.
23. Jane Chance, "Tolkien and the Other: Race and Gender in Middle-earth," in *Tolkien's Modern Middle Ages*, edited by Jane Chance and Alfred K. Siewers (New York: Palgrave Macmillan, 2005), 171–186.
24. Jane Chance, "Subversive Fantasist: Tolkien on Class Difference," in *Proceedings of the Conference on* The Lord of the Rings, *1954–2004: Scholarship in Honor of Richard E. Blackwelder*, edited by Wayne G. Hammond and Christina Scull (Milwaukee: Marquette University Press, 2006), 153–168.
25. Ibid., 161.
26. Jane Chance, "'In the Company of Orcs': Peter Jackson's Queer Tolkien," in *Queer Movie Medievalisms*, edited by Kathleen Coyne Kelly and Tison Pugh (London: Ashgate, 2009), 79–83.
27. Ibid., 95–96.
28. Jane Chance, *Tolkien, Self and Other: "This Queer Creature,"* The New Middle Ages (New York: Palgrave 2016).
29. Ibid., 5. Thanks to Jane Chance for making a version of her book in proof available to us.
30. Jes Battis, "Gazing Upon Sauron: Hobbits, Elves, and the Queering of the Postcolonial Optic," *Modern Fiction Studies* 50.4 (2004): 910. Robin Reid discusses this essay in the context of race; see her essay in this collection "Race in Tolkien Studies: A Bibliographic Essay."
31. Ibid., 915.
32. Lucia Opreanu, "The Inescapable Other—Identity Transitions and Mutations in the Construction of Tolkien's Gollum/Sméagol," *University of Bucharest Review* 1, no. 1 (2011): 151–159.
33. Ibid., 152.
34. Jolanta N. Komornicka, "The Ugly Elf: Orc Bodies, Perversion, and Redemption in *The Silmarillion* and *The Lord of the Rings*," in *The Body in Tolkien's Legendarium: Essays on Middle-earth Corporeality*, edited by Christopher Vaccaro (Jefferson, NC: McFarland, 2013), 83–96. Kormornicka quotes from Jeffrey Jerome Cohen, *Of Giants: Sex, Monsters, and the Middle Ages* (Minneapolis: University of Minnesota Press, 1999), 26, quoted on 89.
35. Benjamin Saxton, "Tolkien and Bakhtin on Authorship, Literary Freedom, and Alterity," *Tolkien Studies* 10 (2013): 167–183.
36. Joseph Tadie, "'That the World Not Be Usurped': Emmanuel Levinas and J. R. R. Tolkien on Serving the Other as Release from Bondage," in *Tolkien Among the Moderns*, edited by Ralph C. Wood (Notre Dame: University of Notre Dame Press, 2015), 219–245.

37. Ibid., 226.
38. Deidre Dawson, "Language and Alterity in Tolkien and Lévinas."
39. Stephen Yandell, "Cruising Faery: Queer Desire in Giles, Niggle, and Smith."
40. "Cinema, Sexuality, Mechanical Reproduction: Peter Jackson's Saruman."
41. Thomas J. West, III, "The Exquisite Queerness of *The Hobbit*," *The Outtake*, April 2, 2015, accessed July 17, 2016, https://theouttake.net/the-exquisite-queerness-of-the-hobbit-7c05ba5a1f60#.secpam930.
42. *Fan Studies Network*, accessed July 17, 2016, https://fanstudies.org/.
43. Smol, 971.
44. Ibid., 972–973, 975.
45. "Race in Tolkien Studies: A Bibliographic Essay."
46. Allen J. Frantzen, "Writing the Unreadable *Beowulf*," chap. 6 of *Desire for Origins: New Language, Old English, and Teaching the Tradition* (New Brunswick, NJ: Rutgers University Press, 1990), 182.
47. James W. Earl, *Thinking about Beowulf* (Stanford, CA: Stanford University Press, 1994), 168.
48. Ibid., 173.
49. Gillian Overing, *Language, Sign and Gender in Beowulf* (Carbondale, IL: Southern Illinois University Press, 1990), xxii.
50. I discuss these authors and their concern with how readers create the poem in my "The Aesthetics of *Beowulf*: Structure, Perception, and Desire," in *On the Aesthetics of Beowulf and Other Old English Poems*, ed. John M. Hill (Toronto: University of Toronto Press, 2010), 227–246. Tolkien's long interest in *Beowulf* is well acknowledged.
51. Letter to Milton Waldman, 1951. Humphrey Carpenter, ed., *The Letters of J. R. R. Tolkien* (Boston: Houghton Mifflin, 1981), 144–145.
52. One fan production space takes this quote in exactly this way, entitling their magazine *Other Minds*, a continuation of another defunct fan production *Other Hands*; *Other Minds*, accessed July 18, 2016, http://otherm indsmagazine.com/about.
53. Tison Pugh, *Queering Medieval Genres* (New York: Palgrave, 2004).
54. Ibid., 5.
55. Ibid., 5–6. He quotes Richard Zeikowitz, "Befriending the Medieval Queer," *College English* 65: 1 (2002): 67–80, at 67.
56. Ibid., 3–4.
57. Ibid., 167, note 56.
58. Ibid., 14.
59. Ibid., 13–14.
60. Ibid., 20.
61. Chance, "'Queer' Hobbits," 34.
62. Ibid., 35.

Bibliography

Battis, Jes. "Gazing Upon Sauron: Hobbits, Elves, and the Queering of the Postcolonial Optic." *Modern Fiction Studies* 50.4 (2004): 908–926.

Brennan, Janet Croft and Leslie A. Donovan, eds. *Perilous and Fair: Women in the Works and Life of J. R. R. Tolkien*. Altadena, CA: Mythopoeic Press, 2015.

Carpenter, Humphrey, ed. *The Letters of J. R. R. Tolkien*. Boston: Houghton Mifflin, 1981.

Chance, Jane. "'In the Company of Orcs': Peter Jackson's Queer Tolkien." In *Queer Movie Medievalisms*, edited by Kathleen Coyne Kelly and Tison Pugh, 79–83. London: Ashgate, 2009.

———. "'Queer' Hobbits: The Problem of Difference in the Shire." Chap. 2 of *The Lord of the Rings: The Mythology of Power*, rev. ed., 26–37. Lexington: University Press of Kentucky, 2001.

———. "Subversive Fantasist: Tolkien on Class Difference." In *Proceedings of the Conference on* The Lord of the Rings, *1954–2004: Scholarship in Honor of Richard E. Blackwelder*, edited by Wayne G. Hammond and Christina Scull, 153–68. Milwaukee: Marquette University Press, 2006.

———. "Tolkien and the Other: Race and Gender in Middle-earth." In *Tolkien's Modern Middle Ages*, edited by Jane Chance and Alfred K. Siewers, 171–186. New York: Palgrave Macmillan, 2005.

———. *Tolkien, Self and Other: "This Queer Creature."* The New Middle Ages. New York: Palgrave, 2016.

Cohen, Jeffrey Jerome. *Of Giants: Sex, Monsters, and the Middle Ages*. Minneapolis: University of Minnesota Press, 1999.

Craig, David M. "'Queer Lodgings': Gender and Sexuality in The Lord of the Rings." *Mallorn* 38 (2001): 11–18.

Croft, Janet Brennan and Leslie A. Donovan. *Perilous and Fair: Women in the Works and Life of J. R. R. Tolkien*. Altadena, CA: Mythopoeic Press, 2015.

Fan Studies Network. Accessed July 17, 2016. https://fanstudies.org.

Frantzen, Allen J. "Writing the Unreadable *Beowulf*." Chap. 6 of *Desire for Origins: New Language, Old English, and Teaching the Tradition*. New Brunswick, NJ: Rutgers University Press, 1990.

Halperin, David. *Saint Foucault: Towards a Gay Hagiography*. New York: Oxford University Press, 1995.

Jagose, Annamarie. *Queer Theory: An Introduction*. New York: New York University Press, 1996.

Kisor, Yvette. "The Aesthetics of *Beowulf*: Structure, Perception, and Desire." In *On the Aesthetics of Beowulf and Other Old English Poems*, edited by John M. Hill, 227–246. Toronto: University of Toronto Press, 2010.

Komornicka, Jolanta N. "The Ugly Elf: Orc Bodies, Perversion, and Redemption in *The Silmarillion* and *The Lord of the Rings*." In *The Body in Tolkien's*

Legendarium: Essays on Middle-earth Corporeality, edited by Christopher Vaccaro, 83–96. Jefferson, NC: McFarland, 2013.

OED Online. "alterity, n." Oxford University Press. Accessed July 05, 2016. http://www.oed.com/view/Entry/5788?redirectedFrom=alterity.

———. "queer, adj.1." Oxford University Press. Accessed July 5, 2016. http://www.oed.com/view/Entry/156236?rskey=QOP7Ov&result=2.

Opreanu, Lucia. "The Inescapable Other—Identity Transitions and Mutations in the Construction of Tolkien's Gollum/Sméagol." *University of Bucharest Review* 1, no. 1 (2011): 151–159.

Other Hands; Other Minds. Accessed July 18, 2016. http://othermindsmagazine.com/about.

Overing, Gillian. *Language, Sign and Gender in Beowulf.* Carbondale, IL: Southern Illinois University Press, 1990.

Pugh, Tison. *Queering Medieval Genres.* New York: Palgrave, 2004.

Reid, Robin Anne. "The History of Scholarship on Female Characters in J. R. R. Tolkien's Legendarium: A Feminist Bibliographic Essay." In *Perilous and Fair: Women in the Works and Life of J. R. R. Tolkien.* Edited by Brennan, Janet Croft and Leslie A. Donovan, 13–40. Altadena, CA: Mythopoeic Press, 2015.

Rohy, Valerie. "On Fairy Stories." *Modern Fiction Studies* 50.4 (2004): 927–948.

Saxey, Esther. "Homoeroticism." In *Reading* The Lord of the Rings*: New Writings on Tolkien's Classic*, edited by Robert Eaglestone, 124–137. London: Continuum, 2005.

Saxton, Benjamin. "Tolkien and Bakhtin on Authorship, Literary Freedom, and Alterity." *Tolkien Studies* 10 (2013): 167–183.

Smol, Anna. "'Oh … oh … Frodo!': Readings of Male Intimacy in *The Lord of the Rings*." *Modern Fiction Studies* 50.4 (2004): 949–979.

Tadie, Joseph. "'That the World Not Be Usurped': Emmanuel Levinas and J. R. R. Tolkien on Serving the Other as Release from Bondage." In *Tolkien Among the Moderns*, edited by Ralph C. Wood, 219–245. Notre Dame: University of Notre Dame Press, 2015.

Timmons, Daniel. "Hobbit Sex and Sensuality in *The Lord of the Rings*." *Mythlore* 89 (2001): 70–79.

Tolkien, J. R. R. *The Fellowship of the Ring*. 2nd ed. Boston: Houghton Mifflin, 1987.

West, Thomas J., III. "The Exquisite Queerness of The Hobbit." The Outtake. April 2, 2015. Accessed July 17, 2016. https://theouttake.net/theexquisite-queerness-of-the-hobbit-7c05ba5a1f60#.secpam930.

Young, Helen. Review. "The Body in Tolkien's Legendarium (2013). Edited by Christopher Vaccaro." Journal of Tolkien Research: 1.1 (2014). Article 5. http://scholar.valpo.edu/journaloftolkienresearch/vol1/iss1/5/.

Zeikowitz, Richard. "Befriending the Medieval Queer." *College English* 65: 1 (2002): 67–80.

CHAPTER 3

Race in Tolkien Studies: A Bibliographic Essay

Robin Anne Reid

Academic discussion on race in Tolkien studies originated fairly recently caused, in part, by the growing influence of cultural studies and the release of the live-action film by Peter Jackson in 2001–2003.[1] For the purpose of this essay, I define Tolkien studies as an inter- and multi-disciplinary field encompassing Tolkien's legendarium as well as adaptations, derivations, and transformative cultural productions arising from his work.[2] My analysis of scholarship dealing with race in Tolkien studies published during the past dozen years reveals two significant patterns of critical approaches and varying, at times oppositional, claims about Tolkien's work and/or Tolkien himself.[3] These patterns tend toward the

I would like to thank Helen Young for her input into this specific essay and for the work she has done generally on race in Tolkien studies. Her review essay on *The Body in Tolkien's Legendarium* inspired this essay, and her feedback during the writing of the essay was invaluable. I would also like to thank Jacob Pichnarcik whose efforts at Interlibrary Loan & Microforms, Texas A&M University-Commerce, have, as always, made my work as a scholar much easier.

R.A. Reid (✉)
Texas A&M University, College Station, TX, USA

C. Vaccaro and Y. Kisor (eds.), *Tolkien and Alterity*, The New Middle Ages, DOI 10.1007/978-3-319-61018-4_3

binary, especially the conflict between those who see Tolkien or his work as racist and those who see Tolkien or his work as celebrating diversity and multi-cultural cooperation.[4] The other conflict is between scholarly periods of specialization, specifically the question of whether approaches developed by medievalists or postmodernists are best suited for analyzing Tolkien's work.[5]

I would argue that these conflicts are based in large part on the assumptions associated with two sets of methodologies.[6] One set is text-based and focuses on interpreting primary sources, centering on developing interpretations based on aesthetic or structural evidence and citing secondary sources using the same method. This methodology uses the literary methods of close reading and explication and may include, at times, philological and linguistic approaches. It is also a methodology used by some film scholarship. The second set focuses on questions concerning interactions between the text and the primary world, drawing on methods from history and the social sciences. While socio-historical information is often conveyed in texts, the secondary sources used in this approach are not limited to analyses of the primary sources. One difference between the two methods is the amount of attention paid to questions about aspects of production and reception of the primary text.[7] Source studies, one important type of Tolkien scholarship, can use either method, depending on the type and nature of the sources used.

The purpose of this essay is not to argue for either side in these debates; work I admire and find of value can be found on both sides. Instead, I would like to point to a third option that involves a synthesis of the methodologies to create an inter- and multi-disciplinary foundation for discussing race in Tolkien studies. This synthesis may offer a path out of the stalemates created by the binary conflicts. I believe the potential for such a synthesis exists because my analysis shows that scholars using either set of methodologies can reach different conclusions concerning racism in Tolkien or his work, and, equally, that neither set is inextricably connected to either medievalist or postmodernist work. Since scholarship on race in Tolkien studies is so recent, both types of methodologies have been present from the start rather than one representing a "new" challenge to a "traditional" method. Finally, scholars, as some have already shown, may draw from both methodologies. The most important point in this essay is the necessity to expand the discussion of race in Tolkien studies in spite of the sense some have that the current state is one of irreconcilable polarization.

The necessity I perceive is shared by other scholars. In 2000, Michael D. C. Drout and Hilary Wynne argued in their bibliographic essay that, while the lack of Tolkien scholarship on gender, race, and class is "simultaneously refreshing and frustrating," failure to engage with these topics carries the danger of "self-marginalization" if Tolkien scholars continue to isolate themselves from the larger discussions of "contemporary literature."[8] An even stronger call for changes in Tolkien studies came from Helen Young in 2015, in a review essay in which she argues that, in spite of the difficulties Tolkien studies have had as an emerging field as well as difficulties (not unique to Tolkien studies) involved in engaging with critical race theory, that:

> At this point in time, however, to not [engage with critical race theory] risks both scholarly marginalization and cultural irrelevance. Given the level of discussion and outright praise of *The Lord of the Rings*—on both novel and film forms—in avowedly white supremacist forums such as Stormfront.org, there is an urgent and particular need to confront and explore potentially troubling questions if *Tolkien Studies* is to maintain its legitimacy.[9]

Young's essay, and her other work, as well as scholarship by other scholars concerning the extent to which white supremacists express admiration for Tolkien's work, provides additional reasons for addressing the issue of race in Tolkien.[10]

The argument that discussions of the social constructions of race, gender, and class are relevant only to contemporary literature rather than work from earlier historical periods is based on the popular conception that the concept of race did not appear in European cultures until the early modern period. That assumption has been challenged by recent medieval scholarship.[11] One scholar's work, in particular, highlights the social consequences of excluding discussions of race from medieval scholarship. Thomas Hahn, in "The Difference the Middle Ages Makes: Color and Race Before the Modern World," describes a paper session on "Race in the Middle Ages" that was held at the Kalamazoo conference in 1996. Michael Awkward, the Director of an African-American Studies Institute rather than a medievalist, was invited to present as a specialist in race studies. Hahn notes how Awkward's presentation highlighted the whiteness of the conference, arguing that:

> his visible presence as a lone black man in an overwhelmingly white milieu, his announced interest in racial discourse, and his status as an outsider/nonmedievalist did more to make difference an issue among these historically engaged scholars than did any of the evidence or argument he offered in his talk.[12]

Awkward's presentation led to a themed issue on "Concepts of Race and Ethnicity in the Middle Ages" with Hahn's essay as the introduction. Hahn identifies as a white academic, a rare moment of identification in academic discourse that foregrounds instead of making invisible the whiteness of academia as an institution, a whiteness that is the result of socio-historical and institutional practices.

While this invisible whiteness is not unique to medieval studies, the extent to which the imagined medieval is seen as a race-free ideal is praised by contemporary white supremacists who politicize and mythologize the vision they see in Tolkien in ways that are similar to Nazi politicization of the Germanic mythos which Tolkien criticized in his 1941 letter to his son, Michael.[13] The idealization of the white Middle Ages in popular culture and among supremacists makes it all the more important to foreground recent changes in scholarship and the implications for Tolkien studies. The historical whiteness of academia and the difficulties of changing the institutional and cultural patterns that created that system are the primary reasons I argue for the necessity of resolving the perceived deadlock and exclusions that have hampered consideration of constructions of race in Tolkien's work, work that has already begun in the scholarship discussed in this essay.

Jane Chance has contributed in major ways to the rise of interdisciplinary Tolkien studies that supports scholarship on race as well as class, gender, and sexuality. She has not only shown through her own scholarship that medievalists can apply postmodern critical theories relating to class, gender, race, and sexuality to Tolkien's legendarium but has also supported the development of others' scholarship in two important ways. First, in 2001, she founded "Tolkien at Kalamazoo," the sponsoring organization for Tolkien studies at the International Congress on Medieval Studies; the group continues to be active to the present day. Second, she published three scholarly anthologies featuring a range of scholarship on Tolkien's work, some of which originated in presentations at Kalamazoo; these anthologies include some of the earliest work on race in Tolkien studies. The anthologies are *Tolkien the Medievalist*

(2003), third in Routledge's series on "Medieval Religion and Culture"; *Tolkien and the Invention of Myth* (2004) from the University Press of Kentucky; and *Tolkien's Modern Middle Ages* (co-edited with Alfred K. Siewers in 2005), from Palgrave Macmillan.

Textual Analysis

In this section, I discuss scholarship published between 2003 and 2013 which focuses primarily on textual analysis for the purpose of analyzing Tolkien's fiction or Jackson's film. The majority of the essays focus on the novel (seven); three focus entirely on the film, and one deals with how the film has impacted perceptions of the book. Primary and secondary sources used in addition to the novel or film include classical and medieval sources, histories, biographies, and Tolkien's letters and scholarly essays. An occasional reference to popular media commentary on racism in Tolkien's work (or in Jackson's film) is made, but primarily for the purpose of debunking charges of racism rather than analyzing the reception of the fiction or film.[14] The organization of this section is chronological until the last four essays. Two of the last four are grouped together because both deal with the question of anti-Semitism in Tolkien's work.[15] The final two essays end the section because, while primarily focusing on texts, they have short sections in which the authors attempt to move beyond interpreting the text to show applicability in the primary world although, as I discuss below, the potential for synthesis is not fully realized. [16]

One of the earliest published articles to move beyond using "race" as a neutral descriptor for different cultures in Middle-earth is Jonathan Evans' "The Anthropology of Arda: Creation, Theology, and the Race of Men" (2003), published in Chance's *Tolkien the Medievalist*.[17] While Evans references briefly "the anthropology of the real world," however, he is referring to linguistic anthropology, specifically ethnocentric group naming, the tendency of human groups to coin names for themselves that reflect their sense of superiority while coining dehumanizing names for outsiders.[18] This discussion of a standard ethnocentrism in all human languages ignores historical specifics of colonialism and racial hierarchies. Evans analyzes linguistic and theological elements from the classical and Germanic world that influenced Tolkien's creation of the various races of Middle-earth. Evans' claim that Tolkien's choice to place humans as one of a number of multiple sentient races creates a sense of "cultural, racial, or *ethnic* depth" has been quoted by a number of later scholars. However, the essay is primarily focused on the theological aspect of Tolkien's work and the question of spiritual hierarchies rather than the socio-historical results of hierarchical constructions of race or ethnicity. Concluding that Tolkien's creation myth does include a spiritual hierarchy based on race, Evans emphasizes that "one central unifying theological theme [is that] – all are *fallen*."[19]

Two essays published in Chance's *Tolkien's Modern Middle Ages* (2005) focus on the influence of medieval European sources about other races in the primary world on Tolkien's work.[20] Brian McFadden's "Fear of Difference, Fear of Death: The *Sigelwara*, Tolkien's Swertings, and Racial Difference," and Jane Chance's "Tolkien and the Other: Race and Gender in Middle-earth" draw on similar medieval sources about the Sigelwara, or Ethiopians, as well as Tolkien's philological scholarship, to discuss the extent to which these medieval texts influenced Tolkien's characters. Despite using similar sources, the two essays make different, though not oppositional, claims. McFadden begins his essay by referencing a contemporary review of the racial patterns in the film; he cites Tolkien's own experiences and works to argue that he opposed racism. McFadden acknowledges some elements of Tolkien's work, including the Orcs, can be seen as racist. Chance's argument is broader in focus, encompassing race, gender, and class issues, and makes a stronger defense of the extent to which Tolkien's scholarship and his subversion of fantasy conventions show readers the danger of discrimination and the need to accept differences. She concludes that marriages between individuals from different species are one of the most important elements of this theme of love and reconciliation.[21] A number of later scholars consider further the conflicting meanings of Tolkien's intercultural marriages in the context of race and postcolonialism.[22]

The impact of Peter Jackson's film upon the discussions of race in Tolkien studies has been remarked upon by a number of scholars. The first published essays on race in Jackson's film appeared in the (2004) publication of the J. R. R. Tolkien issue of *Modern Fiction Studies*.[23] This publication is an important milestone in Tolkien studies since the journal, published by Johns Hopkins University Press, focuses on "theoretically engaged and historically informed articles on modernist and contemporary fiction" (*MFS*) and thus publishes work on a much broader range of genres and topics than specialized journals.[24] The *MFS* issue contains three essays that analyze race from different perspectives.

The first, by Anderson Rearick III, focuses on the question of the impact of the film on perceptions of Tolkien's work rather than interpreting the film.[25] Although Rearick's argument appears to consider a question of reception, his work is primarily based on explication of the primary text, and the purpose of his essay is to defend Tolkien's work and Tolkien himself from the charges of racism. Rearick quotes a fictional discussion about Tolkien's racism between two characters in a novel by Jonathan Coe as evidence that discussion of race in Tolkien has been restricted to fans because of the academic marginalization of his work, and then addresses internet articles by two British critics, one of them an academic, who identify Tolkien's work as racist because of Jackson's film.[26] Summarizing the criticisms in the media, Rearick points out errors caused by critics who are responding primarily to the film rather than Tolkien's work. Rearick notes the lack of analysis of the novel but concludes that the "concerns" should be responded to, and that the "silence of the academy must end."[27] Rearick considers evidence from Tolkien's life and his letters as well as summarizing critics who disagree with those who interpret the work as racist. Rearick's conclusion is that if readers consider the "overall message of the work rather than … particular battles or physical descriptions," they will see that the work's embodiment of the Christian worldview of renouncing power and not focusing on outward appearances proves that it cannot be racist.[28] As Rearick acknowledges, his claim depends on readers distinguishing between "cultural Christianity and the biblical text" in their interpretation of images of light and darkness, a distinction that requires agreement with the assumption that the text can be abstracted from historical and cultural contexts.[29]

Scholarship specifically about Peter Jackson's film, rather than the impact of the film on the reception of Tolkien, can also take a text-based approach with the primary texts being the film and related materials. Two essays analyzing the film appeared in 2006 and 2008. In a 2006 collection on Peter Jackson's film, *From Hobbits to Hollywood*, Cynthia Fuchs' essay analyzes the two "related mythologies" of Gollum in *The Return of the King* film as a "story of race."[30] Fuchs focuses on Gollum as the most extreme Other in a film that deals with many racial constructions, analyzing his loss of self to the Ring and the CGI aspects of the character as markers of his isolation. Although Fuchs mentions postcolonial theories briefly and cites Kim's postcolonial analysis of the film trilogy (discussed in the next section), this essay does not move beyond analysis of the film text to questions of production or reception.

Sean Redmond's "The Whiteness of the Rings" (2008) is the only essay I know of to apply the theory of whiteness studies in Tolkien studies.[31] Focusing on Jackson's *The Fellowship of the Ring*, Redmond acknowledges the binary operation of the racialized images of whiteness as purity and goodness and blackness as an evil Other, but then goes on to argue that the film's construction of whiteness is "contradictory in its representations of whiteness, and more critical of particular forms of whiteness as they are given representational definition."[32] Analyzing in detail the figures of Saruman, Arwen, and Galadriel as embodying both idealized and "hyper-" whiteness, Redmond also considers the extent to which the Ring, by granting invisibility, can be read as the "ideological and political marker of the white race–not to be seen as a race at all."[33] Although Redmond mentions some external evidence—primarily the filmography of Liv Taylor and Cate Blanchett and the CGI techniques used in the film—his primary focus is the analysis of the film as text that reproduces the images/constructions of whiteness.

Focusing on the Orcs, the characters most problematic for many in regard to constructions of race in Tolkien's work, Robert Tally challenges the assumption that they are the most inherently evil of Tolkien's characters. In "Let Us Now Praise Famous Orcs: Simple Humanity in Tolkien's Inhuman Creatures." Tally does not try to argue that Orcs are good. Instead, he attempts to "trouble the facile assumption that they are only and inherently evil."[34] Drawing on Tolkien's different origin stories for the Orcs and on close readings of key scenes (the Orcs' relatively humane treatment of Merry and Pippin, and the conversation between Shagrat and Gorbag) as well as Tom Shippey's arguments about the morality of Orcs, Tally argues that Tolkien takes opportunities to "humanize" the Orcs. While primarily focused on the issues of good and evil, Tally argues that charges of racism in Tolkien's work based on the characters of the Orcs cannot be easily supported because of how differently the Orcs are treated from the different groups, or races, of men who are fighting for Sauron.

One of the more contentious questions relating to race and Tolkien's works is the issue of whether or not similarities between Tolkien's Dwarves and stereotypes of Jews reflect anti-Semitic views. Tolkien's ideas about the Dwarves and the influences on them changed over time as shown by his letters and interviews as well as the multiple drafts of parts of the legendarium developed for *The Lord of the Rings* and in the years afterward.[35] Tolkien's published work, including poetry, fiction, critical and theoretical essays, and posthumously published volumes edited by his son, Christopher, as well as letters, includes epitextual and paratextual writing about his legendarium, enough to complicate any simple attribution of monolithic beliefs. Two scholarly essays deal with the question of anti-Semitism in Tolkien's work. Whether these essays should be included in the discussion on race in Tolkien studies can be debated. One argument would be to set them aside on the grounds that anti-Semitism is a different type of oppression than racism because membership in a religion is not the same as race. However, while I have set aside essays dealing with National Socialism and Fascism, I have chosen to include the conflicting essays on anti-Semitism.[36]

I include these essays for two reasons: first, the two present oppositional views and claims based on the same evidence and attempt to deal with questions of Tolkien's personal beliefs as well as presenting interpretations of his work; however, the second essay is framed as a direct rebuttal to the claims of the first. So, their evidence and rhetorical structures are similar to the scholarship dealing with race that leads to the perception of deadlock because of unacknowledged differences of methodologies. The second reason is the strength of arguments from scholars who maintain that the construction of "Jews" as a raced group has been a part of mainstream Christian culture since the Middle Ages.[37] Differing and indeed oppositional interpretations of texts is the default in literary and cultural studies, but in this case, as Hoiem has noted in regard to other scholarship, the conflict between Brackman and Vink is based to a great extent upon the different methodological assumptions underlying the definition of key terms.[38]

In (2010), Rebecca Brackmann's "'Dwarves are Not Heroes': Antisemitism and Dwarves in Tolkien" was published in *Mythlore*. Brackmann draws on a theoretical approach to "antisemitism" which is signaled by not using the standardized capital letter or hyphen; she cites Gavin Langmuir's argument that the "views originated entirely in the Gentile culture which produced them, and do not reflect Jewish beliefs or cultural values."[39] Scholars such as Langmuir and Hyam Maccoby argue that the category of "Jew" is thus a racialized one. Brackmann traces the development of the characters of Dwarves from Tolkien's early to his later writings, looking at the novels and his letters. She also cites other publications, ranging from Shakespeare to twentieth-century medical essays and popular novels, which she argues also express European "antisemitic" beliefs. Her conclusion is that while there can be critical disagreement on the issue of a "antisemitism", the study of "changes, gaps, alterations, and biases in Tolkien's text" is a legitimate focus of study and should not be dismissed as judging past writers by present standards.[40]

Renée Vink's 2013 article in *Tolkien Studies* makes her opposition to Brackmann's claim clear from the start: her purpose is to "[undermine] Brackmann's thesis and [exonerate] Tolkien from being a (closet) anti-Semite."[41] Vink contrasts arguments made by John Rateliff in 2011 regarding the origin of the Dwarves in *The Silmarillion* with Brackmann's reading, providing detailed summaries of both scholars' work. Vink's use of Rateliff's analysis and her interpretation of the same primary sources that Brackmann uses lead Vink to a different conclusion regarding Tolkien's work. She argues that Brackmann "turns the analogy [that Dwarves resemble Jews] into an allegory," and that "[t]here is no reason to assume that anti-Semitism of any form of Jewish stereotyping contributes to Tolkien's depiction of Dwarves."[42]

The final two articles in this section are examples of the difficulties of my categorization scheme: while both deal largely with Tolkien's text, both also include sections which attempt to move beyond the textual focus and to make claims about applicability in the primary world relating to the reception of Tolkien's novel. Both show the potential for synthesis that I discuss in the third section of this essay, but the limited amount of space given to the issue of applicability, compared to the space dedicated to in-depth explication and analysis of texts in both, show the potential is not fully realized. The first analyzes how the reception of Peter Jackson's film has caused Tolkien's work to be considered in the context of multiculturalism resulting in "a specifically racist interpretation of Tolkien's narrative"; the second considers Tolkien's mixed marriages and their applicability to marriages in the primary world, especially the rise in rates of interracial marriage.[43]

While both essays do an excellent job of interpreting Tolkien's work, the sections on reception and applicability do not move the essays fully into cultural or reception studies for two reasons. The first is that the sections showing the interaction of Tolkien's text(s) with the world are relatively brief and little evidence is provided for the reception claims; the second is that both authors privilege, to different degrees, the question of authorial intentionality. While a wide range of methods and standards can be grouped under the broad category of reception studies, as part of the larger field of cultural studies, one shared assumption is that how an audience receives or interprets a text (whether one is looking at individual reader responses or surveys of film viewers) need not be judged against how well or closely their reception or interpretation conforms to an author's intention, however, that intention may be discerned, a complicated question in itself.[44]

Sandra Baliff Straubhaar's "Myth, Late Roman History, and Multiculturalism in Tolkien's Middle-earth" (2004), published in Chance's *Tolkien and the Invention of Myth*, makes intriguing use of a mixture of classical primary and contemporary secondary sources to move from analysis of Roman influences on Tolkien's work to refuting online critical commentary on *The Fellowship of the Ring* and *The Two Towers*. In the first part of her essay, which is firmly grounded in historical sources, she focuses on how mixed marriages in Gondor and Rohan were influenced by Tacitus' work on Germanic tribes and by the barbarian historians who wrote after the fall of Rome. She then discusses the extent to which Jackson's film resulted in online criticism of Tolkien's work. She analyzes and responds at some length to two popular media examples of critics who argue for "a specifically racist interpretation of Tolkien's narrative" in opinion pieces published in newspapers.[45] The two are academics trained in cultural studies: one, a doctoral student at the University of Stockholm, and the other a faculty member at the University of Warwick. Rather than analyzing the criticism in terms of the theoretical approaches, as Hoiem notes, Straubhaar engages with the arguments in order to refute them, pointing out errors, and evaluating their arguments and evidence against academic criteria as does Rearick, discussed earlier in this section; the interview with Steven Shapiro, a lecturer at the University of Warwick, was also one of two texts chosen by Rearick to discuss. Straubhaar introduces her refutation of claims of racism by stating it "seems to be safe to conclude a polycultured, polylingual world is absolutely central to Tolkien's narrated Middle-earth and is easily perceptible as such by many readers and filmgoers—**while specific topical applicability comes and goes with current events, in addition to clearly running counter to the author's own stated intentions**" (emphasis added).[46] This rhetorical frame implicitly rejects key critical assumptions of reception study and phrases the claim about the "themes of multiculturalism and hybridity" as "indisputable," removing the topic from academic or critical dialog completely. The phrasing implicitly identifies readers who "easily perceive" the "polycultured, polylingual world" as correctly receiving Tolkien's message while those readers who perceive "topical applicability" different from "the author's own stated intentions" as incorrectly receiving the message. Fictional portrayals of polyculturalism and hybridity are assumed to be more powerful than historical and contemporary racist hierarchies.[47]

Hope Rogers' 2013 essay published in *Tolkien Studies*, "No Triumph without Loss: Problems of Intercultural Marriage," focuses on Tolkien's intercultural marriages and their applicability to the primary world. Contextualizing her work within scholarly debates over race in Tolkien studies, she characterizes the state of scholarship as "deadlocked,": "Among scholars analyzing the applicability of Tolkien's races to those of the real world, however, the conversation has become deadlocked, polarized over one of the most common criticisms of *The Lord of the Rings*: Tolkien's supposed racism."[48] Rogers analyzes relevant scholarship and does an extensive close reading of intercultural marriages in Tolkien's legendarium. She identifies problems those in the fictional world who marry outside their culture must face, showing the complexities of Tolkien's narrative constructions of difference.

The majority of Rogers' essay is a textual analysis, but a short section (two and a half pages) focuses on "Applicability." In this section, she references scholarship on the lives and experiences of mixed-race couples and the children of those couples in Britain. She states she will not argue that Tolkien would have been in favor of such marriages during his life and then provides statistical information on the rate of interracial marriage in Britain in the present. Rogers' claims in this section are ambiguous: one reason is her claim that Tolkien "blurs boundaries between race and culture and often addresses [cultural] difference rather than race per se."[49] An intercultural marriage need not be interracial, but the statistical information she provides specifies interracial couples. The second reason relates to the lack of any connection between Tolkien's work and the data on marriage in Britain. Although she discusses Tolkien's work in the section on "Applicability," Rogers does not attempt to claim any causal relationship between Tolkien's work and the growing acceptance of interracial marriages in Britain. However, the lack of any type of connection means that no specific claim about applicability can be made about Tolkien's work despite his exploration of intercultural marriages. The essay is a strong and ambitious attempt to consider the issue of differences including but not limited to racial differences in Tolkien's world and its applicability to the primary world. I wish that the section on "Applicability" could have been extended because the implications are fascinating but acknowledge it would be difficult if not impossible to do in the space of a single essay and would require not only a separate publication but a different methodology. As it stands, Rogers' essay does not make clear the connections between Tolkien's imagined and fictional cultures and the issues around interracial marriages in Britain.

Textual and Primary World Interactions

In this section, I discuss scholarship published between 2003 and 2015 which focuses on how Tolkien's work as well as adaptations and derivative works interact with the primary world. One essay focuses primarily on Tolkien's work while two focus on the film; two consider book and film, and one analyzes race in *The Lord of the Rings* video games. The structure of the section is chronological. Sociocultural and historical evidence in this group of essays includes: online fan responses, the colonial history of New Zealand and the economic context of the production of Jackson's film, Shakespeare's *Othello*, postcolonial histories of Early Modern Europe, the history of Britain's nineteenth-century colonialism, scientific racism, industrialization, and the production of games. The methodologies in the work discussed here include postcolonial, queer theory, and materialist adaptation studies.[50]

In 2003, the same year that Jane Chance published *Tolkien the Medievalist*, Pascal Nicklas' essay "The Paradox of Racism in Tolkien" appeared in *Inklings: Jahrbuch für Literatur und Ästhetik*, a German annual journal.[51] Nicklas argues that Tolkien's work and his expressed opinions on race and anti-Semitism are paradoxical and supports the claim by citing online debates about racism that occurred in response to Jackson's film. Rather than select several online articles to refute, however, Nicklas describes the results of a 2003 Google search that resulted in a list of 6000 sources. Although he does not cite specifics from the search results, his characterization of the range of responses is similar to the range noted by other scholars: "The spectrum stretches from neonazis hailing the advent of caucasian supremacy to terribly concerned p.c. worries."[52] Nicklas, like Rearick and Straubhaar, identifies textual errors in the online commentary but does not locate those errors in any given position on Tolkien's attitudes about race. In addition to the online debate, Nicklas acknowledges the economics of production, noting the extent to which Tolkien's work is a "money-printing machine" for the publishers and the Tolkien estate.[53] Other materialist aspects of the essay include the concept of racism as socially constructed and circulated, the history of scientific racism, and the documented academic resistance to it that developed in Europe during the period between the two World Wars.[54] As well as considering the socio-historical context of Tolkien's lifetime and the current context for Jackson's film, Nicklas explicitly rejects the authority of the author's intentions and privileges the authority of readers in different contexts to create different interpretations: "[t]he intention of the author is no guideline for the reader: there cannot be much debate about that. **What is really interesting about the whole thing is what we make of it** … In Tolkien the racist structures are noticed now because **racism has been a big topic for the past ten, fifteen years**" (emphasis added).[55]

Two of the three essays that discuss race and Tolkien in the *Modern Fiction Studies* Tolkien theme issue (2004) use postcolonial and queer theories. Sue Kim's "Beyond Black and White: Race and Postmodernism in *The Lord of the Rings* Film" argues for the necessity of creating postmodern readings not only about the Jackson film but, by implication, about Tolkien's work as well. She notes an "inability to discuss race," arguing that "in order to understand race in the *The Lord of the Rings* films (a rich and productive discussion has yet to take place on the novels), we find ourselves required to grapple with postmodernism in its many incarnations."[56] In order to do that, scholars have to move beyond the semiotic level to consider "how the films function within and reproduce the logic and process of postmodern, neoliberal global capitalism, both drawing on and burying issues of race."[57] Kim's is the first major production study of either fiction or film that I am aware of that focuses on the impact of race, embedding discussion of the text in an analysis of the how the work "epitomizes postmodernity in a number of significant aesthetic, technical, economic, epistemological, ethical, and political ways"[58] She analyzes how the film's constructions of the Orcs, especially the Uruk-hai, echoes visual and cultural representations of the Maori in the context of New Zealand's colonial history and of the economic impact the loss of manufacturing jobs in the country had on the Maori.[59] Kim's analysis includes the global and transnational aspects of the labor that went into creating, marketing, and distributing the film.

Considering critical and theoretical postmodernisms as well as Tolkien scholars' criticism of postmodernist commentary, Kim argues that a postmodern approach does not require complete relativism of morality or ethics. In the section titled "Selective Applicability," she points out how critics, scholars, and filmmakers can and do associate Tolkien's (and Jackson's) works with specific nineteenth- and twentieth-century political issues, such as industrialism and modern wars, while disallowing applicability of other contemporary political issues such as race and gender.[60] Kim's essay is paired with Rearick's essay as the only two in the section titled "*The Lord of the Rings* and Race." The difference in their claims and methodology is clear although they agree on the necessity for more scholarship on the question of race in Tolkien studies. Also in the *Modern Fiction Studies* issue, though with two other essays in a section titled "Queering *The Lord of the Rings*," Jes Battis presents an intersectional analysis in "Gazing Upon Sauron: Hobbits, Elves, and the Queering of the Postcolonial Optic" (2004).[61] Battis focuses his intersectional study primarily on the Hobbits "as racialized and sexualized" beings.[62] Embedded within his argument concerning the queerness of the Hobbits is a postcolonial reading (drawn from the theoretical concept of Trinh T. Minh-ha's "Inappropriate Other") analyzing Hobbits as "ambivalent colonial subjects."[63]

In the 2006 anthology, *From Hobbits to Hollywood*, Lianne McLarty presents a materialist analysis of Tolkien's novel and Jackson's film. Reading Tolkien's novel after viewing the film, McLarty compares her experience with the preconceptions that had kept her from reading it previously. Believing that the work was no more than a "conservative romantic fantasy," she was surprised by the text which she characterizes as magical but "[anchored]…in the social relations of modernization and industry."[64] She discusses both novel and film in their socio-historical contexts, specifically industrialization, and their interaction with political ideas. McLarty's analysis is multi-layered and multi-topical, focusing on the politics of gender, race, and class in the film and, to a lesser extent, in the novel. Her analysis draws on the materialist concept of the works as products of "popular commodity culture," and her discussion of political ideologies results in an intersectional approach that explores the concept of multiple genders created by the intersections of race and class. McLarty argues that the book and film are similar in examining multiple masculinities in conflict between industrialism and the natural world. Her primary argument concerning race involves the whiteness of the dominant masculinities and the darkness of the opposing masculinities while denying that whiteness/darkness are binary and ahistorical categories:

"[d]egrees of whiteness depend on culture and social class and it is through a class displacement that the 'less than white' character of the army is secured."[65]

Robert Gehl's postcolonial reading of Tolkien's work draws on scholarship done on race and colonialism in Shakespeare's work and in the early modern period in general. In his essay in the 2007 collection on *Tolkien and Shakespeare*, "Something is Stirring in the East: Racial Identity, Confronting the 'Other,' and Miscegenation in *Othello* and *The Lord of the Rings*," Gehl compares the handling of race in both works as examples of the historical attitudes of British culture toward outsiders. Gehl makes a specific disclaimer situating his position within the context of a polarized discourse: "This is not to suggest that Tolkien was virulently racist; I disagree with the critics who argue that *LotR* [sic] is about whites rising against a tide of black-skinned foes. However, I also disagree with critics such as Sandra Straubhaar and Patrick Curry who look to intercultural marriages…as evidence of Tolkien's careful multiculturalism."[66] Gehl's purpose is to argue the importance of race as an area of analysis and to highlight connections between the ways in which race was constructed in Shakespeare's time and the scientific racism of the nineteenth century. He argues for the need to encourage "heightened awareness" of those connections. As do Hoiem, Nicklas, Fimi, Kim, and Young, Gehl argues that the political aspects of race in Tolkien's work, like the political aspects of industrialism and war, should become a part of readers' and scholars' discussions about Tolkien, especially given the affection for Tolkien's work expressed by white supremacist groups, such as the British National Party and the Aryan Nations.

An essay on race in the *Lord of the Rings* games by Helen Young was published in 2015 and analyzes the operation of franchising agreements that dictate structural elements of the games, the narrative conventions of the games, both as adaptations of Tolkien's novel and Jackson's film and in the context of fantasy video games as a genre, and the interactive aspects of gameplay.[67] Young does not analyze any one of the games (twenty-two are listed) in detail; instead, her argument considers broader issues of legalities of ownership affecting narrative conventions and the interactive nature of play, concluding that the franchising of games based on Tolkien's and Jackson's works, with close ties to the film industry, "can perpetuate problematic representations and constructions of race by the extensive reuse of both graphic and narrative elements," but since new content can be created there is the potential for the "[exploration of] not only its imagined world but also its ideologies."[68]

Synthesis

In this section, I consider four works published between 2005 and 2010 in which the scholars blend close readings of Tolkien's text with socio-historical approaches that emphasize the impact of medieval and nineteenth-century constructions of race on Tolkien's work. The four works include the first monograph that deals specifically with race in Tolkien's work, namely, that of Fimi. Unlike the two previous sections, all the works in this section focus primarily on texts from Tolkien's legendarium rather than on Jackson's film. The works are discussed in order of publication. The works, while of different lengths and dealing with a range of topics, have important similarities in approaches: they tend toward conscious and well-developed inter- and multi-disciplinary approaches, drawing from anthropology, art history, intellectual history, and sociology as well as literary studies.

In an essay printed in *Tolkien Studies* in 2005, "World Creation as Colonization: British Imperialism in 'Aldarion and Erendis,'" Elizabeth Massa Hoiem addresses Straubhaar's and Chance's interpretations of Tolkien's marriages in the context of multi- and cross-culturalism in his work. Hoiem references discussions of racism in the wake of the film as an example of "a larger, polarized disagreement in Tolkien studies," but she does not see the conflict as a deadlock around opposing interpretations of racism/celebration of diversity nor does she spend much time on the issue. Instead, she identifies one cause as disciplinary differences between scholars.[69] Hoiem applies postcolonial theory to "Aldarion and Erendis" to argue that Tolkien's critique of imperialism is complicated because of the extent to which his characters who are colonizers are also sub-creators. Acknowledging that postcolonial scholarship focuses primarily on mechanisms of racism and ethnocentrism, she argues that the complexity of Tolkien's work "offers [a] sophisticated criticism of British imperialism even as it makes use of the colonial rhetoric that saturated the literature of its time."[70] This essay opens up possibilities for future work not only on Tolkien, but also on genre fantasy as a contemporary literary form connected to the history of colonization.[71] Hoiem argues that the period in which "Aldarion and Erendis" was written is the late modernist, a period in which anthropological and folkloric interest was focused on the history and culture of the Anglo-Saxons in England rather than the cultures of British colonies. Like Brackmann, although with a different topic and approach, Hoiem emphasizes the importance of the inconsistencies and fictionality not only of literature but of the social and cultural myths that make up dominant narratives such as anti-Semitism (Brackmann) and imperialism (Hoiem).

In the sole monograph on race in Tolkien's work which has been published so far, *Tolkien, Race, and Cultural History: From Fairies to Hobbits* (2009), Dimitra Fimi argues that the impact of cultural studies and related critical theories on literary studies during the second half of the twentieth century has also affected Tolkien studies, allowing for opportunities to widen the scope of methodologies to include theories relating to alterity and intersectionality, including constructions of race. Fimi's in-depth analysis of Tolkien's legendarium from his earliest poems about fairies through the published fictions traces how his work shifted from the genre of myth to history. Her analysis is grounded in cultural and intellectual history including the impact of popular and visual cultural influences of the time on Tolkien's work. I consider this book a requirement for any who wish to consider questions concerning race in Tolkien's work, especially Chap. 9, "A Hierarchical World," which analyzes the changes in constructions of race during Tolkien's lifetime as well as his engagement in the public discourses.

The scientific racism of the nineteenth century is referenced in a number of works discussed in this section, but journal length limits restrict how much time can be spent covering historical background in an essay. Fimi's overview of the intellectual, and cultural, and scientific developments of the nineteenth century, which theorized "race" as a biological reality, reflecting "fixed physical characteristics and mental abilities" as well as the simultaneous challenges to that ideology, is detailed, deep, and convincing. Her monograph is grounded in contemporary historical scholarship on nineteenth-century movements such as Social Darwinism and Eugenics, the role scientific racism played in the genocidal actions of the Nazis, and the way in which later developments in genetics and evolution discredited the earlier ideologies. She also covers primary sources such as Tolkien's letters and commentary published after his death to show his awareness of these cultural conflicts. Fimi analyzes in detail evidence that others have mentioned briefly to show his opposition to "Nazi ideas and even… the use of the term 'race' itself" while pointing out the extent to which the academic fields of philology and

Anglo-Saxon studies included the idea of "race" as important components of national identity and language.[72]

Like Nicklas, Fimi concludes that "there seems to be a contradiction between Tolkien's beliefs concerning race—as these are expressed in his letters and works of scholarship—and the 'racial' ideology found in the Middle-earth cosmos."[73] Fimi's work avoids the simplistic stereotype of "a man of his time" that assumes a homogeneity of the past by providing detailed evidence of the cultural conflicts during his lifetime that are part of the shift in attitudes about race during the twentieth century as well as evidence of how Tolkien's awareness of the changes resulted in shifts in his language and work. I have found no better summary of the complexities of Tolkien's world than: "The blending of all these different strands make Middle-earth complex and unpredictable, a fantasy world that reproduces some of the concepts and prejudices of the 'primary' world while at the same time questioning, challenging and transforming others."[74]

A similar sense of the historical depth and cultural heterogeneity that Fimi conveys about the nineteenth and twentieth centuries' constructions of race can be found in Margaret's Sinex's "Monsterized Saracens: Tolkien's Haradrim and Other Medieval 'Fantasy Products'" concerning the medieval Christian constructions of "Saracens." Published in *Tolkien Studies* in 2010, Sinex's essay covers earlier relevant scholarship on medieval sources for Tolkien's characters as well as Fimi's analysis of theories of race circulating during Tolkien's lifetime. Sinex cites recent postcolonial medieval scholarship to emphasize the extent to which the "Saracens" of the Christian Middle Ages are fictionalized, imaginary characters. She analyzes the influence of the late medieval romances' construction of "Saracens" on Tolkien's work rather than the earlier medieval sources considered by other scholars. Sinex's argument foregrounds the complexity of categories of marginalized groups in medieval thought as well as changes and gaps in those attitudes at the time in addition to changes in contemporary awareness of the past because of changes in historical scholarship since Tolkien's time. Sinex identifies three "othering processes of the Christian West" that she sees as "especially relevant to the Haradrim": the tendency toward binary categories, the belief in the impact of climate and geography on "races," and color imagery, specifically red and gold.[75] As does Hoiem, Sinex applies postcolonial theories to Tolkien's work, specifically the Haradrim. However, Sinex's article utilizes postcolonial scholarship from medievalists. Like Fimi, Sinex considers the impact of visual culture on Tolkien's work, drawing on the work of art historians to discuss the medieval Christian meanings assigned to the use of red and yellow in the portrayal of monstrous "Saracens."

The final essay in this section does not appear in a specialized journal. Helen Young's "Diversity and Difference: Cosmopolitanism and *The Lord of the Rings*" was published in the *Journal of the Fantastic in the Arts.* Her approach draws on genre fantasy studies and contemporary sociological concepts, and she argues that since fantasy as a genre involves worlds populated by "different, often mutually suspicious or inimical species such as elves, dwarves, humans, and goblins," that "[investigations] of racial and cultural difference might be illuminating."[76] Young draws on the sociological concept of cosmopolitanism, which has been developed by scholars such as Robert Fine. The definition of cosmopolitanism provided by Young is of "a set of sociological theories which are concerned with overcoming national prejudices, recognizing the mutual interdependence of global humanity, and advocating world citizenship, justice, and democracy."[77] Applying this concept to a close reading of key elements of *The Lord of the Rings*, Young concludes that the theory "[provides] a positive framework through which *The Lord of the Rings* may be read as a vision of a modern racially and culturally diverse world."[78]

Looking Ahead

As this essay shows, Tolkien scholarship has already begun to engage in those larger discussions relating to race, due in no small part to Jane Chance's contributions to Tolkien studies.[79] The amount of scholarship published over the last twelve years is relatively small although recent years have seen a marked increase. Some are concerned that dealing with the charged topic of race and racisms will lead to polarization (Rogers) or result in conflicts over disciplinary differences relating to methodology (Hoiem, Kim). Those concerns are valid. However, I tend to agree with those who argue that the consequences of refusing to engage with this topic are greater in the long run. I would add that the potential consequences are not solely intellectual, in regard to the scope and quality of published scholarship, but will affect the courses we teach in future and our current and future students. Debates in early 2016 about sexism in Anglo-Saxon and medieval studies, sparked by a post on Allen J. Frantzen's personal blog, resulted in responses by a number of medievalists arguing against the anti-feminist and sexist post. Frantzen, a well-known and recently retired medievalist, titled his post "How to Fight Your Way Out of the Feminist Fog" and incorporated anti-feminist language associated with the misogynistic men's rights online groups.[80] Dorothy Kim, a medievalist at Vassar University, has written about the extent to which calls by scholars of color against racism in medieval studies are treated differently by white medievalists, including white feminists, resulting in the tendency for the field to "[consistently uphold] whiteness as a category."[81] Kim notes that "medievalism and apparently Tolkien is used as a crutch to uphold that whiteness."[82] She continues, asking two questions that have direct implications for Tolkien scholars: "Why are there not attempts to read, research, learn, and decolonize our historical pasts and reframe medieval futures? Why is it so difficult to read critical race theory and the work of historians of race?"[83] Discussing "white supremacist and patriarchal things being written [online] by medievalists in Medieval Studies," she asks "[i]magine what that classroom feels and looks like to an undergraduate or graduate student of color. What exactly are students of color supposed to do with a post like 'Three Cheers for White Men'?"[84] Kim points out that the changing demographics in the USA and Britain mean that there are growing numbers of students of color in our classrooms, yet the faculty teaching those students are overwhelmingly white as well as largely male.

While no accurate studies exist on the demographics of Tolkien fandom, or on the larger science fiction and fantasy fandom, the existence of fans of color of fantastic literature and media can no longer be denied. Major internet debates became visible in 2009 that highlighted the realities and experiences of fans of color, and there are a growing number of writers of color producing science fiction and fantasy.[85] Those writers are also part of the discussion that exists on the issues of race and fantasy, often engaging with the genre and reader expectations as a *Salon* article featuring N. K. Jemison and David Anthony Durham shows. The extent to which the genre of epic fantasy novels is associated with a Eurocentric perspective was established by Tolkien and the white writers who followed him, resulting in epic fantasy written by writers from other countries and cultures being excluded.[86] The increasing numbers and prominence of writers of color writing speculative fiction are also reflected in the work of the Carl Brandon Society which was founded in 1999. The Society is a group dedicated to the mission of "[increasing] racial and ethnic diversity in the production of and audience for speculative fiction."[87] Just as it is clear that (white) women were always readers and fans of Tolkien's work, so too is it clear that people of color have participated in creating a global readership that has caused Tolkien's work and Jackson's film to be considered among the major cultural phenomena of the twentieth century.

There are a number of possibilities for future work, which are already being explored in the scholarship as well as new approaches. These possibilities require moving away from the perceived need to "defend" Tolkien, or Tolkien's work and depend in part upon the rise of interdisciplinary and multi-disciplinary theories and approaches in both "medieval" and "contemporary" period studies as well as the willingness to consider the implications not only of the circumstances of production, already present to some extent in Tolkien studies, but also reception theory which includes the study of Tolkien fans, as well as the willingness to expand the focus of scholarship from Tolkien's fictions to the significant number of adaptations, transformations, and derivative works that have been and continue to be created.

Drout and Wynne made the case in 2000 that, based on Shippey's *Author of the Century*, there was no longer any need to "defend" Tolkien's work in terms of aesthetics or against the claims that its popularity made his work inappropriate for literary scholars to deal with. As they point out, another reason that defensiveness was no longer necessary was the passage of time: "[y]ounger critics, without personal investment in the literary politics of the beginning and middle of the twentieth century, and without memories of 60's Tolkien fanaticism or mania, are less hostile," and added that their colleagues at Wheaton who "specialized in 20th-century literature, modernism, Victorianism, and children's literature are not only open to but frankly excited about using Tolkien to test their own theories and approaches."[88] Similarly, Fimi, in her ninth chapter's conclusion, titled "Tolkien and the charge of racism," notes the impracticality of answering "the question of whether Tolkien can be charged with racism or whether his works reflect racist attitudes," given the historical changes and cultural differences of the cultures of Britain and the USA over the past centuries.[89]

I would add to these arguments the evident fact that, as shown by the existing scholarship, choosing selected letters and invoking authorial intentionality to defend Tolkien has not been sufficient to stop either critical analyses about race or the need for critical analyses of Tolkien's works which are widely perceived as significant cultural phenomena. The growing awareness of the sociological definition of racism as systemic and institutional rather than limited to personal prejudice, and the sociological analysis of types of racism, including unconscious or aversive attitudes, all serve to complicate the idea that authorial intentionality can be used to support the idea of the best interpretation of a text.[90] The wide variety of interpretations of Tolkien's work that exist in scholarly discourse as well as the growing number of disciplinary approaches in recent years—all of which signal the strength of Tolkien studies as an academic sub-field—also proves the extent to which discourses around cultural productions are dialogic, heterogeneous, and change over time.

Scholars who have recently graduated or are currently enrolled in medieval, modern, and postmodern humanities programs that include interdisciplinary programs incorporating critical theories and scholarship on race, class, gender, and sexuality will be familiar with the sociocultural theories informing these programs. Critical race and postcolonial scholarship exist in medieval, early modern, eighteenth century, Victorian, and modernist humanities fields. Additionally, scholarship on neomedievalism(s) includes consideration of a wide range of media and games as well as print texts, many of which were directly influenced by Tolkien's work. A growing body of scholarship in Tolkien studies has begun to examine Tolkien as a modern or postmodern writer, and further work on how his legendarium engages with the cultural changes of the twentieth century will only increase the need to consider issues of race in ways that move beyond the questions of Tolkien's beliefs or the meaning in a single text or small group of texts. Growing scholarship from film and game scholars will add to the work on Tolkien's literary productions. And, finally, the growing field of fan studies and reception studies will allow more direct analysis of the reception of Tolkien's work beyond what academics have previously seen as important.[91]

As scholars whose work I discuss here note, white supremacists' admiration of Tolkien's work is easily found online (Chism, Gehl, Nicklas, and Young). The necessity to consider this aspect of reader response highlights one of the gaps in Tolkien scholarship, specifically the lack of work in reception studies. This lack is common in literary studies which have tended to privilege interpretive work by a single academic reader. That approach will not be replaced by reception studies, nor am I advocating that racist fans become the sole focus of reception work in Tolkien studies although academics who already study the rhetoric and interactions of such groups could well extend their work to consider what fictional texts they claim for their communities. Having participated in online *Lord of the Rings* fandom since 2003, I am aware of the quality and range of interpretive and transformative works created by fans who are actively engaged in communal discussion of Tolkien's and Jackson's works, including a range of discussions on constructions of race in books and film. Those discussions offer the potential for collaborative and multidisciplinary work between and by scholars in Tolkien and fan studies. Of specific interest in such work would be the consideration of fans of color's response to Tolkien's work which I am aware of not only from my personal interactions but through scholarship I have done on internet discussions of race and racisms in online science fiction and fantasy fandom.[92]

Earlier academic defensiveness against Tolkien fans is understandable, but the rise of popular cultural studies and fan studies makes it possible for academics not only to study fandom but to be active in fandom in the twenty-first century. The need during the 1970s for academics studying popular texts to distance themselves from the "cult of fandom" has lessened if not disappeared, and the power and authority of fans of color should be acknowledged as part of the complicated and complex histories of reception of Tolkien's Middle-earth, emphasizing the potential of his work to "[reproduce] some of the concepts and prejudices of the 'primary' world while at the same time questioning, challenging and transforming others" (Fimi 159).

While no demographic studies have been done of online (or offline) science fiction and fantasy fandom, data I collected for an essay, "'The Wild Unicorn Herd Check-in': Reflexive Racialisation in Online Science Fiction Fandom," published in 2014 in Isiah Lavender's anthology, *Black and Brown Planets: The Politics of Race in Science Fiction*, highlights the extent to which fans of color are Tolkien fans. The information below lists some of the race and ethnic identifiers of fans of Tolkien who also discuss the other science fiction and fantasy in multiple media that they love. Many of the fans talk about reading his works from childhood with parents, siblings, and other relatives in their own communities since they were not welcome in the white-dominated fan conventions and gatherings of the time.

The data come from one discussion thread in a LiveJournal community, *Deadbrowalking: The People of Color Deathwatch*. The discussion thread, titled "The Wild Unicorn Herd Check-in," originated in response to a claim made by Lois McMaster Bujold in May 2009 that there were no fans of color in sff fandom until recently. Delux_Vivens, one of the founders and moderators of the community, posted a call for "POC/nonwhite people" and to "native/aboriginal/first nations/ndn" people, especially outside the USA, to discuss their histories of fandom reading and activities. Over a thousand replies give evidence of the extent to which people of color in multiple countries have been reading, for generations, as well as viewing sff media and participating in their own fandom activities outside of the fan conventions which were the basis for Bujold's claim. Complete information about Deadbrowalking and the context for the post can be found in the published essay which describes the multiple and complex linguistic taxonomies of ethnic, race, and national categories created by the fans, but my overall conclusion—that fans of color have been "invisible" to white sff fans in science fiction communities, historically and currently—does, I think, apply to Tolkien readers and fans and academics. To create the list below, I did a search of my electronic file of responses to identify the basic identifiers of the posters whose posts include the words "Tolkien," "The Hobbit," "The Lord of the Rings," "LOTR," or "Silmarillion."

African-American
African-Trinidadian descended Canadian
Anglo-Burmese Brit
Australian-born Chinese
Australian-born Chinese here, female, 22
Bengali/Canadian
Bengali/Canadian living in the USA
Black, American
[B]lack/[A]frican [A]merican
Born of Haitian parents in this country
British Filipino
British Filipino
Caribbean
Chinese
Chinese by race, born in Malaysia, lives in Australia
Chinese descended Australian
Chinese-American child of immigrants
Chinese-Australian
East Indian from Trinidad
East Indian girl who is a proud Trinidadian
Enough Cherokee to get a card
Ethnic Chinese/living in Singapore

Filipino-American
From Trinidad, mainly African and East Indian
half [B]lack twenty-something New Englander
Hawai'i-born mixed-blood enrolled Seneca
Hispanic American
Hispanic second generation fan
[H]ispanic/[B]lack with a dash of [F]rench [C]anadian
Indian in India
Indonesian
Korean (halfie)
Korean-American immigrant (born in Korea, came over as an infant)
Latino, second generation
Malaysian of Chinese descent
Mexican/Guatemalan background and a third generation American
Mixed-race female Asian (Borneo native) and Swiss-American
Multiracial POC
Multiracial: Caucasian, Afro-Caribbean, Amerindian (Arawak/Lokono)
[N]ative
Pakistani-American born in the USA but raised in the Middle East, where I was introduced to SFF by the parents
[P]erson of color, and a female
Singaporean Chinese
South Asian/living in Australia
Southeast Asian
Taiwanese-American
UK via West Indies
Venezuelan indigenous/mestizo (both sides of the family), African-American (both sides of the family), Osage NA (no CDIB), Haitian creole, Cherokee NA (no CDIB), and just a little splish-splash of Scottish and Irish (for flavor!)
West African immigrant living in New Zealand

The world of Tolkien's readers, like Tolkien's world, is much more complex than we have even begun to understand.

Notes

1. See, for example: Dimitra Fimi, *Tolkien, Race, and Cultural History: From Fairies to Hobbits* (Basingstoke, UK: Palgrave Macmillan, 2009); Jes Battis, "Gazing Upon Sauron: Hobbits, Elves, and the Queering of the Postcolonial Optic," *Modern Fiction Studies* 50, no. 4 (2004): 949–979,

accessed March 5, 2013, http://muse.jhu.edu/article/177543; Brian Rosebury, "Race in Tolkien Film," in Michael D. C. Drout, *J. R. R. Tolkien Encyclopedia: Scholarship and Critical Assessment* (New York: Routledge. 2007), 557; and Sandra Ballif Straubhaar, "Myth, Late Roman History, and Multiculturalism in Tolkien's Middle-earth," in *Tolkien and the Invention of Myth: A Reader*, ed. Jane Chance (Lexington, KY: The University Press of Kentucky, 2004), 101–117. Although Jackson's film was released in three parts, paralleling the original release of Tolkien's novel in three volumes, both director and author consider their work to be a single narrative. When I refer to Tolkien's novels in this essay, I mean both *The Hobbit* and *The Lord of the Rings*.

2. Since *Tolkien Studies* is the title of the premier journal in the field of Tolkien studies, I use the capitalization in the body of the essay only when referencing the journal.
3. Other patterns can be observed, including change over time and different disciplinary approaches, but those do not fall into the strong binary/conflicting narratives of the two I focus on.
4. Part of this conflict is perhaps due to conflicting meanings of "racism" as either individual responses or as institutionalized structures. In an entry in the 2007 *J. R. R. Tolkien Encyclopedia*, Christine Chrism summarizes three types of charges: "Critics who accuse Tolkien of racism fall into three camps: those who see him as intentionally racist; those who see him as having passively absorbed the racism or Eurocentrism of his time; and those who, tracing an evolution in his writing, see him becoming aware of racism/Eurocentrism implicit in his early works and taking care to counter it in his later ones:" "Racism, Charge of," in Drout, 558. All three of the "camps" focus on Tolkien's personal feelings or beliefs rather than on the cultural institutions around him. I would note that while these three "camps" are presented as different, all assume an equivalency between the work and the author, which is part of a specific theoretical approach to literary texts.
5. This conflict is complicated by the existence of multiple meanings of "postmodern." I use the term to mean the historical period after the Second World War during which a range of contemporary theories have been developed as opposed to referring to poststructuralist French theories of deconstruction which are often considered "Postmodernism." The debate about postmodern theories and concepts being applied to medieval texts, or to contemporary texts which are influenced by medieval sources, has affected Tolkien studies but has primarily been debated in the larger field of medieval studies. Three recent volumes of *Studies in Medievalism*, 2009–2010, edited by Karl Fugelso, consider the debates over medieval, medievalisms, and neomedievalism: Volumes XVII:

Defining Medievalism, XVIII: *Defining Medievalism(s)* II, and XIX: *Defining Neomedievalism(s)*. The scholars responsible for the majority of scholarship on Tolkien published during the last half of the twentieth century were trained in medieval studies, with others trained in folklore. Recently, more scholarship on Tolkien by academics trained in contemporary fields, using methods associated with postmodernisms, such as critical race theory and postcolonialism, is being published.

6. A similar observation is made by Elizabeth Hoiem in her discussion of the conflict in scholarship on race and Tolkien which she attributes in large part to disciplinary differences, between scholars (like Straubhaar) who work in "source and language work (a strong area in Tolkien criticism)," and critics who consider Tolkien's work racist because of their training in postcolonial theory although Hoiem notes that there is little postcolonial scholarship on Tolkien's work: Elizabeth Massa Hoiem, "World Creation as Colonization: British Imperialism in 'Aldarion and Erendis,'" *Tolkien Studies* 2 (2005): 75. Hoeim's point that debates between scholars in such disparate fields often do not critique the theoretical approaches as much as individual claims contributed to my overall argument in this essay. She and I differ in that I distinguish between text-based and cultural studies approaches which can include but are not limited to postcolonial theory.
7. Christine Chism, "Race and Ethnicity in Tolkien's Works," in Michael D. C. Drout, ed., *J. R. R. Tolkien Encyclopedia: Scholarship and Critical Assessment* (New York: Routledge, 2007), 555–556, identifies two patterns which are similar to mine in that they are organized around an internal/external focus. She distinguishes the two approaches as, first, "[treating] Middle-earth as an autonomous diegetic space and [asking] how each race or ethnicity functions within its total cosmography. The second treats Tolkien's work as literary inventions through which he investigated issues important to him—creativity, morality, friendship, heroism, art, history, language and death—and asks what questions his use of invented races allows him to explore." Her second category is external to the text in the sense of the author choosing to use "race as a literary device for investigating important issues," similar to "character 'types' in medieval works." This category does not move beyond the individual author's choices to consider changes in socio-historical constructions of "race" in European history.
8. Michael D. C. Drout and Hilary Wynne, "Tom Shippey's *J. R. R. Tolkien: Author of the Century* and a Look back at Tolkien Criticism since 1982," *Envoi* 9, no. 2 (Fall 2000): 123. Drout and Wynne specify gender, race, and class as the three "contemporary" issues. Janet Brennan Croft and Leslie A. Donovan, ed., *Perilous and Fair: Women in the Works and Life*

of J. R. R. Tolkien (Albuquerque: Mythopoeic Press, 2014) focus on classic and new scholarship on women and Tolkien. The bibliographic essay I wrote for that volume ends on an optimistic note about the growth of future scholarship based in part of the growing number of women in Tolkien studies, and literary and cultural studies in general, but white women are by far the majority of women in academic disciplines, reflecting the whiteness of academic spaces in general: Robin Anne Reid, "The History of Scholarship on Female Characters in J. R. R. Tolkien's Legendarium: A Feminist Bibliographic Essay," in *Perilous and Fair: Women in the Works and Life of J. R. R. Tolkien*, ed. Janet Brennan Croft and Leslie A. Donovan, 13–40 (Albuquerque: Mythopoeic Press, 2014). Data reported by the American Academy of Arts and Sciences show that, compared to the other fields, humanities award a greater percentage of advanced degrees to white people. With regard to doctoral degrees, the percentage of degrees held by students from minority groups has not yet moved beyond 10%: "In 2013, the share of humanities doctorates completed by students from traditionally underrepresented racial/ethnic groups was 9.9%, almost four percentage points higher than in 1995 but down from the historic high of 10.7% in 2007 (Indicator II-12b)" (para. 4): American Academy of Arts & Sciences. "Racial/Ethnic Distribution of Advanced Degrees in the Humanities," *Humanities Indicators*, April 2015, accessed December 26, 2015, http://www.humanitiesindicators.org/content/indicatordoc.aspx?i=46.

9. Helen Young, Review of *The Body in Tolkien's Legendarium*, ed. Christopher Vaccaro, *Journal of Tolkien Research* 1, no. 1 (2014): 5, accessed June 27, 2016, http://scholar.valpo.edu/journaloftolkienresearch/vol1/iss1/5/. As Young quite rightly notes, the lack of scholarship on raced bodies in the collection is a gap. [I should note that I have an essay on the stylistic constructions of female bodies in this collection. Additionally, I am on the editorial board of *The Journal of Tolkien Research* although I am not involved with the reviews that are overseen by the book reviews editor, Douglas A. Anderson.] Young is particularly qualified to issue this challenge because of her own work on race and fantasy which incorporates critical race theory. Her monograph *Race and Popular Fantasy Literature* begins with an exploration of the work of Tolkien and Robert E. Howard, the two most successful commercial creators of fantasy of their time, and then follows the "habits" of popular fantasy genre into the twentieth and twenty-first centuries: Helen Young, *Race and Popular Fantasy Literature: Habits of Whiteness*, Routledge Interdisciplinary Perspectives on Literature (London: Routledge, 2016). Young's cultural studies approach is informed by sociological theories on race. This monograph, the first to be published on race and fantasy,

is a groundbreaking and multi-disciplinary analysis of the genre, of fan cultures, and of the role digital communications and technology play in today's world.

10. Pascal Nicklas, "The Paradox of Racism in Tolkien," *Inklings: Jahrbuch für Literatur und Ästhetik* 21 (2003): 221–235; Robert Gehl, "Something is Stirring in the East: Racial Identity, Confronting the 'Other,' and Miscegenation in Othello and The Lord of the Rings," in *Tolkien and Shakespeare: Essays on Shared Themes and Language*, ed. Janet Brennan Croft (Jefferson, NC: McFarland, 2007), 251–266.
11. Robert Bartlett, in "Medieval and Modern Concepts of Race and Ethnicity," does an extensive analysis of the different categories of race and ethnicity, arguing that the "medieval terminology of race and ethnicity was no more straightforward than our own. Some of the key terms of medieval Latin usage, such as *gens* and *natio*, imply, etymologically, a concept of races as descent groups. Others, such as *populus*, do not." Robert Bartlett, "Medieval and Modern Concepts of Race and Ethnicity," *Journal of Medieval and Early Modern Studies* 31, no. 1 (2001): 42. While the categories differ (and change over time), both linguistic and historical evidence undercut the concept of a homogeneous medieval European culture with no sense of raced differences.
12. Thomas Hahn, "The Difference the Middle Ages Makes: Color and Race before the Modern World," *Journal of Medieval and Early Modern Studies* 31 no. 1 (Dec. 2001): 2.
13. J. R. R. Tolkien, "Letter 45 to Michael Tolkien," in *The Letters of J. R. R. Tolkien*, ed. Humphrey Carpenter (New York: Houghton Mifflin, 2000).
14. The extent to which an analysis of racist patterns in characterization or imagery of the film is seen as indicting Tolkien or his work of racism deserves further analysis: the connection seems tied to a critical assumption of the strong connection between source and adaptation, an assumption that seems more common among literary scholars who have, arguably, generated the most scholarship on Jackson's film. Kristin Thompson, an academic film historian, notes that while many literary works serve as the source for film adaptations, the response by Tolkien scholars on Jackson's film is unique in scope and purpose: Kristin Thompson, "Gollum Talks to Himself: Problems and Solutions in Peter Jackson's *'The Lord of the Rings,'*" in *Picturing Tolkien: Essays on Peter Jackson's "The Lord of the Rings" Film Trilogy*," ed. Janice M. Bogstad and Philip E. Kaveny (Jefferson, N.C.: McFarland, 2011), 25–45.
15. Rebecca Brackmann, "'Dwarves Are Not Heroes': Antisemitism and the Dwarves in J. R. R. Tolkien's Writing," *Mythlore* 109/110, 28, no. 3–4 (2010): 85–106; Renée Vink, "'Jewish' Dwarves: Tolkien and Anti-Semitic Stereotyping," *Tolkien Studies* 10 (2013): 123–145.

16. Sandra Ballif Straubhaar, "Myth, Late Roman History, and Multiculturalism in Tolkien's Middle-earth," *Tolkien and the Invention of Myth: A Reader*, ed. Jane Chance (Lexington, KY: The University Press of Kentucky, 2004), 101–117; Hope Rogers, "No Triumph without Loss: Problems of Intercultural Marriage in Tolkien's Works," *Tolkien Studies* 10 (2013): 69–87.
17. Jonathan Evans, "The Anthropology of Arda: Creation, Theology, and the Race of Men," in *Tolkien the Medievalist*, ed. Jane Chance, Routledge Studies in Medieval Religion and Culture 3 (London: Routledge, 2003), 194–224. Margaret Sinex mentions an even earlier example: Virginia Luling's 1995 conference paper, "An Anthropologist in Middle-earth," which appeared in the *Tolkien Centenary Conference Proceedings*, as discussing the ways in which the enemies in Tolkien's novel are based on the "inherited" images: Margaret Sinex, "'Monsterized Saracens,' Tolkien's Haradrim, and Other Medieval 'Fantasy Products,'" *Tolkien Studies* 7 (2010): 175.
18. Evans, 194.
19. Ibid., 200.
20. See my review of this collection: Robin Anne Reid, "Tolkien's Modern Middle Ages (Review)." *Tolkien Studies* 4 (2007): 314–323.
21. Jane Chance, "Tolkien and the Other: Race and Gender in the Middle Earth," in *Tolkien's Modern Middle Ages*, ed. Jane Chance and Alfred K. Siewers, The New Middle Ages (Nemia) (New York: Palgrave Macmillan, 2005), 182.
22. Hoiem, 75–92; Rogers, 69–87; and Straubhaar, 101–117.
23. See my review of this issue: Robin Anne Reid, review of *J. R. R. Tolkien Special Issue Mfs: Modern Fiction Studies* 50 no. 4, *Tolkien Studies* 3 (2006): 178–182.
24. My assumption here is not that the journals that focus on broader areas of scholarship are inherently superior to specialized journals, but that scholarship in a larger range of peer-reviewed journals shows growing acceptance of Tolkien's work as part of larger scholarly discussions rather than as a specialized and thus more easily marginalized topic.
25. Anderson Rearick, "Why is the Only Good Orc a Dead Orc: The Dark Face of Racism Examined in Tolkien's World," *Modern Fiction Studies* 40, no. 4 (2004): 861–874. The other two essays are a postcolonial reading (Sue Kim) and a queer studies reading (Jes Battis) which are discussed in the next section: Sue Kim, "Beyond Black and White: Race and Postmodernism in *The Lord of the Rings* Film," *Modern Fiction Studies* 50, no. 4 (2004): 875–907; and Battis, 949–979.
26. Rearick's claim is that: "*The Lord of the Rings* has also found itself open to pop culture scrutiny, especially among contemporary cultural critics

concerned with the racist heritage of Western—and especially American—culture": Rearick, 863. The two critics whose "scrutiny" is discussed are John Yatt, a writer at the *Guardian* and Steven Shapiro, a lecturer at the University of Warwick, who was interviewed for an article in *The Scotsman*. Sandra Ballif Straubhaar's 2004 essay, discussed later in this section, also cites two articles in European publications, one of which is the Shapiro interview cited by Rearick. Shapiro's interview is also cited in Christine Chism's entry on "Racism, Charges of," although credited to "David Shapiro."

27. Rearick, 864.
28. Ibid., 872.
29. Ibid., 870.
30. Cynthia Fuchs, "'Wicked, Tricksy, False': Race, Myth, and Gollum," in *From Hobbits to Hollywood: Essays on Peter Jackson's "Lord of the Rings,"* ed. Ernest Mathijs, Ernest and Murray Pomerance, Contemporary Cinema 3 (Amsterdam, Netherlands: Rodopi, 2006), 249.
31. Sean Redmond, "The Whiteness of the Ring," in *The Persistence of Whiteness: Race and Contemporary Hollywood*, ed. Daniel Bernardi (London: Routledge, 2008), 91–101. Whiteness studies is a recent field of study relating to critical race studies that analyzes whiteness as a racial construct. The Critical Whiteness Study Group's seventy-two page publication, "Towards a Bibliography of Whiteness Studies," references foundational works that started to appear in print in the 1990s: Critical Whiteness Study Group, "Towards a Bibliography of Critical Whiteness Studies," *Center on Democracy in a Multiracial Society, University of Illinois at Urbana-Champaign*, last modified 2006, accessed June 27, 2016, http://archives.library.illinois.edu/erec/University%20Archives/2401001/Production_website/pages/Research/06-07/CriticalWhiteness/Introduction.htm.
32. Redmond, 92–93.
33. Ibid., 100.
34. Robert T. Tally, Jr., "Let Us Now Praise Famous Orcs: Simple Humanity in Tolkien's Inhuman Creatures," *Mythlore* 29, no. 1/2 (2010): 26.
35. One of the best analyses of Tolkien's changing ideas and the changes in British culture during his lifetime can be found in Dimitra Fimi's *Tolkien, Race and Cultural History: From Fairies to Hobbits*, discussed in the next section.
36. Although the discussion of the question between Tolkien's work and the political ideologies of the twentieth century, specifically National Socialism (Nazism) and Fascism is at times referenced in discussions of racism, I see the connection as primarily related to the attempt to defend Tolkien against negative critiques. Thus, for this essay, I do not

discuss these essays because I see them as orthogonal to my primary focus though all are worth considering in the context of twentieth-century history and politics. Chism analyzes in depth Tolkien's response as a scholar and novelist to the Nazi appropriation of the medieval Germanic mythologies that were his love and work and how that response links "aesthetics to politics and ethics:" Christine Chism, "Middle-earth, the Middle Ages, and the Aryan Nation," in *Tolkien the Medievalist*, ed. Jane Chance, Routledge Studies in Medieval Religion and Culture 3 (London: Routledge, 2003), 68. Peter Firchow focuses on the parallels between the culture of Tolkien's Hobbits and specific ideological aspects of fascism, parallels that he argues were neither Tolkien's purpose nor politics. The shared aspects are construction of groups as innately good or evil and the importance of single, charismatic leaders: Peter E. Firchow, "The Politics of Fantasy: *The Hobbit* and Fascism," *Midwest Quarterly: A Journal of Contemporary Thought* 50, no. 1 (Autumn 2008): 15–31. Niels Werber analyzes the popularity of Peter Jackson's films as well as Tolkien's novel in Germany, pointing to the commonalities between the themes of racial constructions and ties between people and land in the context of German geographical and biological ideologies grounded in Romantic Nationalism. While Werber's analysis is about reception in Germany, he argues that the interpretations of conflicts in Middle-earth are applicable to current political issues occurring in other national cultures: Niels Werber, "Geo- and Biopolitics of Middle-Earth: A German Reading of Tolkien's The Lord of the Rings," *New Literary History: A Journal of Theory and Interpretation* 36, no. 2 (2005): 227–246. I would argue Werber's work on reception is important to consider in light of the popularity of Tolkien's work among white supremacists, including Stormfront and the British National Party, popularity that has been noted by Chism, Gehl, Nicklas, and Young.

37. Lynn T. Ramey, in a book-length study on race in the Middle Ages in Europe, acknowledges the importance of the growing scholarship on anti-Semitism in the Middle Ages while noting the need to analyze "a different type and manifestation of racism," specifically the question of "prejudice against darker-skinned persons from non-Western cultures precisely because of their skin color and their usually imagined, always unfamiliar cultural practices" (1). Ramey's work is a valuable addition to medieval scholarship that could be used by Tolkien scholars, medievalists or postmodern, or from any other period, in considering questions relating to race in Tolkien: Lynn T. Ramey, *Black Legacies: Race and the European Middle Ages* (Gainesville, FL: University Press of Florida, 2014).

38. The conflict is shown most clearly in these two contrasting quotes: Brackmann defines her term in the second paragraph of her essay: "I do not limit the meaning of antisemitism to overt violence or discrimination against practitioners of Judaism or Jewish converts to Christianity. Rather, by antisemitism I chiefly mean the underlying assumption that makes such violence and discrimination possible—the claim that there is something about Jews, biologically and psychologically, that marks them as fundamentally different from the Christian cultures that have been dominant in Europe since the Middle Ages:" Brackmann, 85. Brackmann discusses the choice to spell "antisemitism" without the hyphen or capital "S" that is standard style as a specific theoretical approach. Vink's definition does not appear until the sixth page of her essay and is a dictionary definition rather than a specific theoretical one. She agrees with Brackmann that it is possible that people in general "suffer from at least some form of bias or even racism, often unconsciously, and [does] not think Tolkien was very different. But whether there is racism to be found in his works is debatable, although they are certainly rife with **racialism**, or **racial categorization**, defined by *The American Heritage Dictionary of the English Language* as an 'emphasis on race or racial considerations:'" Vink, 129 (emphasis added). The claim that there are separate human races that can be categorized is a racist one. The claim that racism does not consist solely of "overt violence or discrimination" is one reason for some of the conflicts in Tolkien studies as well as other areas of literary and cultural studies.
39. Gavin Langmuir, *Towards a Definition of Antisemitism* (Oakland: University of California Press, 1990), 5–6, quoted in Brackmann, 85.
40. Brackmann, 104.
41. Vink, 123. I do not see Brackmann's argument as focusing solely on Tolkien's personal beliefs, but as always, my interpretation may vary from other readers'.
42. Vink, 142.
43. Straubhaar, 111–112; Rogers, 69–87.
44. Martin Barker and Ernest Mathijs, eds., *Watching "The Lord of the Rings": Tolkien's World Audience* (New York: Peter Lang, 2008) is a collection of essays based on a global survey that resulted in a dataset of responses from 25,000 surveys as well as other materials about the production and marketing of the film. There is no similar reception work done on Tolkien's work since, until recently, literary studies did not make use of social science methodologies. With the advent of cultural studies, that disciplinary exclusion is changing. Two anthologies that may be of use for Tolkien scholars who wish to develop such studies for their research or their courses are: James L. Machor and Philip Goldstein, eds., *Reception*

Study: From Literary Theory to Cultural Studies (New York: Routledge, 2001); and Michael Pickering, ed., *Research Methods for Cultural Studies* (Edinburgh: Edinburgh University Press 2008).

45. Straubhaar, 104.
46. Ibid., 112.
47. Ibid.
48. Rogers, 69.
49. Ibid., 70.
50. This term is drawn from Karen Kline's essays on the four paradigms in adaptation scholarship: translation, pluralist, transformation, materialist: Karen E. Kline, "The Accidental Tourist on Page and on Screen: Interrogating Normative Theories about Film Adaptation," *Literature Film Quarterly* 24, no. 1 (1996): 70–83. The first is the most common, assuming that a film should attempt to "faithfully" translate the novel. The three other paradigms assume a different relationship between film and novel: pluralism allows for differences in media requiring changes be made but asks how true "to the spirit" the film is. The transformation paradigm makes the film the primary work, allowing the scholar to ignore the novel completely, and the materialist paradigm situates both works in their socio-historical and economic contexts rather than privileging one over the other. Kline notes materialist approaches are fairly rare.
51. Nicklas, 221–235. As far as I can tell from searches in Project MUSE and Google Scholar as well as examination of bibliographies, Nicklas' essay is rarely, if ever, cited in later scholarship on race in Tolkien studies, possibly because of its appearance in a German journal which is not easily accessed outside Germany unless scholars have access to a good interlibrary loan office. The essay itself is written in English.
52. Nicklas, 222.
53. Ibid.
54. Scholarship that acknowledges the historical conflicts over constructions of "race" over time rather than assuming a more progressive present exists compared to a homogeneous racist past tends to avoid considering racism (however it is defined) in binary terms, as existing or not existing, and seeing anti-racist resistance to racism as historical and changing over time.
55. Nicklas, 233. While I can see how some aspects of Nicklas' essay can be criticized in regard to diction and handling of evidence, I think his awareness of the importance of online discussions, the quality of the questions he raises at the end of what he acknowledges is a short piece for the topic, and his in-depth analysis of Tolkien's letter to his publisher regarding the German translators' demands for a statement of identity for the German translation of *The Hobbit*, often cited briefly by scholars defending Tolkien, make this essay worth reading.

56. Kim, "Beyond Black and White," 875.
57. Ibid., 876.
58. Ibid.
59. Ibid., 892.
60. Ibid., 881–882.
61. Yvette Kisor also discusses this essay in the context of queerness in Tolkien; see her essay in this collection "Queer Tolkien: A Bibliographical Essay on Tolkien and Alterity."
62. Battis, 901.
63. Ibid., 914.
64. Lianne McLarty, "Masculinity, Whiteness, and Social Class in the Lord of the Rings" in *From Hobbits to Hollywood: Essays on Peter Jackson's "Lord of the Rings,"* ed. Ernest Mathijs and Murray Pomerance, Contemporary Cinema 3 (Amsterdam, Netherlands: Rodopi, 2006), 175.
65. Ibid., 184.
66. Gehl, 264.
67. Helen Young, "Racial Logics, Franchising, and Video Game Genres: *The Lord of the Rings*," *Games and Culture: A Journal of Interactive Media* 10, no. 1 (January 2015): 1–22. The history of rights to film the novels and to create merchandise is a complicated one, and different gaming companies have rights to either only the film content, or to the novel content, or recently, to both, and there are also some games which introduce original content: Young, "Racial Logics," 4–5. As Young notes, the "effects this coupling of innovation and fidelity has had on the representation of race in the games" is complex: Young, "Racial Logics," 5.
68. Young, "Racial Logics," 16.
69. Hoiem, 75.
70. Ibid., 77.
71. Ibid., 76.
72. Fimi, 135–140.
73. Ibid., 157.
74. Ibid., 159.
75. Ibid., 176.
76. Helen Young, "Diversity and Difference: Cosmopolitanism and *The Lord of the Rings*." *Journal of the Fantastic in the Arts* 21, no. 3 (2010): 351.
77. Ibid.
78. Ibid., 367.
79. As the references to conference presentations made by Hahn and Sinex show, presentations do usually precede publication, so work was clearly beginning in the 1990s if not before.
80. Frantzen's post has been deleted but is referenced and summarized in a number of articles responding to his ideas including one by

Rio Fernandes which provides links to responses and quotes some of Frantzen's responses to criticism: Rio Fernandes, "Prominent Medieval Scholar's Blog on 'Feminist Fog' Sparks an Uproar," *The Chronicle of Higher Education*, Jan. 22, 2016, accessed Jan 22, 2016, http://chronicle.com/article/Prominent-Medieval-Scholar-s/235014.

81. Dorothy Kim, "Antifeminism, Whiteness, and Medieval Studies," *In the Middle*, Jan. 18, 2016, accessed Jan. 22, 2016, http://www.inthemedievalmiddle.com/2016/01/antifeminism-whiteness-and-medieval.html.
82. Ibid., para. 9.
83. Ibid., para 23.
84. Ibid.
85. Racefail '09 (or, alternately, the "Great Cultural Appropriation Debate of Doom") took place from January through March 2009 in online spaces, primarily in LiveJournal and individual blogs. The debate originated in questions about cultural appropriation and racism in science fiction and fantasy fandoms and publishing. There have been ongoing public discussions about racism in science fiction since a 1998 article by Samuel R. Delany titled "Racism and Science Fiction" published in *The New York Review of Science Fiction*, so I consider Racefail '09 as representative of political debates that pre-existed it and have continued after it ceased. The article was reprinted: Samuel R. Delany, "Racism and Science Fiction," in *Dark Matter*, ed. Sherree R. Thomas (New York: Warner Books, 2000), 383–397. The conclusion of this particular set of discussions did not end the controversy: other debates came and went, and it is possible to track a fairly coherent line from the events of early 2009 to the most recent events in the science fiction and fantasy community. For an excellent discussion of the events, I highly recommend Nalo Hopkinson's "Ambassador from the Planet Midnight," her Guest of Honor speech from ICFA 2010. Rydra_Wong has links to the original posts although some have been deleted or locked down: Rydra_Wong. "Racefail '09." *The Internet is My Prosthetic Brain*, February 4, 2002, accessed Dec. 26, 2015, http://rydra-wong.dreamwidth.org/148996.html.
86. Laura Miller, "If Tolkien Were Black," *Salon*, Nov. 9, 2011, accessed Jan. 20, 2016, http://www.salon.com/2011/11/09/if_tolkien_were_black/.
87. The Carl Brandon Society, "About the Carl Brandon Society," n.d., accessed December 26, 2015, http://carlbrandon.org/.
88. Drout and Wynne, 116–117.
89. Fimi, 157.
90. Eduardo Bonilla-Silva's work on color-blind racism in the United States is an excellent introduction to the concept: Eduardo Bonilla-Silva,

Racism Without Racists: Color-Blind Racism and the Persistence of Racial Inequality in the United States, 2nd ed. (New York: Rowman & Littlefield, 2006). As Fimi notes, the historical and political aspects of racism in the United States are different from those in Britain, but I consider Bonilla-Silva's work important not so much for understanding Tolkien's work but for understanding the large American readership of the legendarium.

91. Barker's reader-response essay highlights the extent to which the "quite copious writings which have told the story of that first phase of Tolkien fandom" has become a "standard story," one which treats a hugely varied demographic group of readers as homogeneous: Martin Barker, "On Being a 1960s Tolkien Reader," in *From Hobbits to Hollywood: Essays on Peter Jackson's "Lord of the Rings,"* ed. Ernest Mathijs and Murray Pomerance, Contemporary Cinema 3 (Amsterdam, Netherlands: Rodopi, 2006). As someone who read *The Lord of the Rings* in 1965 when I was ten, I know that my own experience of being a "1960s" reader also does not fit the *1960s hippies and youth culture* narrative which dominates most "historical" discussions of Tolkien's first audience.
92. My scholarship on the internet discussions on race and racisms, discussions which have grown since 2009 to include writers and editors as well as fans, has resulted in two essays so far: Robin Anne Reid, "'The Wild Unicorn Herd Check-In': Reflexive Racialisation in Online Science Fiction Fandom," in *Black and Brown Planets: The Politics of Race in Science Fiction*, ed. Isiah Lavender III, 225–240 (Jackson, MS: University Press of Mississippi Press, 2014); and "Bending Culture: Racebending.com's Protests Against Media Whitewashing," in *Bamboo Planets: Racial Representations of Asia in Science Fiction*, ed. Isiah Lavender III (Jackson, MS: University Press of Mississippi, forthcoming).

Bibliography

American Academy of Arts & Sciences. "Racial/Ethnic Distribution of Advanced Degrees in the Humanities." *Humanities Indicators*, April 2015. Accessed Dec. 26, 2015. http://www.humanitiesindicators.org/content/indicatordoc.aspx?i=46.

Barker, Martin. "On Being a 1960s Tolkien Reader." In Mathijs and Pomerance, 81–99.

Barker, Martin, and Ernest Mathijs, eds. *Watching "The Lord of the Rings": Tolkien's World Audience*. New York: Peter Lang, 2008.

Bartlett, Robert. "Medieval and Modern Concepts of Race and Ethnicity." *Journal of Medieval and Early Modern Studies* 31, no. 1 (2001): 39–56.

Battis, Jes. "Gazing Upon Sauron: Hobbits, Elves, and the Queering of the Postcolonial Optic." *Modern Fiction Studies* 50, no. 4 (2004): 949–979. Accessed March 5, 2013, http://muse.jhu.edu/article/177543.

Bonilla-Silva, Eduardo. *Racism Without Racists: Color-Blind Racism and the Persistence of Racial Inequality in the United States.* 2nd ed. New York: Rowman & Littlefield, 2006.

Brackmann, Rebecca. "'Dwarves Are Not Heroes': Antisemitism and the Dwarves in J. R. R. Tolkien's Writing." *Mythlore* 109/110, 28, no. 3–4 (2010): 85–106.

Chance, Jane. "Tolkien and the Other: Race and Gender in the Middle Earth." In *Tolkien's Modern Middle Ages*, ed. Jane Chance and Alfred K. Siewers, 171–186. The New Middle Ages (Nemia). New York: Palgrave Macmillan, 2005.

———, ed. *Tolkien the Medievalist.* Routledge Studies in Medieval Religion and Culture, 3. London: Routledge, 2003.

Chism, Christine. "Middle-earth, the Middle Ages, and the Aryan Nation." In Chance, *Tolkien the Medievalist*, 63–92.

———. "Race and Ethnicity." In Drout, 555–556.

———. "Racism, Charge of." In Drout, 558.

Critical Whiteness Study Group. "Towards a Bibliography of Critical Whiteness Studies." *Center on Democracy in a Multiracial Society, University of Illinois at Urbana-Champaign.* Last modified 2006. Accessed June 27, 2016. http://archives.library.illinois.edu/erec/University%20Archives/2401001/Production_website/pages/Research/06–07/CriticalWhiteness/Introduction.htm.

Chun, W. H. K. *Control and Freedom: Power and Paranoia in the Age of Fiber Optics.* Cambridge, MA: MIT Press, 2007.

Delany, Samuel R. "Racism and Science Fiction." In *Dark Matter*, ed. Sherree R. Thomas, 383–397. New York: Warner Books, 2000.

Delux, Vivens. "The Wild Unicorn Herd Check In." Deadbrowalking. Last modified May 11, 2009. Accessed February 18, 2011. http://deadbrowalking.livejournal.com/357066.html.

Drout, Michael D. C. *J. R. R. Tolkien Encyclopedia: Scholarship and Critical Assessment.* New York: Routledge. 2007.

Drout, Michael D. C. and Hilary Wynne, "Tom Shippey's *J. R. R. Tolkien: Author of the Century* and a Look back at Tolkien Criticism since 1982,"' *Envoi* 9, no. 2 (Fall 2000): 101–167.

Evans, Jonathan. "The Anthropology of Arda: Creation, Theology, and the Race of Men." In Chance, *Tolkien the Medievalist*, 194–224.

Fernandes, Rio. "Prominent Medieval Scholar's Blog on 'Feminist Fog' Sparks an Uproar." *The Chronicle of Higher Education*, Jan. 22, 2016. Accessed Jan 22, 2016. http://chronicle.com/article/Prominent-Medieval-Scholar-s/235014.

Fimi, Dimitra. *Tolkien, Race, and Cultural History: From Fairies to Hobbits.* Basingstoke, UK: Palgrave Macmillan, 2009.

Firchow, Peter E. "The Politics of Fantasy: *The Hobbit* and Fascism." *Midwest Quarterly: A Journal of Contemporary Thought* 50, no. 1 (Autumn 2008): 15–31.

Fuchs, Cynthia. "'Wicked, Tricksy, False": Race, Myth, and Gollum." In Mathijs and Pomerance, 249–265.

Fugelso, Karl. *Defining Medievalism(s).* Studies in Medievalism, XVII. Suffolk, UK: Boydell and Brewer, 2009.

———. *Defining Medievalism(s) II.* Studies in Medievalism, XVIII. Suffolk, UK: Boydell and Brewer, 2009.

———. *Defining Medievalisms(s).* Studies in Medievalism, XIX. Suffolk, UK: Boydell and Brewer, 2010.

Gehl, Robert. "Something is Stirring in the East: Racial Identity, Confronting the 'Other,' and Miscegenation in *Othello* and *The Lord of the Rings.*" In *Tolkien and Shakespeare: Essays on Shared Themes and Language*, ed. Janet Brennan Croft, 251–266. Jefferson, NC: McFarland, 2007.

Hahn, Thomas. "The Difference the Middle Ages Makes: Color and Race before the Modern World." *Journal of Medieval and Early Modern Studies* 31 no. 1 (Dec. 2001): 1–37.

Hoiem, Elizabeth Massa. "World Creation as Colonization: British Imperialism in 'Aldarion and Erendis.'" *Tolkien Studies* 2 (2005): 75–92.

Hopkinson, Nalo. "A Reluctant Ambassador from the Planet of Midnight." *Journal of the Fantastic in the* Arts 21, no. 3 [79] (2010): 339–350.

Jemisin, N. K. "If Tolkien Were…" *Epiphany 2.0 - N.K. Jemisin [Blog]*, Nov. 11, 2011. Accessed Jan. 20, 2016. http://nkjemisin.com/2011/11/if-tolkien-were/.

Kim, Dorothy. "Antifeminism, Whiteness, and Medieval Studies." *In the Middle*, Jan. 18, 2016. Accessed Jan. 22, 2016. http://www.inthemedievalmiddle.com/2016/01/antifeminism-whiteness-and-medieval.html.

Kim, Sue. "Beyond Black and White: Race and Postmodernism in *The Lord of the Rings* Film." *Modern Fiction Studies* 50, no. 4 (2004): 875–907.

Kline, Karen E. "*The Accidental Tourist* on Page and on Screen: Interrogating Normative Theories about Film Adaptation." *Literature Film Quarterly* 24, no. 1 (1996): 70–83.

Luling, Virginia. "An Anthropologist in Middle-earth." In *Proceedings of the J.R.R. Tolkien Centenary Conference*, ed. Patricia Reynolds and Glen H. Goodknight, 53–57. Milton Keynes: The Tolkien Society; Altadena: The Mythopoeic Press, 1995.

Machor, James L. and Philip Goldstein, eds. *Reception Study: From Literary Theory to Cultural Studies.* New York: Routledge, 2001.

Mathijs, Ernest and Murray Pomerance, eds. *From Hobbits to Hollywood: Essays on Peter Jackson's "Lord of the Rings."* Contemporary Cinema 3. Amsterdam, Netherlands: Rodopi, 2006.

McLarty, Lianne. "Masculinity, Whiteness, and Social Class in the Lord of the Rings." In Mathijs and Pomerance, 173–188.

Miller, Laura. "If Tolkien Were Black." *Salon*, Nov 9. 2011. Accessed Jan. 20, 2016. http://www.salon.com/2011/11/09/if_tolkien_were_black/.

Nicklas, Pascal. "The Paradox of Racism in Tolkien." *Inklings: Jahrbuch für Literatur und Ästhetik* 21 (2003): 221–235.

Pickering, Michael, ed. *Research Methods for Cultural Studies.* Edinburgh: Edinburgh University Press, 2008.

Ramey, Lynn T. *Black Legacies: Race and the European Middle Ages.* Gainesville, FL: University Press of Florida, 2014.

Reid, Robin Anne. "Bending Culture: Racebending.com's Protests Against Media Whitewashing." In *Bamboo Planets: Racial Representations of Asia in Science Fiction*, ed. Isiah Lavender III. Jackson, MS: University Press of Mississippi, forthcoming.

———. Review of *J. R. R. Tolkien Special Issue Mfs: Modern Fiction Studies* 50 no. 4. *Tolkien Studies* 3 (2006): 178–182.

———. "Tolkien's Modern Middle Ages (Review)." *Tolkien Studies* 4 (2007): 314–323.

———. "The History of Scholarship on Female Characters in J. R. R. Tolkien's Legendarium: A Feminist Bibliographic Essay." In *Perilous and Fair: Women in the Works and Life of J. R. R. Tolkien*, ed. Janet Brennan Croft and Leslie A. Donovan, 13–40. Albuquerque: Mythopoeic Press, 2014.

———. "'The Wild Unicorn Herd Check-In': Reflexive Racialisation in Online Science Fiction Fandom." In *Black and Brown Planets: The Politics of Race in Science Fiction*, ed. Isiah Lavender III, 225–240. Jackson, MS: University Press of Mississippi Press, 2014.

Rearick, Anderson. "Why is the Only Good Orc a Dead Orc: The Dark Face of Racism Examined in Tolkien's World." *Modern Fiction Studies* 40, no. 4 (2004): 861–874.

Redmond, Sean. "The Whiteness of the Ring." In *The Persistence of Whiteness: Race and Contemporary Hollywood*, ed. Daniel Bernardi, 91–101. London: Routledge, 2008.

Rogers, Hope. "No Triumph without Loss: Problems of Intercultural Marriage in Tolkien's Works." *Tolkien Studies* 10 (2013): 69–87.

Rosebury, Brian. "Race in Tolkien Film." In Drout, 557.

Rydra_Wong. "Racefail '09.' *The Internet is My Prosthetic Brain*, February 4, 2002. Accessed Dec. 26, 2015. http://rydra-wong.dreamwidth.org/148996.html.

Sinex, Margaret. "'Monsterized Saracens,' Tolkien's Haradrim, and Other Medieval 'Fantasy Products.'" *Tolkien Studies* 7 (2010): 175–196.

Straubhaar, Sandra Ballif. "Myth, Late Roman History, and Multiculturalism in Tolkien's Middle-earth." *Tolkien and the Invention of Myth: A Reader*, ed. Jane Chance, 101–117. Lexington, KY: The University Press of Kentucky, 2004.

Tally, Robert T., Jr. "Let Us Now Praise Famous Orcs: Simple Humanity in Tolkien's Inhuman Creatures." *Mythlore* 29, no. 1/2 (2010): 17–28.

The Carl Brandon Society. "About the Carl Brandon Society." N.d. Accessed December 26, 2015. http://carlbrandon.org/.

Thompson, Kristin. "Gollum Talks to Himself: Problems and Solutions in Peter Jackson's *The Lord of the Rings*." In *Picturing Tolkien: Essays on Peter Jackson's "The Lord of the Rings" Film Trilogy*, ed. Janice M. Bogstad and Philip E. Kaveny, 25–45. Jefferson, N.C.: McFarland, 2011.

Tolkien, J. R. R. "Letter 45 to Michael Tolkien." In *The Letters of J. R. R. Tolkien*, ed. Humphrey Carpenter, 54–55. New York: Houghton Mifflin, 2000.

Vink, Renée. "'Jewish' Dwarves: Tolkien and Anti-Semitic Stereotyping." *Tolkien Studies* 10 (2013): 123–145.

Werber, Niels. "Geo- and Biopolitics of Middle-Earth: A German Reading of Tolkien's *The Lord of the Rings*." *New Literary History: A Journal of Theory and Interpretation* 36, no. 2 (2005): 227–246.

Young, Helen. "Diversity and Difference: Cosmopolitanism and *The Lord of the Rings*." *Journal of the Fantastic in the Arts* 21, no. 3 (2010): 351–365.

———. "Racial Logics, Franchising, and Video Game Genres: *The Lord of the Rings*." *Games and Culture: A Journal of Interactive Media* 10, no. 1 (January 2015): 1–22.

———. *Race and Popular Fantasy Literature: Habits of Whiteness*. Routledge Interdisciplinary Perspectives on Literature. London: Routledge, 2016.

———. Review of *The Body in Tolkien's Legendarium*, ed. Christopher Vaccaro. *Journal of Tolkien Research* 1, no. 1 (2014). Accessed June 27, 2016. http://scholar.valpo.edu/journaloftolkienresearch/vol1/iss1/5/.

PART II

Women and the Feminine

CHAPTER 4

Revising Lobelia

Amy Amendt-Raduege

Lobelia Sackville-Baggins seems a thoroughly unlikeable character. From the moment of her introduction near the end of *The Hobbit*, she is set up in direct opposition to the Bagginses of Bag End, whose position and property she covets. She is presented and perceived as a huffy, boorish, social-climbing virago with very little to redeem her. Perhaps for that very reason, Lobelia's character is not often examined by Tolkien scholars, even those of us interested in Tolkien's women. When Lobelia *is* mentioned, it is often only in passing a generic comment on "the greedy and self-aggrandising Sackville-Bagginses,"[1] or merely a footnote, as in Leslie A. Donovan's "The Valkyrie Reflex."[2] She is, in short, everything educated modern women strive *not* to be. For feminist scholars in particular, Lobelia seems more an embarrassment than an asset.

However, as is so often the case in Tolkien's fiction, there is more to Lobelia than meets the eye. Closer examination reveals that her character is more complex and compelling than is generally supposed. She *is* proud, stubborn, unwilling to accept less than her due, and eager to display her status to society: all traits commonly found in the heroes of the medieval poems and sagas that Tolkien so diligently studied. She is also intelligent, forthright, and capable of unexpected generosity.

A. Amendt-Raduege (✉)
Whatcom Community College, Bellingham, WA, US

C. Vaccaro and Y. Kisor (eds.), *Tolkien and Alterity*, The New Middle Ages, DOI 10.1007/978-3-319-61018-4_4

Why, then, do so many readers dislike Lobelia? After all, greed, pride, and stubbornness appear in other characters, many of whom are nevertheless viewed as heroes. The Dwarf-lord Balin was greedy for the *mithril* of Moria, and though it led him to his doom, he is still viewed as courageous for making the attempt. Lobelia attempts to gain Bag End, and she is not. Faramir is justly proud of his Númenorean heritage and honored for it; Lobelia is scorned for putting on airs. And stubbornness, it might be argued, is precisely the trait that allows Frodo and Sam to continue the trudge through Mordor, but Lobelia is simply deemed intractable. But heroic traits are heroic traits, regardless of how they are generally perceived. As Jane Chance has noted, "Tolkien recast the medieval hero in his world in new, unlikely, and multiple forms"[3]—including several female characters. All unlooked-for, Lobelia Sackville-Baggins's flaws become exactly the ingredients necessary to make an unexpected and generally unrecognized hero.

It is widely recognized that Tolkien drew his inspiration from the old heroic legends that he loved. The most obvious example, of course, is Beowulf, whose eponymous poem Tolkien studied for over forty years. Almost equally important and influential texts are *The Battle of Maldon* and *Sir Gawain and the Green Knight*. All these poems received significant scholarly attention from Tolkien. "Beowulf: The Monsters and the Critics" is perhaps one of the most influential pieces of literary criticism yet written, but Tolkien also wrote a play based on *Maldon*, and his translation of *Sir Gawain and the Green Knight*, coauthored with E. V. Gordon, remains a standard in academic classrooms. These works, and more like them, were the subject of many lectures delivered while Tolkien served as a professor at Oxford. The Old Norse sagas, too, played their part; he had begun reading the *Völsungssaga* as a boy,[4] and his fascination with the stories and legends of Scandinavia continued throughout his academic career. All of these stories feature individuals engaged in desperate battles against impossible odds. These men are strong, loyal, and courageous—all features Tolkien found admirable. What he may have found less palatable, as George C. Clark has repeatedly insisted, were the *motives* of medieval heroes: wealth, fame, or revenge.[5] Tolkien knew that such motivation was unlikely to find sympathy with modern readers. And he knew, especially in the aftermath of World War II, an audience was inclined to be skeptical about heroes in general.[6]

All the same, Tolkien had no doubt that heroes existed: He had seen them himself during the Battle of the Somme. These were ordinary men in extraordinary circumstances—an observation that shaped Tolkien's perception of heroism forever after. "I've always been impressed … that we are here, surviving," he said, "because of the indomitable courage of quite small people against impossible odds."[7] The clashing of these forces—medieval, modern, and personal—resulted in a type of hero at once completely new and comfortably familiar: an everyman sort of fellow who is quite literally too small for his task, but the only one great enough to accomplish it. The result, as Flieger puts it, is that "Tolkien has written a medieval story and given it [two] kinds of hero, the extraordinary man to give the epic sweep of great events, and the common man who has the immediate, poignant appeal of someone with whom the reader can identify."[8] But it is Frodo and Sam, the stand-ins for the common man, who save the world, and Tolkien is careful not to let us forget it.

But what to do when the hero is the common *woman*? There are women in both the Anglo-Saxon poems and the Old Norse sagas, but they are usually supporting characters rather than principals in their own right. Nor are they particularly numerous. As Jane Chance has pointed out, the entirety of the *Anglo-Saxon Chronicle* points out only four women who played active roles in the political climate of their day: Seaxburh, Cuthburh, Æthelburh, and Æthelflæd.[9] For the most part, "when Anglo-Saxon documents mention women, […] those women are introduced in passive roles which underscore their subordinate relationships."[10] There are some noteworthy exceptions; *Judith*, for instance, depicts a powerful heroine who saves her people when the men cannot, and she uses physical strength and intelligence in addition to her beauty to do it. Hagiographies provide even more examples; since women can be martyred equally as well as men, many of these stories have female protagonists. *Juliana* tells the story of a young woman who rejected a wealthy and powerful suitor in favor of remaining pure and Christian. The man's response is to try to torture her into submission; she adheres to her faith and is eventually beheaded by her once-potential husband, thus becoming a martyr. Tolkien certainly knew the poem well; he guided one of his students, Simonne d'Ardenne, through her thesis on the poem, and they intended to work together on *Katherine*. But these saints are hardly common: Both women are aristocratic and extraordinary in the extent of their faith. Furthermore, as Huppé has pointed out, the saint is not actually a hero because "the saint is simply too exemplary. He exists to give evidence of things unseen. He is a living miracle, not super-human as the hero is, but supra-human. His battlefield is totally spiritual, and his actions find their motivation not in human, but in divine purpose."[11] But as a general rule, women are not expected to be heroes, and even when they are, they tend to be called "heroines." Heroes are expected to be mighty warriors, great leaders, skilled fighters, and generous benefactors. The Greek concept of a hero was something of a superman,[12] while Germanic heroes were all associated with battle: "war, prowess, courage, bravery, self-defence [sic], and the defence of one's king or nation."[13] But, as so many scholars have pointed out, these are the roles not often available to nor expected of women. "Heroines," instead, are often merely the lead female character in the story; they are the damsels in distress, the women waiting at home; they are bestowers of quests and givers of rewards rather than active participants in their own stories.

Tolkien, then, faced a twofold problem: In the first place, he was trying to create a new kind of hero, and in the second, he was trying to figure out what a female kind of heroism would look like. He already had a foundation upon which to build: His own profound knowledge of the medieval texts he taught and studied, and the re-imagination of medieval chivalry brought about by the Great War. He had traditional models of female heroes before him: warriors like Brunhild or Judith on the one hand, or otherworldly saints like Juliana on the other.[14] The one is represented in Éowyn, and the other in Galadriel. But what about *ordinary* women? If Frodo and Sam demonstrate the principle that anyone can be a hero, then surely that principle must apply to women and men alike. There, Tolkien had some little help: As Damico reminds us, "the heroic temperament is rendered equally appropriate to male and female" in Old English literature,[15] and many of the heroes and heroines of the Old Norse sagas are, in fact, ordinary people, farmers and housewives instead of kings and queens. These female heroes might be less obviously present than their male counterparts, but they are present nonetheless, and model behavior that is seen as "heroic" without regard to status or gender.

He had modern examples, too: the women who participated in WWI. These women are all but lost to history, and yet they, like their male counterparts, went to the front, endured terrible conditions, suffered relentless bombardments, formed enduring bonds with their peers, and died. They were not passive bystanders or mere witnesses, either. The archives at Gloucester, for instance, house a document listing the names of women decorated for valor in the field.[16] Especially after the disasters of 1915, the women of England were called upon to serve in a wide variety of duties. At least forty women doctors served at hospitals or clearing stations near the front. Others took posts as nurses (both in the theater and at home), ambulance drivers, or became members of the VADs (Voluntary Aid Detachments); some even held auxiliary positions at the front.[17] As a young soldier tromping back and forth from the battle, Tolkien must have known some of them. The nurses at least would have cared for him at the front and again at home when he was invalided back to England. John Rateliff is in possession of a letter in which Tolkien speaks with great affection of Mother Mary Michael, whom he calls a "very dear old friend" who befriended him while he was in a military hospital in 1917.[18] I have so far found nothing in Tolkien's published writings about the influence these remarkable women had on his writings; perhaps he himself did not know. All we can say for certain is that he very likely saw for himself the sacrifices and valor of women serving at the front, and that those events happen to coincide with the first germs of the great legendarium. And they were all heroes.

In the end, Tolkien resolved the issue by focusing on the commonalities among all kinds of hero, medieval and modern, male and female: courage, honor, loyalty, and resolve. The heroes portrayed in *The Lord of the Rings* and elsewhere in Tolkien's legendarium universally exhibit these traits. That is not to say that Tolkien deliberately set out to create female heroes palatable to a feminist audience; it does mean that he recognized that true heroism was a path available to anyone. As C. S. Lewis notes, Tolkien has created a hero whose goals "exclude all hope of fame or fear of infamy";[19] instead, his hero is motivated by fellowship and freedom. At a single blow, Tolkien solved the problem of ignoble ends as well as the challenge of gender. Lúthien is hardly less courageous than Beren (she is perhaps even more so); Elwing is not less self-sacrificing than Eärendil; and Éowyn is no less a warrior than Éomer. If heroism is to be found in the most unexpected of places, then what place could be less likely than an ill-tempered, overbearing old lady?

At the start of it, nothing about Lobelia appears heroic at all. Like her husband Otho, she seems to be a greedy, grasping, ungrateful hobbit, anxious for nothing other than to get her hands on Bilbo's property—*any* of his property, even if it is nothing more than a handful of spoons. The problem gets worse in *The Lord of the Rings*, as the Sackville-Bagginses' covetousness becomes ever more pronounced.

A close inspection of Bilbo's family tree, however, makes it clear that the Sackville-Bagginses—or the S-B's, as they are derisively called—have some justification for their behavior. Otho is, after all, Bilbo's first cousin, and Tolkien himself concedes that the headship of the family should have gone to Otho after the death of Laura (neé Grubb) Baggins. Thus, Lobelia actually *is* the matriarch of the Baggins family, but it is a position that nobody acknowledges. And after Bilbo's unexpected disappearance in 1341, the S-B's stood to inherit Bag End, clearly a desirable property. But Bilbo's unexpected return in 1342 threw the entire hobbit legal system into such a tizzy that "no one dared to presume his death again."[20] Then, Bilbo adopted Frodo as his heir, and the hopes of the S-B's seemed to be dashed forever. They had no headship. They had no Bag End. They had no respect. And the people that did get the prestige were Bilbo and Frodo, the family eccentrics.

Seen from this perspective, the Sackville-Baggins' rude behavior begins to make sense. In the heroic world in which *The Lord of the Rings* takes place, family status is important. Almost everyone is initially introduced in terms of their parentage. Boromir is quick to assert that his father is not a common wise man or even a minor noble but "Denethor, Lord of Minas Tirith, wise in the lore of Gondor."[21] Éomer, too, links family and status, listing first his father's name and then the rank it accords him. Most strikingly of all, though in the midst of a deathly battle, Éowyn takes the time to tell the Nazgûl that she is Éomund's daughter—as if that information would mean something to an undead creature that had not dealt with living human beings in centuries. Aragorn, by contrast, is initially careful *not* to announce his family connections precisely because doing so would bring him too much attention. Family, place, position: These things matter in the world of *The Lord of the Rings*.

Hobbits, too, follow this trend. The narrator tells us that "All hobbits were … clannish and reckoned up their relationships with great care. They drew up long and elaborate family-trees with innumerable branches. In dealing with hobbits it is important to remember who is related to whom, and in what degree."[22] Frodo's status as an orphan is addressed early in the book, not by the principals themselves, but by ordinary folk taking their evening's respite at The Ivy Bush. The details of Frodo's family tree are obviously common knowledge, and the Gaffer is able to confidently declare Frodo's complex relationship with Bilbo as being both first and second cousin, in addition to beneficiary and adopted heir. Yet Lobelia declares that Frodo is not even a real Baggins, but a Brandybuck, almost as if "Brandybuck" is the worst insult she could think of.[23] The Brandybucks, for their part, are regarded askance by the hobbits of Hobbiton, mostly because they spent time on rivers and ventured into the Old Forest from time to time. Still, they are one of the oldest, biggest, and most established families in the Shire. The Bagginses were certainly an important family, largely because they were very respectable and never had adventures (until Bilbo and Frodo came along). The Tooks, on the other hand, take pride in their most celebrated member, Bullroarer Took, who famously knocked the Orcish king Golfimbul's head clean off with his club, thus winning the battle and inventing the game of golf at the same time.[24]

Within the context of familial signification, then, Lobelia is acting exactly as she should, asserting her family's place in society. In fact, much of Lobelia's behavior recalls that of women in the Norse sagas particularly, many of whose actions were enacted "on behalf of the *family*, of blood relations, the closest and most basic of all ties."[25] In particular, when family honor was at stake, it is often the woman's job to spur the men into action: She was the one to urge her menfolk to avenge a wrong or revenge a death. These "cold counsels" may seem strange to modern readers, but "as lamenters and whetters to revenge, women … are engaging in one of the few speech acts represented by the literature open to them, and they are speaking on behalf of the customs of their society – not in monstrous aberration from them."[26] So, in *Njal's Saga*, Bergthora actually goads her sons into taking further revenge in a long and costly blood feud[27] against their father's wishes. *Hrolf Kraki's Saga* tells of the Princess Signy, daughter of King Halfdan, who incites her son Hrok to challenge his uncle for possession of a great ring.[28] In both Egil's Saga and Njal's Saga, Queen Gunnhild is portrayed as jealous of her property and careful to protect what she believes is lawfully hers, and questions her husband's manliness when he fails to act as she sees fit. In *Þórðar saga kakala*, Steinvör goads her husband Hálfdan into avenging her father's death by threatening to take up the sword herself, leaving him to do the women's work at home.[29] Even Unn the Deep-Minded, who is continually held up as a thoroughly admirable woman, takes offense when her brother does not offer her what she deems sufficient hospitality.[30] These stories seem to indicate that women were concerned with personal honor as well as family honor: an affront to either was not to be tolerated.

Old English poetry, too, hints at such a role, though here it is more fragmented and subtle. The most obvious example is that of *Waldere*, wherein the heroine, Hildegyð, encourages him to do battle with his onetime friend Atla for the sake of honor:

is se dæg cumen
þæt ðu scealt aninga   oðer twega
lif forleosan   oððe l. . . . gne dom
agan mid eldum, ælfheres sunu. (ll. 8–11)

(The day is come when you must [do] one of two [things]: forsake life or achieve [lasting?] glory among men, son of Ælfhere.)
And later,

Weorða ðe selfne
godum dædum   ðenden ðin god recce (ll.22–3)

(Bring honor to yourself with good deeds while God cares for you)[31]

Even the regal Wealhþeow might carry an echo of the older Germanic tradition, as Murphy suggests: "only after she has spoken to Beowulf and he has vowed to her publicly is the hero certain of his acceptance as a functionary of the Danes."[32] The *Nibelungenlied* shows that "women still responded to personal grievances according to the old Germanic method of inciting men to take revenge on their behalf,"[33] most obviously when Guðrún encourages her brothers to seek revenge for the murder of Siegfried. None of these women's actions were frivolous or self-serving; they reflect the damage done to the family[34] and the need to correct it. In fact, Zoe Borovsky speculates that "women were responsible for maintaining the honor of the household to which they belonged."[35] If these interpretations are correct, then it was a woman's job to ensure that justice was served and that the family's place in society remained stable.

Given Tolkien's long familiarity with the Old Norse sagas, Old English poetry, and the *Nibelungenlied*, it seems perfectly plausible that these models of womanhood might well have been swimming in the soup when he was writing Lobelia. He knew perfectly well that characters in the old heroic stories tend to be "prickly: stiff, on their dignity, ready to take offense, therefore requiring careful handling"[36]—an apt description of Lobelia if ever there was one. Furthermore, Lobelia is also one of the few characters in the Legendarium known to be modeled on a real, live woman. In a letter to Rayner Unwin, Tolkien confesses that part of his inspiration came from "one elderly lady" who would "certainly set about Auden (and others) had they been in range of her umbrella."[37] It is hard not to hear some measure of amused respect in his words and harder still to imagine that a character created out of such affection should be complete without merit. Certainly, Lobelia belongs in the long list of "indomitable hobbit matrons"[38] that linger in the background of Tolkien's fiction; she is far more formidable than her husband, whose most memorable action is to snap his fingers under Frodo's nose and huff, "Spoons? Fiddlesticks!"[39] Lobelia is both more pragmatic and more intelligent; she gets Bilbo's jibe at once—but she also gets the spoons.

Humble and everyday as they are, spoons are rich with symbolism. First and most obviously, they are linked with that which hobbits love best of all: food. The "Allegory of the Long-Handled Spoons," found in Jewish, Christian, Muslim, and Buddhist cultures, symbolizes the difference between heaven and hell—in heaven, people feed each other; in hell, everyone starves because no one thinks beyond themselves. Spoons, then, represent the bonds of community and fellowship. Even today, two spoons in a cup signal an upcoming wedding,[40] while two spoons given to the same person during a meal indicate that someone will arrive hungry.[41] Spoons are also symbols of wealth and family, as is hinted at in the proverb "born with a silver spoon in your mouth." Folklore also records the important tradition of giving spoons at Christenings, particularly "apostle spoons." These spoons contained an image of an Apostle on the shaft; a full set includes the twelve Apostles and a master spoon with an image of Jesus or, in one case, the Virgin Mary. Poorer folk contented themselves with only one, but more opulent individuals gave a whole set.[42] Thus, in a way, Lobelia's possession of the full set of spoons reasserts her status and symbolically allows her to reclaim her "rightful" position as the matriarch of the Baggins family.

Perhaps, on some level, Bilbo's relinquishment of the spoons indicates that he has recognized that position all along (though not enough to give her Bag End). Still, symbolic recognition is not real recognition, and Lobelia knows it. It is an affront to her pride that Frodo inherits what she and Otho think should have been theirs. So it is no particular surprise when they show up the day after the Party, demanding to see Frodo and being "rather offensive": offering bad bargain prices, insinuating that "the whole affair was fishy," and finally demanding to see Bilbo's will. Otho leaves, but Lobelia is more persistent, and even attempts to make off with several small but valuable items that had somehow fallen inside her umbrella.[43] This behavior is far more than asserting her place in the family; it is just plain rude, and that makes her harder to stomach than other characters in *The Lord of the Rings*. But for Tolkien's heroes, that is part of the process. They have to grow into their roles. Frodo is not a hero yet, either. Neither is Sam, nor Merry, nor Pippin. They are simply people, going about their individual lives in their individual ways. None of them has confronted evil. And until that time, all their vices and virtues are only seeds in the soil, with the potential to be used for good or for ill. Lobelia is difficult, certainly; heroes often are. She is impolite and ungracious, acutely aware of any slight to her family or to her dignity. These are precisely the characteristics that mark Grettír, the eponymous hero of *Grettír's Saga*, or Egil of *Egil's Saga*. In Lobelia's case, those character flaws are also the very characteristics that will ultimately make her a hero.

When the Shire is invaded by Sharkey and his Men, Lobelia alone has the courage to attack them directly. Confronted with a lot of ruffians who seem about to invade Bag End, the home she had desired for so long, she does not step aside and obey quietly, as so many of the hobbits do; she "ups with her umbrella and goes for the leader, near twice her size."[44] The story is told with a kind of grudging respect; it is hard for the hobbits (and readers) to acknowledge that Lobelia got anything right. Until the arrival of the Travelers, hers is the only direct action taken in Hobbiton. True, the Tooks wage their own rebellion, but it is both more violent and more isolated, and has little effect on the rest of the Shire. Poor Old Will, the Mayor, tries a peaceful means of resistance, but he never even makes it to Bag End to lodge his protest. By contrast, Lobelia's action seems more immediate and more heroic. She did not attack without provocation, but neither did she step aside and let herself be bullied. And that is the moment of transformation for Lobelia.

The text does not state so explicitly, but it seems that Lobelia's actions shift the hobbits' general dislike of the Sackville-Baggins from the family in general to Lotho in particular, who is resentfully called "Pimple," as if he were a blemish on the face of hobbit society. Although it is not clear at what point Lotho earned his unattractive nickname, it *is* clear that by the time the Travelers return, its use has become commonplace, while no one speaks ill of Lobelia again. In Icelandic literature, it seems that *marginalized* women are called in specifically "to represent communitas [sic] and the performances that bond the local community (or the family) together,"[45] and such seems to be the case in the Shire, too. Lobelia moves, literally at one blow, from a resented figure to an admired one. Young Tom's admission that "she showed more spirit than most" at last recognizes that flaws can become strengths. The traits that made her so repellent in the beginning—her stubbornness, her unwillingness to accept any affront to her dignity, and her clear understanding of social position—transform into the traits that revise Lobelia, in the hobbits' minds, from a harridan into a hero. When she emerges from the Lockholes, pride and stubbornness are still evident, but now they are read as signs of strength and determination: "She insisted on hobbling out on her own feet; and she had such a welcome, and there was such clapping and cheering when she appeared, leaning on Frodo's arm but still clutching her umbrella, that she was quite touched, and drove away in tears. She had never in her life been popular before."[46]

If Lobelia had not had the irascibility to stand up to Sharkey's thugs, her innate courage might never have been recognized, and she might have died alone and unloved. As it is, after her release from the Lockholes, Lobelia returns to her family of origin, the Bracegirdles, to live out the rest of her life. When she dies, she does so with one of the most unexpected gestures of love in the book: She leaves all her money, and Lotho's, to Frodo, "to use in helping hobbits made homeless by the troubles."[47] She has the grace to set aside old grudges, accept her responsibility for the tragedy, and do what she can to make it right. That takes its own kind of courage. Moreover, the text explicitly states that Lobelia's bequest ends the rivalry between the two families: "So that feud was ended."[48] Her unexpected generosity, even if it is rooted in grief and sorrow, at last allows Frodo—who has been through much on his journey and learned that people are often capable of much more than they are expected to be—to set aside his lingering grudges. But it is *her* example, *her* willingness to let go of the past that precipitates the end of hostilities. In Tolkien's Middle-earth, heroes are not those who fight with weapons, though those who fight with weapons may still be heroes. Instead, Tolkien's heroes are those who put themselves at risk for the sake of others. The qualities they exhibit are not self-aggrandizing quests for glory but self-effacing quests for justice. And so it goes with Lobelia. Her final act—willing what remains of her worldly goods to help those whom her son had hurt—reveals an entirely different interpretation of

Lobelia: a generous, loving spirit that had been too long repressed by a society that made her into an enemy.

As is so often the case in Tolkien's fiction, heroes come from exactly those people who ought not be heroes at all. From the start, Lobelia possesses qualities once regarded as heroic, but that have since been suppressed and misinterpreted by the society around her. And yet, when that society is threatened, her flaws turn out to be exactly what is required to resist that threat. In the end, Lobelia's actions are those of a hero: She challenges those who threaten her homeland, refuses to be cowed by bullies, and—maybe most importantly of all—does so with no expectation of fame or recognition. *She* is the one who ends the feud, not by killing off all challengers but by an act of unsolicited generosity. Her actions do not represent a *change* of character, but a *growth* of character. While Lobelia's doings are not always admirable, they *are* in keeping with the heroic tradition, and once again assert Tolkien's belief that anyone can be a hero—even if she is a woman.

Notes

1. Jane Chance Nitzsche, *Tolkien's Art* (London: Macmillan, 1979), 106.
2. Leslie A. Donovan, "The Valkyrie Reflex in J.R.R. Tolkien's *The Lord of the Rings*: Galadriel, Shelob, Éowyn, and Arwen," in *Tolkien the Medievalist*, ed. Jane Chance (New York: Routledge, 2003), 106–132.
3. Jane Chance, "Tolkien's Women (and Men): The Films and the Book," *Mallorn* 43 (July 2005): 30. For further coverage by Chance on this subject, see Chapter 7 "'Usually Slighted': Gudrún, Other Medieval Women, and *The Lord of the Rings*, Book 3 (1925–1943)" in her *Tolkien, Self, and Other: "This Queer Creature."* (New York: Palgrave, 2016).
4. Cf. Humphrey Carpenter, *J.R.R. Tolkien: A Biography* (New York: Houghton Mifflin, 2000), 54.
5. Cf. Timmons' interview of Clark in *The Hero Recovered*, or Clark's own entry in *J.R.R. Tolkien and His Literary Resonances*, eds. George Clark and Daniel Timmons (Westport, Connecticut: Greenwood Press, 2000).
6. Cf. Stefan Goebel's *The Great War and Medieval Memory*, where he notes that "'modern memory' was the product of the Second World War rather than the First" (12). The result was that "[m]edievalism was the ultimate casualty of the Second World War" (13), including the diction that honored both fighters and fallen: heroes. Even if it is true, as most critics believe, that the process was begun in the First World War (cf. Shadi Neimneh, "The Anti-Hero in Modernist Fiction"), WWII certainly did

not improve the situation. The result was that, for most of the twentieth century heroes were viewed with a certain skepticism. See also Shippey, *The Road to Middle*-earth (Boston: Houghton Mifflin, 2003), 71 for his particular take on Tolkien's heroes.

7. Carpenter, *A Biography*, 180.
8. Verlyn Flieger, "Frodo and Aragorn: The Concept of the Hero," in *Understanding* The Lord of the Rings: *The Best of Tolkien Criticism*, ed. Rose A Zimbardo and Neil D. Isaacs (Boston: Houghton Mifflin, 2004), 124.
9. Jane Chance, *Woman as Hero in Old English Literature* (Eugene, OR: Wipf & Stock, 1986), 60.
10. Ibid., 61.
11. Bernard F. Huppé, "The Concept of the Hero," in *Concepts of the Hero in the Middle Ages*, ed. Norman T. Burns and Christopher Reagan (Albany, NY: State University of New York Press, 1975), 2. Note the exclusive use of the masculine pronoun.
12. Leo Carruthers, "Kingship and Heroism in Beowulf," in *Heroes and Heroines in Medieval English Literature: A Festschrift Presented to André Crépin on the Occasion of His Sixty-Fifth Birthday*, ed. Leo Carruthers (Woodbridge, Suffolk: D.S. Brewer, 1994), 22.
13. Ibid., 24.
14. Cf. Coline Covington's "In Search of the Heroine," *Journal of Analytical Psychology* (1989): 243–254.
15. Helen Damico, "The Valkyrie Reflex in Old English Literature," in *New Readings on Women in Old English Literature*, ed. Helen Damico and Alexandra Hennessey Olsen (Bloomington, IN: Indianapolis University Press, 1990), 182.
16. Gloucester Archives D4/180 3, which also contains, according to its records, a photograph of one of those forty doctors. Though the documents themselves cannot be seen online, the Archives can be contacted at http://www.gloucestershire.gove.uk/archives.
17. Susan Kingsley Kent, "Feminists at the Front: Reinventing Masculinity," in *Making Peace: The Reconstruction of Gender in Interwar Britain* (Princeton: Princeton University Press, 1993), 52.
18. John Rateliff, "The Missing Women: J.R.R. Tolkien's Lifelong Support for Women in Higher Education," in *Perilous and Fair: Women in the Works and Life of J.R.R. Tolkien*, ed. Janet Bennet Croft and Leslie A. Donovan (Altadena, CA: Mythopoeic Press, 2015), 51.
19. C. S. Lewis, "The Dethronement of Power," in *Understanding* The Lord of the Rings: *The Best of Tolkien Criticism*, ed. Rose A. Zimbardo and Neil D. Isaacs (New York: Houghton Mifflin, 2004), 13.
20. J. R. R. Tolkien, *The Letters of J.R.R. Tolkien*, ed. Humphrey Carpenter (New York: Houghton Mifflin, 2000), 294.

21. J. R. R. Tolkien, *The Fellowship of the Ring*, 2nd ed. (Boston: Houghton Mifflin, 1987), II, ii, 259.
22. Tolkien, *Fellowship of the Ring*, I, Prologue, 16.
23. Tolkien, *Fellowship of the Ring*, I, i, 48.
24. J. R. R. Tolkien, *The Hobbit* (New York: Ballantine, 1994), 18.
25. Michael Murphy, "Vows, Boasts and Taunts, and the Role of Women in Some Medieval Literature" *English Studies* (1985): 111. Original emphasis.
26. Sarah Anderson, with Karen Swenson, "Introduction: 'og eru köld kvenna ráð'" in *Cold Counsel: Women in Old Norse Literature and Mythology* (New York: Routledge, 2002), xii–xiii.
27. *Njal's Saga*, trans. Robin Cook (New York: Penguin Books, 2011), 270.
28. *The Saga of King Hrolf Kraki*, trans. Jesse L. Byock (London: Penguin Books, 1998), 16.
29. Zoe Borovsky, "Never in Public: Women and Performance in Old Norse Literature," *The Journal of American Folklore* 112 no. 443 (Winter 1999): 16, doi:10.2307/541400.
30. *The Saga of the People of Laxardal*, trans. Keneva Kunz, in *The Sagas of the Icelanders*, preface by Jane Smiley, introduction by Robert Kellogg (New York: Penguin Publishing, 2000), 279.
31. Marian Dexter Learned, "Versions of the Walther Saga" *PMLA* 7 no. 1 The Saga of Walter of Aquitaine (1892): 3. My translation.
32. Murphy, 111.
33. Jenny Jochens, *Women in Old Norse Society* (Ithaca: Cornell University Press, 1995), 11.
34. Carol. J. Clover, "Hildigunnr's Lament," in *Cold Counsel: Women in Old Norse Literature and Mythology* (New York: Routledge, 2002), 23.
35. Borovsky, 32.
36. Tom Shippey, "Principles of Conversation in Beowulfian Speech," in *Techniques of Description: Spoken and Written Discourse,* ed. John M. Sinclair, Michael Hoey, and Gwyneth Fox (New York: Routledge, 1993), 120.
37. Tolkien, *Letters*, 229. This imaginary reaction was in response to Auden's assertion that anybody who disliked *The Lord of the Rings* lacked literary taste, a sentiment with which Tolkien himself disagreed.
38. John D. Rateliff, *The History of the Hobbit* Part One: *Mr. Baggins* (New York: Houghton Mifflin, 2007), 47.
39. Tolkien, *Fellowship of the Ring*, I, i, 47.
40. Jacqueline Simpson and Steve Roud, "Spoons," in *The Oxford Dictionary of English Folklore* (Oxford: Oxford University Press, 2001), 340.
41. Mary A. Chamberlain, "Certain Common Superstitions," *Journal of American Folklore* 6 no. 21 (April–June 1893): 145.

42. John Brand, *Brand's Popular Antiquities of Great Britain: Faiths and Folklore*, Vol. 3 (London: Reeves and Turner, 1905), 10.
43. Tolkien, *Fellowship of the Ring*, I, i, 47–82.
44. J. R. R. Tolkien, *The Return of the King* (Boston: Houghton Mifflin, 1987), VI, viii, 293.
45. Borovsky, 15
46. Tolkien, *Return of the King*, VI, ix, 301.
47. Ibid.
48. Ibid.

Bibliography

Anderson, Sarah, with Karen Swenson. "Introduction: 'og eru köld kvenna ráð'." *Cold Counsel: Women in Old Norse Literature and Mythology*. New York: Routledge, 2002.

Borovsky, Zoe. "Never in Public: Women and Performance in Old Norse Literature." *The Journal of American Folklore* 112 no. 443 (Winter 1999): 6–39.

Brand, John. *Brand's Popular Antiquities of Great Britain: Faiths and Folklore*. Vol. 3. London: Reeves and Turner, 1905.

Carruthers, Leo. "Kingship and Heroism in Beowulf." In *Heroes and Heroines in Medieval English Literature: A Festchrift Presented to André Crépin on the Occasion of his Sixty-fifth Birthday*, ed. Leo Carruthers, 19–29. Woodbridge, Suffolk: D.S. Brewer, 1994.

Chamberlain, Mary A. "Certain Common Superstitions." *Journal of American Folklore* 6 no. 21 (Apr–Jun 1893): 144–146.

Chance, Jane. "Tolkien's Women (and Men): The Films and the Book." *Mallorn* 43 (July 2005): 30–37.

———. *Woman as Hero in Old English Literature*. Eugene, OR: Wipf & Stock, 1986.

Chance Nitzsche, Jane. *Tolkien's Art*. London: Macmillian, 1979.

Clark, George. "Tolkien and the True Hero." In *J. R. R. Tolkien and His Literary Resonances: Views of Middle-earth*, eds. George Clark and Daniel Timmons, 39–52. Westport, CT: Greenwood Press, 2000.

Clover, Carol. J. "Hildigunnr's Lament." *Cold Counsel: Women in Old Norse Literature and Mythology*, 15–54. New York: Routledge, 2002.

Damico, Helen. "The Valkyrie Reflex in Old English Literature." In *New Readings on Women in Old English Literature*, eds. Helen Damico and Alexandra Hennessey Olsen, 176–192. Bloomington, IN: Indianapolis University Press, 1990.

Donovan, Leslie A. "The Valkyrie Reflex in J.R.R. Tolkien's *The Lord of the Rings*: Galadriel, Shelob, Éowyn, and Arwen." In *Tolkien the Medievalist*, ed. Jane Chance, 106–132. New York: Routledge, 2003.

Egil's Saga. In *The Sagas of the Icelanders*, trans. Katrina C. Attwood with a preface by Jane Smiley, and introduction by Robert Kellogg, 3–184. New York: Viking, 2000.

Flieger, Verlyn. "Frodo and Aragorn: The Concept of the Hero." In *Understanding* The Lord of the Rings: *The Best of Tolkien Criticism*, eds. Rose A. Zimbardo and Neil D. Isaacs, 122–145. Boston: Houghton Mifflin, 2004. Reprinted in *Green Suns and Faërie: Essays on J.R.R. Tolkien*. Kent, OH: The Kent State University Press, 2012.

Frederick, Candice and Sam McBride. "Against Insubordination: Women in Inklings Fiction." In *Women Among the Inklings: Gender, C.S. Lewis, J.R.R. Tolkien, and Charles Williams*, 107–158. Westport, CT: Greenwood Press, 2001.

Goebel, Stefan. *The Great War and Modern Memory: Wars, Remembrance and Medievalism in Britain and Germany, 1914–1940*. Cambridge, UK: Cambridge University Press, 2007.

Huppé, Bernard F. "The Concept of the Hero." In *Concepts of the Hero in the Middle Ages*, eds. Norman T. Burns and Christopher Reagan, 1–26. Albany, NY: State University of New York Press, 1975.

Jochens, Jenny. *Women in Old Norse Society*. Ithaca: Cornell University Press, 1995.

Kent, Susan Kingsley. "Feminists at the Front: Reinventing Masculinity." In *Making Peace: The Reconstruction of Gender in Interwar Britain*. Princeton, New Jersey: Princeton University Press, 1993.

Learned, Marian Dexter, "Versions of the Walther Saga." In *The Saga of Walter of Aquitaine*. Ed. Marian Dexter Learned. PMLA 7.1, (1892): 1–129, 207–208.

Lewis, C.S. "The Dethronement of Power." In *Understanding* The Lord of the Rings: *The Best of Tolkien Criticism*, eds. Rose A. Zimbardo and Neil D. Isaacs, 11–15. New York: Houghton Mifflin, 2004.

Murphy, Michael. "Vows, Boasts and Taunts, and the Role of Women in Some Medieval Literature." *English Studies* (1985): 105–112.

Niemneh, Shadi. "The Anti-Hero in Modernist Fiction: From Irony to Cultural Renewal." *Mosaic: A Journal for the Interdisciplinary Study of Literature* 46.4 (2013): 75–90.

Njal's Saga. Translated by Robin Cook. New York: Penguin Books, 2011.

Rateliff, John D. *The History of the Hobbit*. Part One: *Mr. Baggins*. New York: Houghton Mifflin, 2007.

———. "The Missing Women: J.R.R. Tolkien's Lifelong Support for Women in Higher Education." In *Perilous and Fair: Women in the Works and Life of J.R.R. Tolkien*, eds. Janet Bennet Croft and Leslie A. Donovan, 41–69. Altadena, CA: Mythopoeic Press, 2015.

The Saga of the People of Laxardal. In *The Sagas of the Icelanders*, trans. Keneva Kunz, with a preface by Jane Smiley, and introduction by Robert Kellogg. New York: Penguin Publishing, 2000.

Simpson, Jacqueline and Steve Roud. "Spoons." In *The Oxford Dictionary of English Folklore*. Oxford: Oxford University Press, 2001.

Shippey, Tom. "Principles of Conversation in Beowulfian Speech." *Techniques of Description: Spoken and Written Discourse*, eds. John M. Sinclair, Michael Hoey, and Gwyneth Fox, 109–26. New York: Routledge, 1993.

———. "The Bourgeois Burglar." *The Road to Middle-earth*, 55–93. New York: Houghton Mifflin, 2003.

Timmons, Daniel. "Heroes and Heroism in the Fiction of Tolkien and the Old Norse World: An Interview with George Clark." In *The Hero Recovered: Essays on Medieval Heroism in Honor of George Clark*, eds. Robin Waugh and James Weldon. Kalamazoo, MI: Medieval Institute Publications, 2010.

Tolkien, J.R.R. *The Fellowship of the Ring*. 2nd ed. Boston: Houghton Mifflin, 1987.

———. *The Hobbit*. 1937. New York: Ballantine, 1994.

———. *The Letters of J.R.R. Tolkien*. Ed. Humphrey Carpenter. New York: Houghton Mifflin, 2000.

———. *The Return of the King*. 2nd ed. Boston: Houghton Mifflin, 1987.

CHAPTER 5

Medieval Organicism or Modern Feminist Science? Bombadil, Elves, and Mother Nature

Kristine Larsen

In her introduction to *Tolkien the Medievalist*, Jane Chance explains that Tolkien "responded to his modern contexts by retelling his medieval sources and adapting his medieval scholarship to his own voice. Tolkien was, over time, influenced by his own personal medievalism."[1] Indeed, a leisurely perusal of Tolkien scholarship in general (e.g., as cataloged by West[2] and Johnson,[3] and recounted in Jane Chance's edited volumes[4]) leaves no doubt as to the indelible mark Tolkien's training, teaching, and scholarship in medieval literature, language, culture, and mythology left on his subcreation.

It is also well-known among Tolkien scholars that Tolkien utilized a tremendous amount of the scientific understanding of his day in fleshing out the details of the cosmology,[5] geology,[6] paleontology,[7] botany,[8] and other aspects of Middle-earth. It is therefore clear that Tolkien was not anti-science; he did, however, make a clear distinction between science and pseudoscience, e.g., between astronomy and astrology, and was a vehement critic of the misuse and overuse of technology that he saw

K. Larsen (✉)
Central Connecticut State University, New Britain, CT, USA

C. Vaccaro and Y. Kisor (eds.), *Tolkien and Alterity*, The New Middle Ages, DOI 10.1007/978-3-319-61018-4_5

as the corrupt legacy of the Scientific and Industrial Revolutions.[9] For example, Tolkien famously wrote of *The Lord of the Rings* in a 1956 draft to a letter to Joanna de Bortadano:

> Of course my story is not an allegory of Atomic power, but of *Power* (exerted for Domination). Nuclear physics can be used for that purpose. But they need not be. They need not be used at all. If there is any contemporary reference in my story at all it is to what seems to me the most widespread assumption of our time: that if a thing can be done, it must be done. This seems to me wholly false.[10]

While Tolkien actively integrated modern scientific knowledge about the natural world into his largely medieval universe—leading to stylistic and consistency problems that he was ultimately not able to reconcile[11]—is also true that medieval views of science also played a central role in shaping Middle-earth, most importantly the concept of *organicism*. In this philosophical perspective, the natural world is viewed as alive and part of the gods' domain.[12] Every creature is "responsible for maintaining its own place and expressing itself within the natural order;" it is a "necessary part of the whole, but [is] not the whole itself."[13] Organicism therefore defines alterity in a relational way, whereby something is defined as "other" in that it has an identity that is definable other than as the whole (the whole meaning the natural world) but each individual is inextricably linked to the whole (and hence to all other individuals).

The well-documented tension in Western culture between gender and science can be found as early as ancient Greece, specifically in the organicist perspectives of Plato and Aristotle. The views of their respective schools differed in how they incorporated gender into this view of the world. Plato envisioned a feminine "world soul" that was "the source of motion in the universe," in other words, the active power or source of agency.[14] Aristotle, on the other hand, viewed action as a masculine property, while the feminine aspect of nature served in a passive role.[15] Within the Platonic view, the central image was that of a nurturing Mother Nature who provided humans and all living things the resources necessary for survival. However, there was simultaneously a secondary interpretation of this feminine force, as the uncontrollable chaos of storms and natural disasters. Carolyn Merchant explains these viewpoints as "projections of human perceptions" of female sexuality "onto the external world."[16] Feminist author Sandra Harding points out that our views of nature and the scientific endeavor are fluid and "have been highly influenced by the political strategies used in historically identifiable battles between the genders. Gender politics has provided resources for the advancement of science, and science has provided resources for the advancement of masculine domination."[17]

In her seminal work *The Death of Nature*, Carolyn Merchant argues that this medieval concept of the "nurturing earth" was "superseded by new controlling imagery" in the Scientific Revolution.[18] Observation—a passive, and in Aristotelian terms, feminine, scientific method—was replaced by active experimentation, where agency was the embodiment of the masculine principle.[19] Since nature was seen as gendered, specifically female, this domination of nature paralleled a dominion over women and female sexuality. Gone was the nurturing Mother Nature, supplanted by the previously secondary characterization of nature as feminine chaos that must be tamed. As Lisa Stenmark reflects, "Women threatened man's innocence, nature threatened his dominion. And, just as God intended that man should dominate and control women, God intended man should dominate and control nature."[20]

In *The Death of Nature*, Merchant masterfully uses the words of Francis Bacon, one of the fathers of the Scientific Revolution, to demonstrate the depths of the misogyny and mechanistic heartlessness in so-called Baconian science. For example, in *The Masculine Birth of Time*, Bacon explains that his methodology is "leading you to nature with all her children to bind her to your service and make her your slave… We have no right to expect nature to come to us… Nature must be taken by the forelock, being bald behind."[21] Nature is to be dissected, "forced out of her natural state and squeezed and molded" by the (presumably male) "scientist's 'hard facts,' 'penetrating mind' or the 'thrust of his argument'."[22] Bacon felt that "there are still laid up in the womb of nature many secrets of excellent use […]… only by the method which we are now treating can they be speedily and suddenly and simultaneously presented and anticipated."[23] Merchant explains, "As woman's womb had symbolically yielded to the forceps, so nature's womb harbored secrets that through technology could be wrested from her grasp for use in the improvement of the human condition."[24] She refers to Bacon's attitude toward nature as the "'rape' of nature for human good."[25] Similar language is effectively employed in Mary Shelley's famous cautionary tale *Frankenstein* when, early in the work, the titular character delights in a college lecture concerning modern scientists.

He is inspired by the idea that they are said to "penetrate into the recesses of nature and show how she works in her hiding-places… They have acquired new and almost unlimited powers; they can command the thunders of heaven, mimic the earthquake, and even mock the invisible world with its own shadows."[26]

In the Scientific Revolution, nature also became viewed as a machine rather than a living being; therefore, since it had "no spirit and no animation, it could be exploited at will."[27] A prime example of this was mining. Previously, the image of nature as a "nurturing mother" had prevented the wholesale destruction of the environment, as often happens in large-scale commercial mining operations. One does not simply mutilate the body of Mother Earth. With this anthropomorphized viewpoint gone, replaced with a vision of the Earth as nothing more than spiritless dirt and stone, the need for metals and minerals easily superseded environmental concerns. In Bacon's words, "the truth of nature lies hid in certain deep mines and caves"; therefore, in order to study nature, scientists should "sell their books and build furnaces" and forsake "Minerva and the Muses as barren virgins" for the forges of Vulcan.[28]

In his subcreated world, Tolkien purposefully and eloquently rejected the power-seeking scientific establishment of the Scientific and Industrial Revolutions. We witness such exploitation of nature fueling the industrial fires of Saruman—who has a "mind of metal and wheels"[29]—in Isengard as well as in Sharkey's Shire. When Saruman succumbs to his lust for power through technology, he transforms the beautiful tower of Isengard where "wise men" had once engaged in observing the heavens (an example of pure science) into a "child's model or a slave's flattery, of the vast fortress, armory, prison, furnace of great power, Barad-dûr, the Dark Tower."[30] Even earlier in the history of Middle-earth, Fëanor, "the most subtle in mind and the most skilled in hand" of all the Noldor developed great artificial jewels "greater and brighter than those of the earth," the most acclaimed of these being the three Silmarils.[31] In a letter to Milton Waldman, Tolkien explains that Fëanor "imprisoned" the light of the Two Trees within the jewels, clearly a work of subjugating nature.[32] It is should therefore be no surprise to the first-time reader of *The Silmarillion* that Fëanor's obsessive lust for this technological feat is the ultimate downfall of both him and his house and is the cause of much pain and suffering over the centuries.

The contrast between a pursuit of knowledge through patient, passive observing versus an unquenchable hunger for power over nature through the action of technology is eloquently voiced in the short cautionary piece called "The Tale of Adanel" found in Tolkien's commentary to the "Athrabeth Finrod ah Andreth." Here, it is accounted how the disembodied Voice of Ilúvatar spoke to the newly awakened humans with words quite reminiscent of Genesis: "In time ye will inherit all this Earth, but first ye must be children and learn."[33] At first, humans obeyed the Voice of their Creator, but as often happens, Ilúvatar's human students discovered that "learning was difficult" and sought the easy and immediate answers from Ilúvatar. In response, Ilúvatar cautioned them to "First seek to find the answer for yourselves. For ye will have joy in the finding, and so grow from childhood and become wise."[34] The first humans became impatient and "desired to order things to our will; and the shapes of many things that we wished to make awoke in our minds. Therefore we spoke less and less to the Voice."[35] This yearning left humans open to the machinations of Melkor, who was all too happy to give them what they desired most, but at a price. Thus humanity fell from science into technology, from the satisfaction of merely understanding into a desire for practical uses; as a result, their personal relationship with their Creator suffered. Is this, therefore, to be interpreted as Tolkien's morality play concerning the outcome of the Scientific Revolution?

Contrast the language used in the above tale with Gimli's organicist feelings concerning the Glittering Caves of Aglarond:

> No dwarf could be unmoved by such loveliness. None of Durin's race would mine those caves for stones or ore, not if diamonds and gold could be got there. Do you cut down groves of blossoming trees in the springtime for firewood? We would tend these glades of flowering stone, not quarry them.[36]

This juxtaposition of the organic with the inorganic is found throughout Tolkien's legendarium, for example in his description of the Silmarils themselves as "indeed living things."[37] In *The Hobbit*, Thranduil's throne room is described as "a great hall with pillars hewn out of the living stone,"[38] while the halls of Erebor features stairs that "were smooth, cut out of the living rock broad and fair."[39] Gandalf recounts his battle with the Balrog as beginning "far under the living earth" and describes how they climbed up the Endless Stair to "Durin's Tower carved in the living rock of Zirakzigil."[40] In *The Silmarillion*, it is said that the gate of the harbor of Alqualondë "was an arch of living rock sea-carved"[41] and that the dwarves delved for Thingol an underground abode of "high halls and chambers… hewn in the living stone," the Thousand Caves of Menegroth.[42] Indeed, the literal and metaphorical connections between the lithic and the living in Tolkien's works are legion.[43]

These efforts of the Elves to celebrate the beauty of the natural world, especially within their own dwellings, reflect one of the fundamental defining characteristics of elven philosophy. In a 1956 letter to Michael Straight, Tolkien notes that the Elves "represent, as it were, the artistic, aesthetic, and purely scientific aspects of the Humane nature raised to a higher level than is actually seen in Men. That is: they have a devoted love of the physical world and a desire to observe and understand it for its own sake and as 'other' [namely] as a reality derived from God in the same degree as themselves—not as a material for use or as a power-platform."[44] Seen through the lens of organicism, we note that the Elves understand that while they are not synonymous *with* the world, they are *of* the world; therefore, study of the natural world is a laudable endeavor in and of itself, even in (Tolkien would say especially in) the absence of any directed endgame.

An elf also understood that he or she occupied a precarious position within Arda, the world: his or her spirit, or *fëa*, "was imperishable within the life of Arda, and that its fate was to inhabit Arda to its end."[45] Therefore, not only was an elf other than Arda (being an identifiable being within it) but at the same time intimately related to it, as his or her life span was determined by the very fate of the natural world. Liam Campbell notes that there is a "clear interconnection" between the Elves' "position as creatures bound to the Earth in an immortal state and their devotion for and love of the Earth. Because of their bond with nature and the Earth, the elves are consumed by a deep sense of loss when part of the world's natural beauty is lost."[46] The Elves' serial longevity (until the world's end) also defines humans as "other" to elvenkind, despite the fact that they and humanity are "evidently in biological terms one race, or they could not breed and produce fertile offspring."[47] Whereas Elves remain in the world until its end, being bound to it, humans are heirs to the Gift of Ilúvatar, mortality, and upon death their spirits are removed from the world and are sundered from it at least until the end of Arda, if not permanently.

The Elves' deep association with nature is also demonstrated in their relationship with the Ents, whom they originally taught to talk, another set of intelligent beings who are deeply rooted in their relationship with the natural world as being simultaneously both "other" and part of the whole. Treebeard explains to Merry and Pippin that "Ents are more like Elves; less interested in themselves than Men are, and better at getting inside other things."[48] The distinction between pure science and applied technology is also illustrated through the fate of the Ents and their sundering from the Entwives. For while the Ents were content to be the shepherds of the forests and speak with the trees, the Entwives "did not desire to speak with these things"; but they wished them "to grow according to their wishes, and bear leaf and fruit to their liking, for the Entwives desired order, and plenty, and peace (by which they meant that things should remain where they had set them). So the Entwives made gardens to live in… Many men learned the crafts of the Entwives and honoured them greatly."[49]

The Scientific Revolution (and its direct offspring, the Industrial Revolution) was founded on the dual concepts of "order and power," power being an "ominous and sinister word" in Tolkien's tales.[50] We see in the fate of the Entwives (their disappearance from the face of Middle-earth) a cautionary tale for the fate of technologists. In an interesting note to a 1955 letter to W.H. Auden, Tolkien explains that the difference between the Ents' and Entwives' approach to growing things represented "the difference between the 'male' and 'female' attitude to wild things, the difference between unpossessive love and gardening."[51] While Tolkien's assignment of these specific genders to these traits is interesting in and of itself, the main lesson is, again, that the exertion of power for domination over nature (the modern scientific perspective) is inferior to the organicist perspective.

One final character whose actions clearly demonstrate an organicist perspective is Tom Bombadil. When asked by Naomi Mitchison if there was a connection between Tom and the Entwives, Tolkien replied that Bombadil "is almost the opposite, being say, Botany and Zoology (as sciences) and Poetry as opposed to Cattle-breeding and Agriculture and practicality."[52] This philosophy is echoed in a number of Tolkien's letters. For example, in a 1954 letter to Peter Hastings, Tolkien explains that Tom Bombadil is "an 'allegory,' or an exemplar, a particular embodying of pure (real) natural science: the spirit that desires knowledge of other things, their history and nature, *because they are 'other'*… and entirely unconcerned with 'doing' anything with the knowledge: Zoology and Botany not Cattle-breeding` or Agriculture."[53] Bombadil has "no desire of possession or domination at all. He merely knows and understands about such things as concern him in his natural little realm."[54] Again, Bombadil embodies the organicist understanding of alterity as being different from yet a part of nature. Campbell describes him as representing "the harmony of nature itself—the spirit of humanity as it was meant to be: in complete union with the natural world, seeking understanding without control."[55]

But power is not the sole pursuit of modern science. C.P. Snow offers that the two explicit motivations of modern science are the understanding of the natural world as well as its domination.[56] Marx Wartofsky adds that "scientific innocence consists in the pure pursuit of truth for its own sake, in a selfless inquiry detached from consideration of personal advantage, practical consequence, or ideological prejudice."[57] Patrick Curry agrees, noting that "some scientists are more oriented to the wonder of the natural world (i.e. enchantment) than its manipulation and exploitation (i.e. magic)."[58] Specifically, Curry,[59] Dickerson and Evans,[60] Campbell,[61] and Jeffers[62] have noted in Tolkien's works modern twentieth-century ecological threads. Merchant explains that modern ecology very much has its "roots in medieval organicism—the idea that the cosmos is an organic entity, growing and developing from within, in an integrated unity of structure and function."[63]

Another viewpoint developed in the late twentieth century is the idea of "feminist science" or "feminist epistemology," based in large part on the work of Fausto-Sterling,[64] Harding,[65] and Keller.[66] This revisioning of the scientific method places "emphasis on intuition, on feeling, on connection and relatedness."[67] Nobel Prize-winning biologist Barbara McClintock's research style perhaps best epitomizes this view of science. She attributes her great success in understanding plant genetics as due to her ability to devote "the time to look, the patience to 'hear what the material has to say to you,' the openness to 'let it come to you.' Above all, one must have 'a feeling for the organism'."[68] Evelyn Fox Keller makes the important distinction that here *organism* is not to be understood in the narrow modern sense of a biological entity, but rather in a classical organicist view, as a piece of the natural world that is to be understood. She also notes that McClintock believes that the goal of science is "not prediction per se, but understanding; not the power to manipulate, but empowerment."[69]

Feminist views of science therefore hearken back to a medieval viewpoint of the interconnectedness of a nurturing cosmos that is knowable through respectful interactions with it. These viewpoints parallel Tolkien's views of science, and Barbara McClintock would have been right at home in Rivendell. Interestingly, an organicist view of the world is also found in the Gaia hypothesis of James Lovelock and Lynn Margulis, which argues that living things and the wider geological, physical, and chemical environment interact in such a way as to self-regulate, just as the organs and systems of any living creature would in order to stay alive.[70] Liam Campbell offers the Ents' attack on Isengard as an example of this concept.[71] Another example is the anthropic principle in physics, which, in its weakest form, acknowledges that if the universe were such that it did not have the conditions necessary to nurture human life, we would not be here to observe it in the first place. More controversial versions of the hypothesis suggest that the universe had no choice in its fine-tuning because the eventual existence of intelligent observers was a necessity. Rather than merely to note that the fine-tuning of the universe makes our existence possible, these extensions seek to answer "why" the universe is fine-tuned by appealing to our very existence itself.[72]

Maria Mitchell, the first American woman astronomer, wrote in 1870 concerning observing sunspots that "the true observer will study Nature because he loves her, and seeking neither reward nor renown, will open his heart to her wonderful revelations."[73] Her words not only reflect an organicist or feminist viewpoint of both nature and the scientific endeavor, but resonate quite loudly with the great theme of the song of Ilúvatar in which the divine relationship between sentient beings and nature was determined before the creation of Middle-earth. It is only due to the discord of Melkor that the Scientific and Industrial Revolutions entered into the world of Tolkien's subcreation. In modern times, naming something as "Other" has taken on a negative, oppositional connotation. In the medieval world, both in its primary and Tolkienian forms, one could recognize, respect, and celebrate both the Otherness of the natural world and simultaneously our connection to it. Tolkien echoes this quite clearly in the creation story of the Dwarves by Aulë; while the Vala was rightly rebuked by Ilúvatar for his attempt to manufacture unnatural beings, his goal was neither power nor dominion: "I desired things other than I am, to love and to teach them, so that they too might perceive the beauty of Eä, which thou has caused to be."[74]

To identify something as Other clearly does not preclude one from being in an intimate relationship with it. As Stenmark summarizes this feminist epistemology, nature is "not a 'thing,' separate or separable from a speaking and knowing 'we.' What people know about nature they know because they interact with and are embedded in it. People know the world, because they are a part of the world and because they are in a relationship with it."[75] It is in the revealing of the depth and beauty of this relationship between self and other that we learn not only about the other, but about ourselves as well. In this author's mind, this is not only the ultimate goal of science, but one of the most fundamental rewards of immersing oneself in Middle-earth.

Notes

1. Jane Chance, ed., *Tolkien the Medievalist* (New York: Routledge, 2008), 4.
2. Richard C. West, *Tolkien Criticism: An Annotated Checklist* (Kent: The Kent State University Press, 1981).
3. Judith A. Johnson, *J.R.R. Tolkien: Six Decades of Criticism* (Westport: Greenwood Press, 1986).
4. Jane Chance, ed., *Tolkien and the Invention of Myth: A Reader* (Lexington: The University Press of Kentucky, 2004); Chance, *Tolkien the Medievalist.*
5. Kristine Larsen, "'It Passes Our Skill in These Days': Primary World Influences on Durin's Day," in The Hobbit *and Tolkien's Mythology*, ed. Bradford Lee Eden (Jefferson: McFarland, 2014), 40–58; "A Little Earth of His Own: Tolkien's Lunar Creation Myths," in *The Ring Goes Ever On: Proceedings of the Tolkien 2005 Conference, Vol. 2, ed.* Sarah Wells (Coventry: The Tolkien Society, 2008), 394–403.
6. Gerard Hynes, "'Beneath the Earth's Dark Keel': Tolkien and Geology," *Tolkien Studies* 9 (2012): 21–36.
7. Kristine Larsen, "'A Creature of an Older World': Tolkien and the Mythology of the Prehistoric," *Lembas Extra* (2015): 167–190.
8. Dinah Hazell, *The Plants of Middle-earth: Botany and Sub-creation* (Kent: The Kent University Press, 2006).
9. Kristine Larsen, "'Alone Between the Dark and the Light': 'The Lay of Aotrou and Itroun' and Lessons from the Later Legendarium," in *Author of the New Century: T. A. Shippey and the Creation of the Next Canon*, eds. John William Houghton, Janet Brennan Croft, Nancy Martsch, John D. Rateliff, and Robin Anne Reid (Jefferson: McFarland, 2014), 226; 232.
10. Humphrey Carpenter, *The Letters of J.R.R. Tolkien* (Boston: Houghton Mifflin, 2000), 246.

11. Kristine Larsen, "The (Nearly) Discarded Image: Tolkien's Later Tinkerings with his Medieval Cosmology," paper presented at the 49th International Congress on Medieval Studies, Western Michigan University, Kalamazoo, MI, May 2014.
12. Sandra Harding, *The Science Question in Feminism* (Ithaca: Cornell University Press, 1986), 113.
13. Carolyn Merchant, *The Death of Nature: Women, Ecology and the Scientific Revolution* (San Francisco: Harper and Row, 1989), 6.
14. Ibid., 10.
15. Harding, *The Science Question*, 114.
16. Merchant, *The Death of Nature*, 2.
17. Harding, *The Science Question*, 112.
18. Merchant, *The Death of Nature*, 189.
19. Evelyn Fox Keller, *Reflections on Gender and Science* (New Haven, CT: Yale University Press, 1985), 37.
20. Lisa Stenmark, "Feminisms and Science," in *The Encyclopedia of Science and Religion*, ed. Wesley J. Wildman (New York: Macmillan Reference USA, 2003), 324.
21. Merchant, *The Death of Nature*, 170.
22. Merchant, *The Death of Nature*, 171.
23. Merchant, *The Death of Nature*, 169.
24. Ibid.
25. Ibid., 171.
26. Mary Shelley, *Frankenstein, or The Modern Prometheus* (New York: Signet Classics, 2000), 32–33.
27. Stenmark, "Feminisms and Science," 324.
28. Merchant, *The Death of Nature*, 171.
29. J.R.R. Tolkien, *The Two Towers*, 2nd ed. (Boston: Houghton Mifflin, 1987), III, iv, 76.
30. Ibid., III, viii, 160–161.
31. J.R.R. Tolkien, *The Silmarillion* (Boston: Houghton Mifflin, 2001), 64.
32. Carpenter, *Letters*, 148.
33. J.R.R. Tolkien, *Morgoth's Ring* (Boston: Houghton Mifflin, 1993), 346.
34. Ibid., 345–346.
35. Ibid., 346.
36. Tolkien, *The Two Towers*, III, viii, 153.
37. Tolkien, *The Silmarillion*, 68.
38. J.R.R. Tolkien, *The Hobbit* (Boston: Houghton Mifflin, 2007), 158.
39. Ibid., 220.
40. Tolkien, *The Two Towers*, III, v, 105.
41. Tolkien, *The Silmarillion*, 61.
42. Ibid., 93.

43. Kristine Larsen, "'Ore-ganisms': The Myth and Meaning of 'Living Rock' in Middle-earth," paper presented at the Popular Culture Association/ American Culture Association National Conference, New Orleans, LA, April 2015.
44. Carpenter, *Letters*, 236.
45. Tolkien, *Morgoth's Ring*, 219.
46. Campbell, *Ecological Augury*, 189.
47. Carpenter, *Letters*, 189.
48. Tolkien, *The Two Towers*, III, iv, 71.
49. Ibid., III, iv, 79.
50. Carpenter, *Letters*, 152.
51. Ibid., 212.
52. Ibid., 179.
53. Ibid., 192.
54. Ibid.
55. Campbell, *Ecological Augury*, 80.
56. C.P. Snow, *The Two Cultures: And A Second Look* (New York: Cambridge University Press, 1963), 64–65.
57. Marx W. Wartofsky, "The Critique of Impure Reason II: Sin, Science, and Society," *Science, Technology, and Human Values* 6, no. 33 (1980): 5.
58. Patrick Curry, *Defending Middle-Earth: Tolkien, Myth and Modernity*, 2nd ed. (Boston: Houghton Mifflin, 2004), 63.
59. Curry, *Defending Middle-earth.*
60. Matthew T. Dickerson. and Jonathan Evans, *Ents, Elves, and Eriador: The Environmental Vision of J.R.R. Tolkien* (Lexington: The University of Kentucky Press, 2011).
61. Campbell, *Ecological Augury.*
62. Susan Jeffers, *Arda Inhabited: Environmental relationships in* The Lord of the Rings (Kent: The Kent State University Press, 2014).
63. Merchant, *The Death of Nature*, 100.
64. Anne Fausto-Sterling, *Myths of Gender: Biological Theories about Women and Men* (New York: Basic Books, 1985).
65. Harding, *The Science Question.*
66. Evelyn Fox Keller, *A Feeling for the Organism* (New York: W.H. Freeman and Co., 1983); Keller, *Reflections.*
67. Keller, *Reflections*, 173.
68. Keller, *A Feeling*, 197–198.
69. Keller, *Reflections*, 166.
70. James E. Lovelock and Lynn Margulis, "Atmospheric Homeostasis by and for the Biosphere: The Gaia Hypothesis," *Tellus* Series A 26, no. 1 (1974): 3.
71. Campbell, *Ecological Augury*, 40.

72. Brandon Carter, "Large Number Coincidences and the Anthropic Principle in Cosmology," in *Confrontation of Cosmological Theories with Observational Data: Copernicus Symposium 2*, ed. M. S. Longair (Dordrecht: D. Reidel, 1974), 291–298.
73. Maria Mitchell, "Watching the Sun." *Hours at Home* 11, no. 3 (1870): 236.
74. Tolkien, *The Silmarillion*, 43.
75. Stenmark, "Feminisms and Science," 325.

Bibliography

Campbell, Liam. *The Ecological Augury in the Works of J.R.R. Tolkien*. Zurich: Walking Tree Publishers, 2011.

Carpenter, Humphrey, ed. *The Letters of J.R.R. Tolkien*. Boston: Houghton Mifflin, 2000.

Carter, Brandon. "Large Number Coincidences and the Anthropic Principle in Cosmology." In *Confrontation of Cosmological Theories with Observational Data: Copernicus Symposium 2*, edited by M. S. Longair, 291–298. Dordrecht: D. Reidel, 1974.

Chance, Jane, ed. *Tolkien and the Invention of Myth: A Reader*. Lexington: The University Press of Kentucky, 2004.

———. *Tolkien the Medievalist*. New York: Routledge, 2008.

Curry, Patrick. *Defending Middle-Earth: Tolkien, Myth and Modernity*, 2nd ed. Boston: Houghton Mifflin, 2004.

Dickerson, Matthew T. and Jonathan Evans. *Ents, Elves, and Eriador: The Environmental Vision of J.R.R. Tolkien*. Lexington: The University of Kentucky Press, 2011.

Fausto-Sterling, Anne. *Myths of Gender: Biological Theories about Women and Men*. New York: Basic Books, 1985.

Harding, Sandra. *The Science Question in Feminism*. Ithaca: Cornell University Press, 1986.

Hazell, Dinah. *The Plants of Middle-earth: Botany and Sub-creation*. Kent: The Kent University Press, 2006.

Hynes, Gerard. "'Beneath the Earth's Dark Keel': Tolkien and Geology." *Tolkien Studies* 9 (2012): 21–36.

Jeffers, Susan. *Arda Inhabited: Environmental Relationships in* The Lord of the Rings. Kent: The Kent State University Press, 2014.

Johnson, Judith A. *J.R.R. Tolkien: Six Decades of Criticism*. Westport: Greenwood Press, 1986.

Keller, Evelyn Fox. *A Feeling for the Organism*. New York: W. H. Freeman and Co., 1983.

———. *Reflections on Gender and Science*. New Haven, CT: Yale University Press, 1985.

Larsen, Kristine. "'A Little Earth of His Own: Tolkien's Lunar Creation Myths." In *The Ring Goes Ever On: Proceedings of the Tolkien 2005 Conference. Vol. 2, edited* by Sarah Wells, 394–403. Coventry: The Tolkien Society, 2008.

———. "Alone Between the Dark and the Light': 'The Lay of Aotrou and Itroun' and Lessons from the Later Legendarium." In *Author of the New Century: T. A. Shippey and the Creation of the Next Canon,* edited by John William Houghton, Janet Brennan Croft , Nancy Martsch, John D. Rateliff, and Robin Anne Reid, 221-36. Jefferson: McFarland, 2014.

———."'It Passes Our Skill in These Days': Primary World Influences on Durin's Day." In The Hobbit *and Tolkien's Mythology*, edited by Bradford Lee Eden, 40–58. Jefferson: McFarland, 2014.

———. "The (Nearly) Discarded Image: Tolkien's Later Tinkerings with his Medieval Cosmology." Paper presented at the 49th International Congress on Medieval Studies, Western Michigan University, Kalamazoo, MI, May 2014.

———. "'A Creature of an Older World': Tolkien and the Mythology of the Prehistoric." *Lembas Extra* (2015): 167–190.

———. "'Ore-ganisms': The Myth and Meaning of 'Living Rock' in Middle-earth." Paper presented at the Popular Culture Association/American Culture Association National Conference, New Orleans, LA, April 2015.

Lovelock, James E. and Lynn Margulis. "Atmospheric Homeostasis by and for the Biosphere: The Gaia Hypothesis." *Tellus* Series A 26, no. 1 (1974): 2–10.

Merchant, Carolyn. *The Death of Nature: Women, Ecology and the Scientific Revolution*. San Francisco: Harper and Row, 1989.

Mitchell, Maria. "Watching the Sun." *Hours at Home* 11, no. 3 (1870): 231–236.

Shelley, Mary. *Frankenstein, or The Modern Prometheus*. New York: Signet Classics, 2000.

Snow, C.P. *The Two Cultures: And A Second Look*. New York: Cambridge University Press, 1963.

Stenmark, Lisa. "Feminisms and Science." In *The Encyclopedia of Science and Religion*, edited by Wesley J. Wildman, 323–326. New York: Macmillan Reference USA, 2003.

Tolkien, J.R.R. *The Two Towers*. 2nd ed. Boston: Houghton Mifflin, 1987.

———. *Morgoth's Ring*. Boston: Houghton Mifflin, 1993.

———. *The Silmarillion*. Boston: Houghton Mifflin, 2001.

———. *The Hobbit*. Boston: Houghton Mifflin, 2007.

Wartofsky, Marx W. "The Critique of Impure Reason II: Sin, Science, and Society." *Science, Technology, and Human Values* 6, no. 33 (1980): 5–23.

West, Richard C. *Tolkien Criticism: An Annotated Checklist*. Kent: The Kent State University Press, 1981.

PART III

The Queer

CHAPTER 6

Cinema, Sexuality, Mechanical Reproduction

Valerie Rohy

To many critics, Peter Jackson's *The Lord of the Rings* film trilogy is a queer story indeed; while the *Village Voice* called the third film "gayer than anything in *Angels in America*," another review observed that "the relationship between the Hobbits, particularly fat Sam and saucer-eyed Frodo, is played like a teenage crush."[1] In one sense, these remarks are pure camp, but they also tell the truth: Their "absurd" assertion describes a real erotic vector of the films. Tolkien scholars such as Jane Chance and Esther Saxey have agreed that Jackson amplifies the homoerotic aspects of the novel, even as Anna Smol rightly observes that the films labor to diminish the novels' suggestions of same-sex love.[2] Ambivalent though it may be, Jackson's trilogy shows a degree of male intimacy seldom seen in Hollywood blockbusters, from the bedroom reunion of Sam and Frodo at Rivendell to the Grey Havens sequence, with a deliberate kiss and intimation of an unheard message. So confident were the filmmakers of their audience's tolerance for tenderness between men that a key promotional image for *The Return of the King* showed Sam, on the slopes of Mount Doom, cradling Frodo in his arms.

V. Rohy (✉)
University of Vermont, Burlington, VT, USA

C. Vaccaro and Y. Kisor (eds.), *Tolkien and Alterity*, The New Middle Ages, DOI 10.1007/978-3-319-61018-4_6

But far from urging the viewer to acknowledge the same-sex love that is, after all, no small part of Tolkien's novel, such images work *in the opposite way*: Their direct and public presentation of male–male intimacy, like the critics' winking reviews, works to inoculate the films against that recognition. In a potent example of what Eve Sedgwick calls the open secret, the more insistently commentators note the films' homosexual valence, the more effectively they show that it cannot exist.[3] If it is so plainly visible, then of course we must be imagining it. Whatever is happening between Sam and Frodo cannot be queer, because it is overt, not covert, and literal, not ironic—hidden in plain sight, like the purloined letter whose place is, as Poe writes, "a little *too* self-evident."[4]

The production team that invented such images also sought to guard against the perception of same-sex love in films destined for box office gold. In a series of interviews, writer Philippa Boyens rejected the possibility of any sexual bond between Sam and Frodo; instead, she said they share "a genuine friendship. It's quite clean and pure."[5] But efforts to deny what looks exactly like, but *cannot possibly be*, homosexuality in *The Lord of the Rings* may only confirm it, for in the realm of queer meaning, to protest at all is always to protest too much. Such headlines as "Hobbits Are Not Gay Lovers Says Wood"—with which the Internet Movie Database glossed Elijah Wood's rather more ambiguous remarks on the subject—serve also to suggest that they might well be.[6] So the effort to straighten Tolkien's tale must also come in the diegesis, where all three films enhance Tolkien's attenuated, lightly outlined marriage plots, enlarging the Aragorn-Arwen and Sam-Rosie stories with freshly scripted scenes. Thus, Jackson's *The Return of the King* concludes with a wedding, never glimpsed in the book, that fulfills Sam's sudden conversion to heterosexuality at Mount Doom—the moment when, stranded with Frodo at "the end of all things," Sam is stricken by regret that he did not marry a girl whose existence he had quite forgotten during the boys' extended camping trip.[7]

Knowing full well that the novel's same-sex bonds, *pace* Boyens, can never register cinematically as "clean and pure," Jackson's compensatory efforts go further. Even as they augment *The Lord of the Rings*' limited heterosexual possibilities, the films shift the focus of non-normative sexuality from object-choice to reproduction. Through this cinematic sleight of hand, perversity comes to mean monstrous birth, not misdirected desire: The films foreground the figure of the child as a sentimental emblem of proper love and introduce, by contrast, the threat of unnatural reproduction.[8] In this, Jackson follows the logic of heteronormative discourse, which has no need for scrupulous distinctions among same-sex desire, the abnegation of heterosexual fertility, and the unnatural proliferation of perversion. While the novel's horror of sterility makes it no less chary of actual children, Jackson and collaborator Fran Walsh seize every opportunity to film round-faced, wide-eyed youngsters, including but not limited to their own. In Bilbo's storytelling session in *Fellowship*, the young refugees from the Westfold in *Two Towers*, the cuts to frightened women and children during the battle of Helm's Deep, and Arwen's vision of the son she will have with Aragorn—again and again the films' children conventionally represent the hope of futurity as threatened by Sauron, and the material confirmation of straight love's accomplishment.[9] By the end of the trilogy, we learn that Bilbo's remark to a mother trailing a brood of hobbit children in the extended edition of *Fellowship*—"good gracious, you have been productive"—represents the films' own view *literally*, that is, stripped of the sarcasm that marks Bilbo as an exile from the fertile future the films promote.[10]

If normative sexuality means the sacralized figure of the child, the non-normative appears as unnatural reproduction, as Saruman, taking his cue from *Frankenstein*, engineers the oozing birth of Uruk-hai soldiers, "bred for a single purpose," out of inanimate matter.[11] In *Fellowship*, we see orcs extract a newborn Uruk-hai from the earth, scraping away a film of mud to reveal a face moving grotesquely under a glistening caul. This is a distinct departure from the novel, whose references to Saruman's orcs suggest hideous crossbreeding, not asexual mass production. As Tolkien has it, Gamling observes "creatures of Isengard, these half-orcs and goblin-men that the foul craft of Saruman has bred."[12] Jackson's depiction of the Uruk-hai does have a precedent in Tolkien's writing, in a text that predates *The Lord of the Rings* by decades. "The Fall of Gondolin," written in 1917, states that Orcs are "bred by Melko of the subterranean heats and slime."[13] But Tolkien explicitly forecloses this possibility in later work; in *The Lord of the Rings* Frodo explains that evil "can only mock, it cannot make: not real new things of its own," and *The Silmarillion* notes that Orcs "multiplied after the manner of the children of Ilúvatar."[14]

If for Tolkien the Ring is the sole emblem of sexual perversity—the voracious force that distorts desire, drawing all lust and longing to itself and suspending normative coupling—Jackson's account of Saruman's parthenogenic project adds another index of deviance. Born with adult size and strength, the Uruk-hai find their lifespan is truncated at both ends, as if they inhabit a different register of time. Richard Taylor, co-director of the film's special effects workshop, explains on the *Two Towers* extended edition DVD that over time the Uruk-hai's "genetic lineage begins to corrupt," producing "significant acceleration in their aging." Like the replicants in *Blade Runner*, the Uruk-hai are subject to "accelerated decrepitude," and their rapid decay betrays the shoddy workmanship of their unnatural origin.[15] It is no wonder, then, that Jackson chooses to include in *The Two Towers* Tolkien's obscure, unfunny joke about dwarf women. When Gimli earnestly refutes "the belief that there *are* no dwarf women and that dwarves just spring out of holes in the ground," his protest against such "ridiculous" notions is a serious bit of business, since the film has minutes earlier reprised the sequence showing Uruk-hai entering the world in exactly this way.[16] Inside a torch-lit cave beneath Isengard, the camera finds a smaller cave, from which two orcs drag a brown, gelatinous sac, slitting its membrane to reveal a slimy head. The newborn's roaring mouth forms a perfect O, replicating the O of the obscene hole from which he emerged, the O of the One Ring whose interest he will serve—and the apparition of Sauron's eye, which Jackson renders in the shape of the ring.[17] "Nothing will come of nothing," says Shakespeare's Lear, and Jackson shows precisely how: This creature is born from the sheer emptiness of the Ring itself, one devouring negativity delivered out of another.[18]

Just what that void signifies for Jackson is no mystery: The neonate Uruk-hai seems to emerge from the wrong orifice, an O more anal than vaginal, as the cavern discharges its burden. The Uruk-hai are, to put it crudely, born as shit. Naming this aperture as anal, we may recall how that term, as Lacan reminds us, etymologically names a *ring*, and thus how the O, the nothingness, from which the Uruk-hai are born repeats not only the shape but also the function of the One Ring.[19] To borrow Lee Edelman's words, it is "emptied of meaning except for its residual meaning as waste and its consequent association with that very emptying or wasting of meaning."[20] If Rosie's complaint to Sam at the end of the novel—"Well, you've wasted a year" (to which Sam replies "I wouldn't call it that")—construes same-sex love as *a waste of time*, Jackson's films translate non-normative desire into *waste matter*. Where the novel finds in homosexual meandering a nonproductive waste of time, the film imagines perversity as an indecent *form of* reproduction, an endlessly proliferating sterility, which will, if unchecked, lay waste to the world.

It is either from the wedding ring or from the gaping hole of the One Ring, the films tell us, that the future will be born.

Begetting offspring made not in his own image but in the image of his murderous desire, Saruman becomes the queerest figure in the *Rings* films, the figure whose depravity makes all of Sam and Frodo's hand-holding look, by comparison, almost innocent. But sentimentalized, sublimated homosexuality and monstrous, queer reproduction turn out to represent two sides of the same coin: The Uruk-hai are not only a convenient distraction from Sam and Frodo's relationship, but also its grotesque analog, its secret logic. Saruman manifests his villainy in the same crass impersonation with which the queer is eternally charged, the same second-rate imitation of a norm whose own contingent status is strategically concealed. As a travesty of organic life, that is, the Uruk-hai recall the phobic notion of homosexuality as an impersonation of heterosexuality—as, in Judith Butler's words, "a copy, an imitation, a derivative example, a shadow of the real."[21] The tropes of sterile proliferation and corrupt mimesis are so indelibly linked to homosexuality that even, *or more to the point, especially*, without any suggestion of erotic coupling, such unnatural reproduction can only signify as queer. Homosexuality, Guy Hocquenghem argues, constitutes "the ungenerating-ungenerated terror of the family, because it produces itself without reproducing." Indeed, he continues:

> the transmission of homosexuality has something faintly mysterious about it, like the production of desire: a prefect of Police quoted by Gustav Macé defines homosexuals as "people who, though not procreating, have a marked tendency to multiply."[22]

In this hetero-familial logic, Hocquenghem suggests, homosexuality threatens a contagious transmission of deviance not merely because it refuses normative reproduction but also because it constitutes an unnatural *form* of reproduction. Jackson's fantasy of parthenogenesis, which seems to remove the Uruk-hai from the realm of sexuality as such, succeeds only in obviating their dangerous proximity to *heterosexuality*. Here queer multiplication functions to divide, cordoning off the morbidity against which the heterosexual family, its own endless self-replication notwithstanding, will triumphantly define itself.

Such matters of imitation and imposture concerned Tolkien as well: While the scenes in the caverns of Isengard are Jackson's invention, they obliquely dramatize Tolkien's paratextual comments on Saruman and illegitimate reproduction. After Houghton Mifflin published hardcover editions of *The Lord of the Rings* in 1954–1955, the American paperback edition was delayed, allowing Ace Books to exploit a copyright loophole and print an unauthorized edition in 1965. When Ballantine Books issued the authorized paperback later the same year, a new section in Tolkien's "Foreword" denounced the piracy:

> It seems to me a grave discourtesy, to say no more, to issue my book without even a polite note informing me of the project: dealings one might expect of Saruman in his decay rather than from the defenders of the West.[23]

The distributors of the pirate edition resemble "Saruman in his decay," to Tolkien, because they proliferate bad copies whose decline in quality bespeaks their status as impostures. (Promising "the only complete and authorized paperbound edition, containing all of the original text and maps," Ballantine's front matter suggests that the pirate edition is not only unethical but also incomplete.) Although it was the novel's trolls, not the Uruk-hai, that Tolkien named as "counterfeits" in a 1954 letter, the term aptly describes both the literary counterfeiters whose treachery the Ballantine foreword condemns and Jackson's Saruman, whose false reproductions mock legitimate creation.[24]

As Saruman's monster-making works within the narrative to defuse the problem of queer sexuality, this mechanical reproduction extends to the films' own creative work. Although it may seem that Jackson's camera has more in common with Sauron, the Great Eye, whose unblinking gaze is echoed in the films' long, bravura pans around Orthanc and Barad-Dur, in fact the camera's place is Saruman's. After all, Jackson's films copy Tolkien's text, producing an ingenious simulacrum, which, however well-crafted, will always seem to "mock, not make." Unlike the American Ace edition of the novel, Jackson's film adaptation of *The Lord of the Rings* is authorized by the Tolkien estate; but that legal status did not alter fans' complaints about the accuracy of its reproduction—a topic of obsessive attention even before the start of filming. Perhaps any film adaptation of a novel must seem mechanical beside the comparatively organic book, but the *Lord of the Rings* films make matters worse in their effort to solve the problem of same-sex love. The invented subplot about Saruman's perverse reproduction itself enacts the revisionary "bad copying" (always, like Saruman, in the pursuit of perfection) that *the subplot itself* portrays as perverse wizardry. That is, Jackson's effort to defuse the problem of same-sex love in Tolkien's novel leads to the invention of a story about unnatural reproduction; yet that invention itself symptomatizes the widespread revisions that make the films themselves simulacra, implicated in Saruman's parthenogenic reproduction and thus in the queer sexuality they seek to avoid.

This mimicry of Saruman, while hinted in the films' narrative revisions, is most obvious visually. As we have seen, Jackson imagines unnatural reproduction as industrial production: In *The Two Towers* and *The Fellowship of the Ring*, the camera's tour of Isengard's satanic mills cuts from sword-making assembly lines in what Saruman calls his "fires of industry" to the mass production of the soldiers who will wield them. In each film, shots of "the machinery of war" in the caves of Isengard—the molten metal cast into swords, the gears and scaffolding, the row of identical helmets—link the Uruk-hai's creation to industrial processes, as if to literalize what Walter Benjamin calls mechanical reproduction. The iconic figures of Saruman's ambition, the giant cog-wheels driving his subterranean machinery—Tolkien writes of Isengard, "iron wheels revolved there endlessly"—resemble nothing so much as the reels of a film projector, and the processes those wheels serve are equally cinematic.[25] As Benjamin observes, cinema both exemplifies art transformed by massification and multiplication, and to some degree transcends its own mechanical means of production. Unlike other mass-produced art, cinema erases the apparatus upon which it relies, offering an illusory but potent glimpse, Benjamin writes, of "an aspect of reality which is free of all equipment."[26] Ironically, the equipment of twenty-first-century cinematic production that allows Jackson to visualize Tolkien's pre-industrial fantasy "free of all equipment" does so only through a version of Saruman's craft. Jackson's production team drew life out of inanimate matter and multiplied such beings through the "fissiparous" techniques of digital animation. Tolkien writes of the elemental force of darkness in his universe, "Evil is fissiparous. But itself barren. Morgoth could not 'beget', or have any spouse."[27] From the computer-generated Gollum who mimics and replaces Andy Serkis' performance to the trolls, fell beasts, oliphaunts, and Balrog created entirely through digital technology, and the MASSIVE software that, as if obeying Sauron's instructions to "build me an army worthy of Mordor," produce phalanxes of artificial intelligence "agents," the films, no less than Saruman, mechanically and asexually manufacture the semblance of living beings.[28] The cinematic mechanism is implicated in the perversity it represents as monstrous.

If, as Benjamin recognizes, cinema is always a technology of mechanical reproduction, we might regard the way in which Jackson's *The Lord of the Rings* exploits that technology as an act of bad faith. Only through technological artifice do the films produce a vision of a pre-industrial world in which that same artifice, working as a site of displaced queer sexuality, appears as a future-negating abomination. But Jackson is surely not the only one to inhabit that paradox, and the truth, as usual, is more complicated. Born out of the O, the open mouth, the gaping hole, the nothingness of the Ring are Jackson's films themselves: Straight narrative is a function of queer magic. At the least, then, the way the films' own practice of mechanical reproduction finds its mirror image in Saruman's corrupt wizardry suggests the profound complicity of the normative and the perverse in the very machinery that subtends fantasies of normative desire. Where sexuality is concerned, as Foucault argues, in a society of "blatant and fragmented perversion" the perversity of the law does not mitigate its disciplinary power, but the perversity of the law is also never wholly reducible to a form of discipline.[29] Jackson's vision of Saruman may serve to deny the unnaturalness of straight familialism, but it also exposes just how that mass-marketed familial ideology depends upon the artificial reproduction of cinema itself—and on the queer sexuality located at the heart of the machine.

Notes

1. J. Hoberman, "Final Fantasy," *Village Voice*, December 15, 2003, C62; Alastair McKay, "Disappointing Turn of the Ring," *The Scotsman*, December 12, 2003, accessed December 13, 2003, http://www.news.scotsman.com/entertainment.cfm?id=1359622003.
2. Jane Chance, "'In the Company of Orcs': Peter Jackson's Queer Tolkien," in *Queer Movie Medievalisms*, ed. Kathleen Coyne Kelley and Tison Pugh (Burlington, VT: Ashgate, 2009), 89; Esther Saxey, "Homoeroticism," in *Reading* The Lord of the Rings: *New Writings on Tolkien's Classic,* ed. Robert Eaglestone (New York: Continuum, 2005), 124; Anna Smol, "'Oh … oh … Frodo!': Readings of Male Intimacy in *The Lord of the Rings*," *Modern Fiction Studies* 50: 4 (2004): 967. Chance both acknowledges Frodo's "tenuous queer relationship" with Sam (84) and argues that the hobbits in Jackson's film are queer in a gendered

sense, feminized in comparison with Aragorn's ideal masculinity and the orcs' sadistic hypermasculinity (82–83).

3. Eve Kosofsky Sedgwick, *Epistemology of the Closet* (Berkeley: University of California Press, 1990), 165.
4. Edgar Allan Poe, *The Tell-Tale Heart and Other Writings* (New York: Bantam, 1982), 109.
5. Bob Longino, "Off-Screen Friendship Creates On-Screen Bond," *Fort Worth Star-Telegram*, December 8, 2003, accessed September 4, 2004, http://www.dfw.com/mld/dfw/living/7429681.htm?1c.
6. "Hobbits Are Not Gay Lovers Says Wood," *IMDb*, November 19, 2002, accessed January 12, 2004, http://us.imdb.com/news/wenn/2002-11-19.
7. *The Lord of the Rings: The Return of the King*, directed by Peter Jackson (New Line, 2003), DVD. On Sam's relationships with Rose and Frodo in the novel, see Smol (966), and Jes Battis, "Gazing Upon Sauron: Hobbits, Elves, and the Queering of the Postcolonial Optic," *Modern Fiction Studies* 50:4 (2004): 914–915.
8. This shift from object-choice to reproduction recalls the contemporary debates around marriage equality in the USA, which suggested that same-sex love may be tolerated as long as normative familial structures continue unaltered.
9. I discuss the novel's similar insistence on heteronormative futurity in "On Fairy Stories," *Modern Fiction Studies* 50:4 (2004): 936–938.
10. *The Lord of the Rings: The Fellowship of the Ring: Extended Edition*, directed by Peter Jackson (New Line, 2002), DVD.
11. *The Lord of the Rings: The Two Towers*, directed by Peter Jackson (New Line, 2002), DVD.
12. J. R. R. Tolkien, *The Two Towers*, 2nd ed. (Boston: Houghton Mifflin, 1987), III, vii, 142. Appendix F notes that "Orcs were first bred by the Dark Power of the North in the Elder Days" and in the Third Age, "That Sauron bred them none doubted, but from what stock was not known"; see *The Return of the King*, 2nd ed. (Boston: Houghton Mifflin, 1987), App. F, 409, 410. In another text, published posthumously in *Morgoth's Ring*, Tolkien underscores the biological nature of orcs' reproduction, when Saruman "in his lust for mastery committed this, his wickedest deed: the interbreeding of Orcs and Men, producing both Men-orcs large and cunning, and Orc-men treacherous and vile"; see *Morgoth's Ring*, ed. Christopher Tolkien (Boston: Houghton Mifflin, 1993), 418.
13. J. R. R. Tolkien, *The Book of Lost Tales, Part Two,* ed. Christopher Tolkien (Boston: Houghton Mifflin, 1984), 159.
14. Tolkien, *The Return of the King*, VI, i, 190; and J.R.R. Tolkien, *The Silmarillion* (New York: Ballantine Books, 1977), 50.

15. Richard Taylor, "Commentary," Disc 3, *The Lord of the Rings: The Two Towers: Extended Edition*, directed by Peter Jackson (New Line, 2003), DVD. Throughout Jackson's *The Two Towers* and *The Return of the King*, the Uruk-hai grow progressively more grotesque, though no less powerful.
16. *The Lord of the Rings: The Two Towers*, directed by Peter Jackson (New Line, 2002), DVD.
17. Viewers more commonly take the heteronormative path, linking Jackson's depiction of Sauron's eye to female sexuality, even in readings that acknowledge the films' queer bonds among men; see Chance (95) and Ruth Goldberg and Krin Gabbard, "'What Does The Eye Demand': Sexuality and Forbidden Vision in *The Lord of the Rings,* in *From Hobbits to Hollywood: Essays on Peter Jackson's Lord of the Rings*" (Amsterdam: Rodopi, 2006), 270. But as I argue in "Fairy Stories," Tolkien's mythology is more Lacanian than Freudian, reflecting the symbolic insufficiency for which female genital lack is merely a strategic displacement—an emptiness, that is, embodied in the Ring as the hollow signifier around which *The Lord of the Rings* is organized.
18. William Shakespeare, *King Lear. The Riverside Shakespeare*, ed. G. Blakemore Evans (Boston: Houghton Mifflin, 1974), 1. 1. 90.
19. Quoted in Lee Edelman, "*Rear Window*'s Glasshole," in *Out Takes: Essays on Queer Theory and Film*, ed. Ellis Hanson (Durham, NC: Duke University Press, 1999), 84.
20. Edelman, 75. Edelman also reminds us of the fantasy of anal birth in Freud's Wolf Man case (77, 79).
21. Judith Butler, "Imitation and Gender Insubordination," in *The Lesbian and Gay Studies Reader,* ed. Henry Abelove, Michéle Aina Barale, David M. Halperin (New York: Routledge, 1993), 312.
22. Guy Hocquenghem, *Homosexual Desire*, trans. Daniella Dangoor (Durham: Duke University Press, 1993), 107, 109.
23. J.R.R. Tolkien, "Foreword," *The Lord of the Rings* (New York: Ballantine Books, 1965), xiii.
24. J.R.R. Tolkien, *The Letters of J.R.R. Tolkien*, ed. Humphrey Carpenter (Boston: Houghton Mifflin, 1981), 191.
25. Tolkien, *The Two Towers,* III, viii, 160.
26. Walter Benjamin, *Illuminations*, trans. Harry Zohn, ed. Hannah Arendt (New York: Schocken Books, 1969), 234.
27. Tolkien, *Morgoth's Ring*, 405.
28. *The Lord of the Rings: The Fellowship of the Ring,* directed by Peter Jackson (New Line, 2001).
29. Michel Foucault, *The History of Sexuality: An Introduction*, trans. Robert Hurley (New York: Vintage, 1990), 47.

Bibliography

Battis, Jes. "Gazing Upon Sauron: Hobbits, Elves, and the Queering of the Postcolonial Optic."*MFS: Modern Fiction Studies* 50: 4 (2004): 908–926.

Benjamin, Walter. *Illuminations*. Translated by Harry Zohn. Ed. Hannah Arendt. New York: Schocken Books, 1969.

Butler, Judith. "Imitation and Gender Insubordination." In *The Lesbian and Gay Studies Reader*, eds. Henry Abelove, Michéle, Aina Barale, David M. Halperin, 307–320. New York: Routledge, 1993.

Chance, Jane. "'In the Company of Orcs': Peter Jackson's Queer Tolkien." In *Queer Movie Medievalisms*, eds. Kathleen Coyne Kelley and Tison Pugh, 79–96. Burlington, VT: Ashgate, 2009.

Edelman, Lee. "*Rear Window*'s Glasshole." In *Out Takes*, ed. Ellis Hanson, 72–96. Durham, NC: Duke University Press, 1999.

Foucault, Michel. *The History of Sexuality: An Introduction*. Translated by Robert Hurley. New York: Vintage, 1990.

Hoberman, J. "Final Fantasy," *Village Voice* (December 15, 2003): C62.

Hocquenghem, Guy. *Homosexual Desire*. Trans. Daniella Dangoor. Durham: Duke University Press, 1993.

IMDb. "Hobbits Are Not Gay Lovers Says Wood," (November 19, 2002). Accessed January 12, 2004, http://us.imdb.com/news/wenn/2002-11-19.

Peter Jackson. *The Lord of the Rings: The Fellowship of the Ring*. New Line, 2001.

———. *The Lord of the Rings: The Return of the King*. New Line, 2003.

———. *The Lord of the Rings: The Two Towers: Extended Edition*. New Line, 2003.

———. *The Lord of the Rings: The Two Towers*. New Line, 2002.

Longino, Bob. "Off-Screen Friendship Creates On-Screen Bond." *Fort Worth Star-Telegram* (December 8, 2003) Accessed September 4, 2004, http://www.dfw.com/mld/dfw/living/7429681.htm?1c.

McKay, Alastair. "Disappointing Turn of the Ring." *The Scotsman* (December 12, 2003) Accessed December 13, 2003. http://www.news.scotsman.com/entertainment.cfm?id=1359622003.

Rohy, Valerie. *Lost Causes: Narrative, Etiology, and Queer Theory*. New York: Oxford University Press, 2015.

———. "On Fairy Stories." *Modern Fiction Studies* 50: 4 (2004): 927–948.

Saxey, Esther. "Homoeroticism." In *Reading* The Lord of the Rings: *New Writings on Tolkien's Classic*, ed. Robert Eaglestone, 124–137. New York: Continuum, 2005.

Sedgwick, Eve Kosofsky. *Epistemology of the Closet*. Berkeley: University of California Press, 1990.

Shakespeare, William. *The Riverside Shakespeare*. Ed. G. Blakemore Evans. Boston: Houghton Mifflin, 1974.

Smol, Anna. "'Oh … oh … Frodo!': Readings of Male Intimacy in *The Lord of the Rings*." *Modern Fiction Studies* 50: 4 (2004): 949–979.

Tolkien, J. R. R. *The Book of Lost Tales, Part One*. Ed. Christopher Tolkien. Boston: Houghton Mifflin, 1984.

———. *The Book of Lost Tales, Part Two*. Ed. Christopher Tolkien. Boston: Houghton Mifflin, 1986.

———. *The Fellowship of the Ring*. 2nd ed. Boston: Houghton Mifflin, 1987.

———. "Foreword." *The Lord of the Rings*. New York: Ballantine Books, 1965.

———. *The Letters of J. R. R. Tolkien*. Ed. Humphrey Carpenter. Boston: Houghton Mifflin, 1981.

———. *Morgoth's Ring*. Ed. Christopher Tolkien. Boston: Houghton Mifflin, 1993.

———. *The Return of the King*. 2nd ed. Boston: Houghton Mifflin, 1987.

———. *The Silmarillion*. New York: Ballantine Books, 1977.

———. *The Two Towers*. 2nd ed. Boston: Houghton Miflfin, 1987.

CHAPTER 7

Saruman's Sodomitic Resonances: Alain de Lille's *De Planctu Naturae* and J. R. R. Tolkien's *The Lord of the Rings*

Christopher Vaccaro

In this essay, I intend to explore the ethical scaffolding of two neoplatonic mythopoeic texts: the twelfth-century *De Planctu Naturae*, by Alain de Lille and J. R. R. Tolkien's widely known *The Lord of the Rings*. On March 28, 1958, in Rotterdam, the Netherlands, J. R. R. Tolkien gave a toast at the "Hobbit Dinner" at which he spoke of the hobbits' resilience while making an important distinction between the evil of Sauron and that of Saruman:

> "I look East, West, North, and South, and I do not see Sauron; but I see that Saruman has many descendants. We Hobbits have against them no magic weapons. Yet, my gentlehobbits, I give you this toast: To the Hobbits. May they outlast the Sarumans and see spring again in the trees."[1]

C. Vaccaro (✉)
University of Vermont, Burlington, VT, USA

C. Vaccaro and Y. Kisor (eds.), *Tolkien and Alterity*, The New Middle Ages, DOI 10.1007/978-3-319-61018-4_7

Tolkien's reference to Saruman here is due to more than just speech-making artistry; it reveals a sustained reading of Saruman as a blight upon nature. The metaphorical application of his name relies on a well-recognized set of attributed meanings, which—while not allegorical in the strict sense of the term—appear so fixed in Tolkien's mind that explanation is hardly necessary. While Sauron's threat has been nearly eliminated, Saruman has, through profligate means we can be sure, effectively given birth to a line of "descendants"; from him issues much that plagues humankind today. Tolkien likens Saruman to a long winter during which fecundity has been suppressed. To outlast him is to experience the revivification brought about by spring's renewal.

Beginning his existence as the Maiar Curunír, Saruman is a being that, as Fangorn complains, "ought to know better" when it comes to morality.[2] As a member and eventually the leader of the Istari and chief of the White Council, he was charged with working ceaselessly to defend Middle-earth and to protect Iluvatar's children from Morgoth's lieutenant, Sauron.[3] Sadly, his fate is more in line with those who had fallen.[4] Ultimately, Saruman is transformed into something monstrous through a discourse of "sodomitic" vices, which multiply until the formerly white wizard becomes the locus of them all.

The following argument developed out of a conference session titled "Queer Tolkien." Its intervention at that time was to argue for the maintenance of the relationship between queer theory and queer sexual practice, for the sustained inclusion of a liberated sexuality within the parameters of the term "queer" alongside the efficacious and powerful deployment of its use as "difference."[5] In *The Trouble With Normal*, Michael Warner effectively points out the challenges of today's LGBT culture built around a normalized, sanitized, and socially acceptable sexuality (void of sex!).[6] There is good sex (monogamous, procreative, private, in a relationship, non-pornographic, and vanilla) and bad sex (promiscuous, non-procreative, public, casual, pornographic, and kinky). Also, the struggle has shifted to how homo-sex can be naturalized (the search for a "gay gene" or "gay brain" is an example). Yet legitimizing as normal and natural, a certain range of sexual variants inevitably leads to the exclusion of everything outside it. New and creative forms of sex are categorized as "out there," and the thought of sex as recreational is met with disapproval if not disdain. Yet, as Warner brilliantly argues "sex does not need to be primordial in order to be legitimate… And new sexualities, including learned ones, might have as much validity as ancient ones, if not more."[7]

With such concerns in mind, the question for queer critics then becomes how to apply such a sexually liberatory lens to their disciplines.

Readers of Tolkien's fiction find themselves in challenging territory. There is a clear evidence of Tolkien's acceptance of difference and of physical pleasure. But for a liberated sexuality, Tolkien has little sympathy. In a letter to his son Michael in 1941 on the subject of marriage, he gives a very hard line:

> The dislocation of sex-instinct is one of the chief symptoms of the Fall. The world has been "going to the bad" all down the ages. The various social forms shift, and each new mode has its special dangers: but the 'hard spirit of concupiscence' has walked down every street, and sat leering in every house, since Adam fell.[8]

Suffice it to say that through a comparison with Alain de Lille's twelfth-century *De Planctu Naturae*, an acknowledgment of Tolkien's exceptional empathy toward the marginalized and oppressed is here coupled with scrutiny over his intolerance of a liberated *eros*, itself an increasingly marginalized yet nonetheless important component of the inclusive and deliberately elusive concept we call the "queer."[9]

Before beginning such an argument, I must first address the discipline of source identifications and comparisons. Jason Fisher provides astute guidance in this area of Tolkien scholarship.[10] At certain times, we can be very sure of a direct borrowing; take the case of the Finnish *Kalevala* or of *Beowulf*. At other times, we can speak with confidence about a text to which Tolkien refers in his letters or in his scholarship, say *Sir Gawain and the Green Knight*. But we do not always have such definitive evidence. A text may possess resonances and not appear in proximity to Tolkien's legendarium.[11] Alain de Lille's allegorical *De Planctu Naturae* is just such a text.

It is inconceivable that Tolkien would not have known about Alain's treatise. In his *The Allegory of Love: A Study in Medieval Tradition* (1936), C.S. Lewis examines the shifts in the expressions of courtly love over the centuries; it is a book Tolkien knew and read. In it, Lewis speaks at length about Alain's *Anticlaudianus* and translates two substantial passages of *De Planctu*.[12] Moreover, Alain's works circulated very widely throughout Europe during the later medieval period. Tolkien drew upon and wrote on works by Geoffrey Chaucer, who refers to Alain directly in his *Parliament of Fowls*.[13] The certainty that Tolkien knew of the text is high.

Aside from Chaucer, Tolkien relied on other medieval authors for his ethical framework as Charles Nelson makes clear:

> In the tradition of Gower, Langland, and Chaucer, then, Tolkien did indeed 'reflect and contain in solution elements of moral and religious truth' in an effort to foster virtuous behavior as some medieval writers did through the ancient device of the figures embodying the Seven Deadly Sins.[14]

In addition to the Deadly Sins, I will suggest Tolkien might have also been inspired by a popular medieval figure of ethics, Goddess Natura, which traces its origins back to the Platonic tradition. Plato does not personify Nature in his *Timaeus*, but this work informs those like Aristotle, who speak of Nature (*Physics*) as working alongside God. According to George Economou, Macrobius is the first to personify Natura as a creator [*artifex*]. Calcidius's commentaries on the *Timaeus* fix Natura as intermediary between the celestial and worldly[15]; in this, she will share something significant with the figure of the Virgin Mary. Boethius employs the celestial figure of Lady Philosophy and supplies a prosimetra, a text of alternating verse and prose, that will be used by many who come after him including Alain.

There is much in Alain's text that Tolkien would have enjoyed. *De Planctu* contains a naturalized Christianity championed by a female divinity through the employment of reason. Alain expresses through a fairly proverbial language the author's concern over and rebuke of misguided *eros*. He employs the intellectual construct of the goddess Natura, which symbolizes an accord between human behavior and God's law, in order to admonish those who would give their lives over to vice. Links between astronomy, astrology, environmental conservation, and moral guidance fasten the text's ethical framework.

The inner workings of the seemingly pagan mythology are inextricably linked to the Christian reform movement of the twelfth through fourteenth centuries. The goddess floats down to greet the "dreamer" and explains to him why she is in such deep sorrow. She had recently given her charge over human behavior to Venus, who displayed great irresponsibility and wantonness. Now that practices such as same-sex fornication, masturbation, and unsanctioned love out of wedlock have become rampant, she is forced to gather her virtues and send an epistle through

Hymen to the figure of Genius, asking the latter to formally expel the practitioners. The text describes the attire and signification of each figure and concludes with the excommunication.

De Planctu lends itself to a fascinating comparison with *The Lord of the Rings* when examining the prominent motifs and imagery. Given the focus of this argument around Saruman, I will briefly summarize here what I cover more comprehensively in another essay.[16] An immediately recognizable trait is that of the *ubi sunt* motif found in many works of northwestern Germanic and Romano-Mediterranean literatures. The nostalgic and elegiac voice laments the inevitable degradation of the world; things are not (nor can they ever be again) as beautiful as they once were. Like much of the imagery in Tolkien's legendarium, *De Planctu*'s events are set against a greater cosmological backdrop containing the music of the heavens and divine assemblies.[17] The goddess Natura, resplendent in her golden tresses,[18] is surrounded by imagery of light, stars, gems, and stones[19] much like Varda.[20] Her nature imagery[21] is linked thematically to the anvil and hammer,[22] something we find in Tolkien's goddess Yavanna[23] and her consort Aulë. With her fountains set in the deep woods[24] and her mirror,[25] she reminds one of Galadriel. Tolkien's emphasis on morality can be recognized in Alain's allegorical pantheon of virtues, those "lonely lamps in human darkness," and "*morning stars* of a setting world" [emphasis mine].[26] Gandalf's wizened and hoary features are similar to those of the figure of Genius, as is his excommunication of the debased from the community of the wise.[27] And lastly, Saruman finds resonances in those anathematized due to their vices and debasement, and it is this that the following pages will now examine in detail.

A Sodomitic Saruman

In Alain's *De Planctu*, the goddess Natura focuses her lengthy diatribe on the practice of "sodomy," a term that—within the biblical and patristic traditions—is often linked to sexual activities, to excess or *luxuria*, and to inhospitality. Suggestive of a moral weakness, *luxuria* grouped together a number of sexual sins.[28] Texts that describe the destruction of Sodom do not focus equally on the sexual sins of that city. Sodom and sodomy were then as they are today associated with "general sinfulness, or non-specific sexual sin"[29] often targeting non-procreative sexual behavior. Through the influence of Philo of Alexandria among others, the phrase *contra natura* was used as a means of defining these behaviors as morally bankrupt, unhealthy, and contrary to God's harmonious plan. The degree to which it referred to sexual behaviors specifically or to a broad range of acts is the subject of thorough scholarship.[30] Often the sins related to Sodom were linked to gluttony, sloth, and pride; the sexual sins were a by-product of these more ruinous vices.[31] Any and all sexual acts performed outside of marriage were categorized as commonsensically against "nature" (read against "church-sanctioned behavior") as were certain acts within marriage. While non-procreative, these practices were paradoxically seen as spawning a figurative form of progeny. This discourse is central to Alain's text.

The anathematized in *De Planctu* are first and foremost identified by their host of vices. Greed and pride, themselves symptoms of prodigality's excess, produce the ideal moral conditions for lust to exist, and thus, the three are inextricably linked. Alain spends considerable time elaborating on the effects of all three, supplying proverbial phrases that serve to elucidate his points. He does this through Natura's "naturalized" and rationalized Christian discourse, which establishes the credibility of a "Natural Law."

In his book *Following Gandalf*, Matthew Dickerson highlights the existence of an absolute and objective morality or "Natural Law" in Middle-earth, emphasizing that the authority comes from the creator of Nature not just nature itself.[32] Characters are judged against this moral register. Laura Garcia points out Tolkien's reliance on an Aristotelian view of virtue and morality stating: "His highest praise is reserved for the virtuous, for characters of character, so to speak, and those folks make their decisions by considering what would be the loyal, courageous, or just thing to do."[33] The likes of Saruman despise those displaying such virtue. John Treloar locates six vices in *The Lord of the Rings* and attributes them to specific characters in the story. According to Treloar, Saruman is the best example of "pride and its related vices of anger and envy."[34] Charles Nelson argues that Saruman displays the vices of pride and greed.[35] Both argue that Saruman becomes a nexus of these vices in the text. Moreover, Aeon Skoble explores the characters of the novel through the lens of "virtue ethics" and finds Saruman lacking in virtue entirely.[36]

The effect of similar vices is visible within *De Planctu*. In a lengthy sermon, Alain describes greed as a primary manifestation of a soul at odds with Natura's principles. In addition, the greedy often display vindictive and malevolent behavior, enjoying the poverty and financial distress of others: "He laughs at the tears of the poor and feasts on the toil of the wretched."[37] And the greedy, like all others in opposition to Natura ("Othered" by Natura?), ironically find themselves bereft of that which they so excessively desired. She informs the dreamer-narrator that "the individual covets everything, and by that very covetousness is made poor."[38] God being just will give suitable punishments to fit the crime.

Much like those in *De Planctu*, Saruman covets material things. He falls to the allure of the One Ring, envies the mighty tower of Barad Dûr, and hoards the resources of the Shire for his personal use. By the novel's end, he has become so covetous that he finds joy only in destroying what others have: "You have doomed yourselves, and you know it. And it will afford me some comfort as I wander to think that you pulled down your own house when you destroyed mine."[39] And like Alain's excommunicated, Saruman enjoys witnessing the poverty of others. He becomes an active agent of this destruction again and again, as we see toward the novel's end. Precisely, as Alain's Natura would predict, Saruman's covetousness leads to his impoverishment, until in the final instance, he is a beggar "clothed in rags of grey or dirty white"[40] passed on the road.

Linked to the sodomitic practices abhorred in the text, pride holds its position as the worst of the sins for Alain's Natura and most deserving of severe punishment. "[A]nathematized with the mark of excommunication, and condemned to banishment and uttermost destruction,"[41] the proud call divine wrath upon themselves.[42] In seeking dominion over others, the proud are cast out of the community and left to live in exile. As the greedy become beggars, so too the proud "sink while they bear themselves aloft."[43] The more they exalt themselves, the more rapidly they fall.

John Rateliff reminds us that pride is the worst of sins in Tolkien's ethos.[44] Found in Elf, Dwarf, and Man alike, it stymies one's reverence to the Valar and respect for one's peers. Aside from Sauron himself, Saruman struggles the most with his hubris out of all other characters. Gandalf makes it a significant point when talking to Frodo: "He is great among the Wise. He is the chief of my order and the head of the Council. His knowledge is deep, but his pride has grown with it, and he takes ill any meddling."[45] Saruman raises himself up above Elves and Men and other Istari only to fall to great depths of isolation and exile. Each time he engages with Gandalf, it becomes clear that Saruman sees himself as superior. During his first attempt to persuade Gandalf, Saruman arrogantly asserts that he is more than fit to rule Middle-earth.[46] And when his schemes and fortifications are dismantled following the battle of Helm's Deep, he fails to conceal his arrogance and contempt when talking to the victorious army of Rohan and its allies.[47]

De Planctu's main focus, however, is "depraved" sexual practice and the destructive results of its ungoverned expression. Alain associates lust with a near Ovidian transformation in which behaviors have permanent effects on one's soul and psyche. Contrasting it with reason, which converts man into a god and "illuminates the darkness of the brain by the light of contemplation,"[48] lust "changes him into a beast." Reason illuminates, lust obfuscates. Reason is celestial, lust filthy, and primitive. Alain extends this contrast, comparing lustful humans to brutes that "roam and riot along the breadth of the whole earth."[49] Beyond direct personal effects, the binary also regulates social interactions: "reason makes man to talk with angels, lust forces him to wanton with brutes."[50] Sensuousness here mars the world through its excess and precludes healthy and acceptable fecundity while paradoxically giving unnatural "birth" to depraved creations, the vices. Alain gives a literal and literary example from Ovid's *Metamorphoses*, describing the monstrous birth of the Minotaur.[51]

Alain also supplies figurative examples of this monstrous generation. Vice gives birth to vice; monstrosity breeds monstrosity. Sloth, belying its own name, "is wont to form its abundance of misshapen offspring."[52] Drunkenness "exposes man to the darkness of brutish sensuality"[53] and situates him "among those who are like brutes in bestial sensuality."[54] The ironic logic here, of course, is that not only do these vices reduce human faculties to the point of nonexistence, but also they perpetuate and even generate additional vices monstrously. The unmistakable conclusion is that sexual behaviors outside the parameters of procreation and the vices linked to these behaviors manifest a wrongful and harmful fecundity that paradoxically reads as sterility. The target of Natura's rebuke demonstrates a lack of control over his sexuality by choosing the path of lust over that of reason. Forsaking the latter, he "slips down into the decline of things of earth"[55] and dishonors himself.

On the surface, bodily lust seems conspicuously absent not only from *The Lord of the Rings*, but also from its earliest scholarship, as if this one particular vice was somehow absent in Middle-earth. Only a very few critics acknowledge its existence. Charles Nelson argues for the presence of lechery in Grima's "lascivious looks" at Eowyn, and Jes Battis detects a non-heteronormative eroticism throughout the text.[56] Around the more theoretical subject of desire, important recent work has been done. Evoking Slavoj Žižek, Valerie Rohy points to the One Ring's function as *point de capiton* within the text, anchoring the symbolic order around itself and making desire ubiquitous throughout the story.[57] Gergely Nagy recognizes the Ring as a signifier of physical desire and hence as "lack" in his essay "The 'Lost' Subject":

> The Ring generates desire for itself by amplifying desire for other things: it catalyzes desires and offers an (illusory) power for their achievement if used.[58]

Jane Chance likewise agrees that desire circulates around the One Ring. It satisfies Bilbo's desire for "specialness" and power within the economy of the Shire.[59] Saruman is caught up within this diffuse and pervasive *eros* along with everybody else, but he also personally and directly desires the Ring. Speaking of it to Gandalf, "a lust which he could not conceal shone suddenly in his eyes."[60] Its Saruman's lust for it that sets the course for much of the novel.

Unlike Alain's anathematized, Tolkien never depicts Saruman's desire as sexually perverse, nor would we expect him to; he is opposed to moralizing. Rather, it is deemed monstrous[61] and an opposition to reason.[62] His own alterity coalesces around his making of the Uruk-hai, where his lust links him to their brutishness. Alain's Natura speaks of the instances where men surrender to their sexually "depraved" acts despite her gifts.[63] As examples, she refers to the disaster caused by Helen's misdirected love, to the mating of Minos' wife, Pasiphaë, with the bull the king should have given to Poseidon, to Myrrha's sexual union with her father, and to Narcissus' love with himself:

> Such a great body of foul men roam and riot along the breadth of the whole earth, by whose seducing contact chastity herself is poisoned.[64]

In his misguided desire for control and knowledge, Saruman behaves much like those in Alain's text; he gives himself over to his desire for the One Ring and attacks nature not only when cutting down the forest but also when breeding Orcs with Men. And it is by this depravity that he is drawn closer to a community of brutes.

This "unnatural" activity undergirds Saruman's plans for domination and inserts into the text's moral landscape all that the Orc represents: an unspoken and repressed yet powerful sexuality. Citing Randel Helms' *Tolkien's World*, Chance reminds us that, "*The Lord of the Rings* can… be seen as a political fantasy expressed in covert sexual symbols."[65] Randel Helms recognized Tolkien's need to contain the erotic energies seething just below the surface, arguing that "Tolkien wants Orc-hood sealed in precisely the same underworld of the mind from which Blake wants it to erupt." This "Orc-hood" lurks in the text's sodomitic shadows. I use the term "shadow" here as it is defined by Allen Frantzen to mean an interpretive mode that sees homosexual relations not hidden in a closet so much as "always there, always present" and always "adjacent to the ordered world."[66] The text allows us to locate shadowy traces of the sodomitic. Not only is Saruman's unnatural fecundity paradoxically coded as a type of sterility (in a manner similar to that of Alain's vices), but his behavior repels him from the celestial light of reason and casts him among the brutes.

Tolkien's Orcs represent our primitive instincts, which fight with our divinely inspired reason. Barely restrained in the text, this aggressive sexuality is amplified in Peter Jackson's cinematic representation, as Jane Chance again points out in a queer reading sensitive to the traces of sex:

> Orcs, as manifestations of repressed sexuality, brute animality, and the hypermasculine Other, represent the queer polar opposite of the Hobbit as a desexualized and even idealized feminine Other.[67]

Chance argues here and elsewhere that this is true of the films and the novel. The animality of the Orc is pitted against the anality of the virtuous and desexualized hobbits, against the act of "natural" procreation epitomized by Sam's post-plot fecundity.[68] They are "Othered" by their hyper-masculinized gender and barely containable sexuality. Even the scene where Grishnákh searches Merry and Pippin for the Ring is "disturbingly sexualized."[69] In Tolkien's *The Lord of the Rings*, the unsublimated *eros* and the queer, excessive behavior of Saruman's Uruk-hai are set against the "sentimentalized" (Rohy's term) and desexualized desire between Frodo and Sam.

Gríma Wormtongue, Saruman's surrogate, is likewise associated with this form of alterior *eros.* As his name suggests, Gríma worms his way into the great hall of Rohan and whispers Saruman's lies into the ears of the king. He incarcerates loyal thanes in order to dismantle the power of the king's house and spreads lies concerning the Lady of the Wood. When Gandalf arrives at Meduseld, light is literally shed upon Gríma's affiliations in a scene comparable to the excommunication at the very end of *De Planctu.* In that scene, Natura's priest performs his role as her surrogate:

> Then Genius after laying aside his common garment, and being adorned more honorably with the higher ornaments of the sacerdotal vestment, called out from the secret places of his mind the order of excommunication.[70]

Gríma's arrogant insult of Galadriel (who bears some resemblance to Natura) sets up Gandalf's first presentation of himself as her ally and acolyte:

> In Dwimordene, in Lórien
> Seldom have walked the feet of Men,
> Few mortal eyes have seen the light
> That lies there ever, long and bright.
> Galadriel! Galadriel!
> Clear is the water of your well;
> White is the star in your white hand;
> Unmarred, unstained is leaf and land
> In Dwimordene, in Lórien
> More fair than thoughts of Mortal Men.

Thus, Gandalf softly sang, and then suddenly he changed. Casting his tattered cloak aside, he stood up and leaned no longer on his staff. Only Gandalf could be seen, standing white and tall before the blackened hearth.[71]

The inclusion of both verse and prose echoes Alain's Boethian structure, and the rhyming couplets establish a structural unity to the matter of Gandalf's verse: Galadriel's purity. Her light and power are now associated with Gandalf, who uncovers here his "sacerdotal vestment" in order to cleanse Meduseld. The term *Dwimordene* translates as "vale of phantoms" in the language of Rohan. However, the *Bosworth-Toller*

Anglo-Saxon Dictionary, Supplement, supplies the additional reading of the Old English *dwimor* as "portent," which is also relevant in this scene.[72] A change is coming to Edoras and to Middle-earth as Gandalf here plays the Genius to Galadriel's Natura.[73]

Gríma's haunting "lasciviousness" (Nelson's term), the sole example of an overtly sexualized desire in the novel, is yet another "monster" born from Saruman's prodigality. Gríma desires Éowyn, who serves here as a form of treasure; his lust for her is recognized by Gandalf:

> "Down on your belly! How long is it since Saruman bought you? What was the promised price? When all the men were dead, you were to pick your share of the treasure, and take the woman you desire? Too long have you watched her under your eyelids and haunted her steps."[74]

The attainment of Éowyn is contingent upon the death of all those who would protect her from Gríma's unwanted advances. Associated only with Gríma in the novel, overt sexual desire is read as impure and depraved and is contrasted against the brotherly love of Éomer and the noble love of Faramir to come later. It is a form of lust that reflects the deterioration of morality in Middle-earth and a presage of what is to come if Saruman succeeds in his plans. Moreover, Gríma evinces a secondary desire equally as abject in the novel, submitting to Saruman's sadistic treatment as he gives over to the masochistic desire to submit to his master in spite of (or because of?) the cruelty manifest over the course of their relationship.

A similar *eros* exists around Saruman's (a.k.a. Sharkey's) ruffians, who serve as conduits of the wizard's power and desire. His seductive voice echoes in their minds as they destroy the beauty of the Shire and brutalize (and figuratively sodomize) its inhabitants. Frodo astutely comments on the position of the Hobbits and their land: "The ruffians are on top, gathering, robbing, and bullying, and running or ruining things as they like."[75] As Saruman's actions perform a rape of Middle-earth,[76] their act of defilement is a rape of the land and, in some ways, those who work on it. Of those who live in the Shire almost everyone, Merry tells us, hates what's been done: "all of them except perhaps one or two rascals, and a few fools that want to be important."[77]

At this moment, a queer reader may, as Frodo did on the stairs to Cirith Ungol, feel compelled to employ his/her imagination in order to underscore an alternative narrative thread. Frodo's fantasy relates to his homo-amorous and interdependent relationship with Sam: "I want to hear more about Sam, dad."[78] But other questions could be posed to Merry regarding a more (sodo)masochistic and alterior desire that respond to Michael Warner's call for the inclusiveness of sexual variation: "What about them rascals in the Shire, Merry? I want to hear more about them. Were they rough and dangerous lookin? Did they lurk in the woods after curfew to exchange stashes of pipe-weed and ale? Did they brawl with each other or maybe serve as sadistic guards at the Lockholes prison at Michel Delving? And what would they do to you if they were defied"? These are meant to be more than provocative and (potentially) arousing questions. Theorists Alexander Doty and Elizabeth Cowie both assert that queer readers may find an agency in the manner of their interpretations and in the fulfillment of their own fantasies.[79] Such questions give voice to the alterior *eros* that can draw a reader in that threatens to break through the very surface of *The Lord of the Rings*, an *eros* that lurks *pace* Allen Frantzen in the text's sodomitic "shadows." It is a "trace" hidden within the neo-platonic Christian morality upon which it is contingent. Such is the *eros*, the company of lascivious brutes and the amalgam of vices with which Saruman is associated.

Contra Natura

A broader motif that corresponds interestingly to what we find in Alain's *De Planctu* is depravity's oppositional relationship toward nature. The most obvious example in *The Lord of the Rings* is found in Saruman's destruction of trees and his war with the Ents. No longer caring for growing things, he has for some time before the War of the Ring commanded his "foul folk" to "cut down and leave to rot" many good trees on the borders of the ancient forest.[80] Treebeard testifies to this firsthand, remarking to Merry and Pippin that "[t]here are wastes of stump and bramble where once there were singing groves." Later in the heart of the Shire, Saruman continues his attack on trees well after his defeat by the Ents: "The trees were the worst loss and damage, for at Sharkey's bidding they had been cut down recklessly far and wide."[81] As Chance observes, Treebeard's ire is important since, "signifying the principles of reason and order inherent in Nature," the Ents "join with the Men of Rohan …to combat the evil represented by "Cunning Mind."[82] Both Alain and Tolkien recognize these "principles of reason and order inherent in Nature" and use the pen to come to their defense.

Also relevant is Saruman's relationship with others in the White Council. Despite there being a number of important differences, the comparison offers some fascinating and important insights. If—as I argue elsewhere—Galadriel possesses the physical traits, the unblemished purity, the associations with light, stars, and nature, and the desire for preservation of Alain's Natura, and Gandalf finds correspondences in the figures of Genius and Hymen, then Saruman's ongoing battle with these two speaks to his further likeness to Alain's anathematized.[83] A direct confrontation with Galadriel in the novel's final chapters reveals a long-existing enmity as Saruman states to Gandalf: "And as for the Lady here, I do not trust her: she always hated me, and schemed for your part."[84] Convinced that Galadriel finds pleasure in his recent impoverishment, Saruman rebukes her as he had Gandalf, her Grey Pilgrim.

As for Gandalf, Saruman has little love for the wizard whose earlier approach to Isengard was greeted not with affection but with condescension and hostility. He imprisons his angelic guest in a move that recalls the inhospitality of the Sodomites.[85] Even then, Saruman no longer considered Gandalf an equal. It took little time for him to reveal to Gandalf his true designs, which are made evident in his comments at Isengard:

> "For I am Saruman the wise, Saruman Ring-maker, Saruman of Many Colours!"

Gandalf then notices the true nature of Saruman's robes:

> "I looked then and saw his robes, which had seemed white, were not so, but were woven of all colours, and if he moved they shimmered and changed hue so that the eye was bewildered."[86]

Such attire appears again after the Ents attack Isengard, when a defeated Saruman is described as "an old man, swathed in a great cloak, the colour of which was not easy to tell, for it changed if they moved their eyes or if he stirred."[87]

In Alain's *De Planctu*, the figures of Nature and Venus both wear garments of "many colors" that shift and bewilder the dreamer of the poem. Nature's garments display the richness of the animal kingdom with birds, beasts, and creatures of the sea. They start off white, but take on multiple hues:

> A garment, woven from silky wool and covered with many colors, was as the virgin's robe of state. Its appearance perpetually changed with many a different color and manifold hue. At first it startled the sight with the white radiance of the lily.[88]

Saruman, of course, sneers that white light can be broken and the white page can be rewritten. To which Gandalf responds: "In which case, it is no longer white. And he who breaks a thing to find out what it is has left the path of wisdom."[89] As a figure of prodigality and *luxuria* Saruman now serves as a perfect antithesis of all for which Galadriel and Gandalf strive. His kaleidoscopic robes appear to be a mockery of their solid white garments.

Even more relevant are the shifting garments of Alain's Venus, which are associated with the wicked potential of rhetoric. The narrator observes that "[s]he changes her art by gaudy ornaments of rhetoric into artifice, and her artifice into viciousness."[90] In James J. Sheridan's translation, Venus is "discolouring herself with the colours of Rhetoric."[91] Much like Venus who wears a grotesque counterfeit of Natura's robes in her disregard and direct assault on the virtues celebrated in Alain's poem, Saruman's opposition to the novel's ethics and to the Natural Law promoted by the White Council is startlingly visible. Moreover, his perversion of Nature is linked to the colorful rhetoric and he is able to employ to sway others. In opposition to the priest of the rational mind, which steers those who see the light of the "morning stars" (virtues) toward noble action, rhetoric is comprised of flourish and superfluity, perversity, and excess.

The signification of robes to distinguish between Good and Evil appears once again when the two wizards engage each other at Orthanc. Arriving at Isengard after the victory of the Ents, Gandalf once again takes on the mantle of cleric as he had done at Edoras:

> 'Behold, I am not Gandalf the Grey, whom you betrayed. I am Gandalf the White, who has returned from death. You have no colour now, and I cast you from the order and from the Council.'
>
> He raised his hand, and spoke slowly in a clear cold voice. 'Saruman, your staff is broken.' There was a crack, and the staff split asunder in Saruman's hand, and the head of it fell down at Gandalf's feet. 'Go!' said Gandalf. With a cry Saruman fell back and crawled away.[92]

Saruman's excommunication by Gandalf occurs in a chapter titled "The Voice of Saruman," an interesting choice given that the words "voice" and "vice" are homophones in certain (and relevant) historical dialects of English.[93] This chapter is about both Saruman's power and his pride. Gandalf reveals his sacerdotal robe while rendering Saruman's garments irrelevant. Casting him out of the community of the faithful, Gandalf's most immediate authority comes from Galadriel and then, of course, Ilúvatar.

Conclusions

Between the legalization of "gay marriage" in the USA and the astounding effectiveness of pre-exposure HIV medications, the LGBT communities find themselves struggling with issues of assimilation, identity, activism, and (hetero- and homo-) normalcy. Efforts to legitimize a sentimental sexuality compress the range of what is considered acceptable often at the expense of more recreational and creative attitudes toward sex. "Slut-shaming" has become a familiar practice across the community as judgments abound over an individual's indulgence in desire.[94] Yet, a liberated sexuality, at odds with most religious traditions, is an equally valid element of however we come to define the "queer."

While Tolkien accepted and even embraced difference and despised regulations of "apartheid" as Chance compellingly argues in her most recent work,[95] his religious views restricted his acceptance of sexual desire to only those behaviors understood as virtuous. For him, surrendering to sexual appetites amounts to giving oneself over to the "hard spirit of concupiscence." As Nelson has argued, Tolkien wrote in the tradition of medieval authors who sought to "foster virtuous behavior" in their readers. In a text, where renunciation, sacrifice, and the deferment of sexual performance are persistent themes, where discipline, heroic fortitude, chastity, and pity are paramount, Saruman's association with the most damning of vices marks him as Other in ways similar to those found in Alain de Lille's *De Planctu Naturae*. A comparison of Alain's text to *The Lord of the Rings* provides useful insights into Tolkien's complicated reaction to sexual alterity.

Jane Chance astutely observes that Saruman's pride "so puffs him up that to him all others appear diminished. To the proud, all outside the Self *is* Other, different."[96] His pride precludes his acceptance of difference. And, as critics have recognized, he is made monstrous ("Othered") through the story's moral logic. Ultimately, Saruman becomes a nodal point of all the vices Tolkien makes alterior, particularly a sodomitic *eros* the novel positions as *contra natura*. Yet perhaps, it is even more complicated than this, as Tolkien's early drafts sketching out Saruman's possible pardon and change of heart would suggest. But that, if the reader would permit, would be the subject for another essay.

Notes

1. Humphrey Carpenter, *J. R. R. Tolkien: A Biography* (London, HarperCollins, 1978), 255.
2. J. R. R. Tolkien, *The Two Towers*, 2nd ed. (Boston: Houghton Mifflin, 1987), III, iv, 89.
3. See "Of the Rings of Power and the Third Age," in *The Silmarillion* (Boston: Houghton Mifflin, 1977), 299.
4. *Unfinished Tales* (Boston: Houghton Mifflin, 1980), 396. "Whereas Curunír was cast down, and *utterly humbled*, and perished at last by the hand of an oppressed slave; and his spirit went whithersoever it was doomed to go, and to Middle-earth, whether naked or embodied, came never back." [Emphasis mine.]
5. Session 324: Queer Tolkien, sponsored by the Society for the Study of Homosexuality in the Middle Ages, Presider, Graham N. Drake, International Medieval Studies Conference, Kalamazoo, Michigan 2013. "Queer" sexual practice here is meant to specify a particular link between promiscuity and politics.
6. Michael Warner, *The Trouble with Normal: Sex, Politics, and the Ethics of Queer Life* (New York: Free Press, 1999). Warner finds it timely to remind us that "sex is an occasion for losing control, for merging one's consciousness with the lower orders of animal desires and sensation, for raw confrontations of power and demand, it fills people with aversion and shame" (2).
7. Warner, *The Trouble with Normal*, 11. Warner borrows his categorization from Gayle Rubin's essay "Thinking Sex: Notes for a Radical Theory of the Politics of Sexuality," in *Pleasure and Danger: Exploring Female Sexuality*, ed. Carole S. Vance (Boston: Routledge and Kegan Paul, 1984), 3–44.
8. Letter 43. Tolkien, *The Letters of J. R. R. Tolkien*, ed. Humphrey Carpenter (Boston: Houghton Mifflin, 2000), 48.
9. I will use the term *eros* throughout to mean sexuality either expressed or unexpressed.

10. "One must always keep in mind that source studies require a *causal* relationship, or at the least, the probability of one. The proposed source must have been available to Tolkien, and we would like to be able to demonstrate he actually read it. Without that, we may still observe similarities between two works—Tolkien's and another author's—but the best we can hope for, and all we should aim for in such cases, is a comparative study." Jason Fisher, *Tolkien and the Study of His Sources: Critical Essays* (Jefferson, NC: McFarland, 2011), 37.
11. Similarly, Nicholas Birns brings to light the possible influence of Gilgamesh in his "The Stones and the Book: Tolkien, Mesopotamia, and Biblical Mythopoeia," in *Tolkien and the Study of His Sources*, 45–68.
12. C.S. Lewis, *Allegory of Love: A Study in Medieval Tradition* (New York: Oxford University Press, 1958), 98–109. Begun in 1929, first published in 1936, *Allegory of Love* covers Alain for twenty pages. In his Preface, Lewis credits Tolkien for commenting on the first chapter. Lewis comments on Moffat's 1908 translation, which he likely used to supplement his reading of the 1872 edition by Wright. It is tempting to consider that Tolkien did the same though we have no evidence of this, and it is hazardous to make assumptions solely on what Lewis read. This essay seeks solely to expose the unintentional resonances. Douglas M. Moffat, *The Complaint of Nature*, Yale Studies in English 36. (New York, 1908). Thomas Wright, *The Anglo-Latin Satirical Poets and Epigrammatists of the Twelfth Century*, Vol II. (London: Longman, 1872), 429–522.
13. Geoffrey Chaucer, "And right as Aleyn, in the Pleynt of Kynde/Devyseth Nature of aray and face" (l316–1317), "The Parliament of Fowls," in *The Riverside Chaucer* 3rd Edition, ed. Larry Benson (Oxford: Oxford University Press, 2008), 389.
14. Nelson, Charles. "The Sins of Middle-earth: Tolkien's Use of Allegory," in *J. R. R. Tolkien and His Literary Resonances*, edited by George Clark and Daniel Timmons (Westport, Connecticut and London: Greenwood Press, 2000), 94.
15. *DeCaelo* I. iv. 271a. George D. Economou, "The Character Genius in Alain de Lille, Jean de Mein, and John Gower," *Chaucer Review* 4.3 (1970): 13. See Macrobius Ambrosius Theodosius, *Commentary on the Dream of Scipio*, trans. William Harris Stahl, vol. 48 of Records of Civilization: Sources and Studies (New York: Columbia University Press, 1990) and Calcidius, *Commentary on Plato's* Timaeus, trans. John Magee (Boston: Harvard University Press, 2016).
16. I give a full comparison of the two texts in my essay "'Morning Stars of a Setting world': Alain de Lille's *De Planctu Naturae* and Tolkien's Legendarium" (forthcoming in *Mythlore*, fall 2017).
17. Alain de Lille, *De Planctu Naturae*, Prose 1, 7.

18. Alain de Lille, *De Planctu Naturae*, Prose 1, 5.
19. Alain de Lille, *De Planctu Naturae*, Prose 1, 7–9.
20. Tolkien, *The Silmarillion*, 26.
21. Alain de Lille, *De Planctu Naturae*, Prose 1, 11–13.
22. Alain de Lille, *De Planctu Naturae*, Prose 5, 45.
23. Tolkien, *The Silmarillion*, 28.
24. Alain de Lille, *De Planctu Naturae*, Meter 3, 23.
25. Alain de Lille, *De Planctu Naturae*, Prose 8, 85.
26. Alain de Lille, *De Planctu Naturae*, Prose 8, 83.
27. Alain de Lille, *De Planctu Naturae*, Prose 9, 90; 94–95.
28. Allen Frantzen, *Before the Closet: Same-sex Love from* Beowulf *to* Angels in America (Chicago and London. University of Chicago Press, 1998), 186.
29. David Clark, *Between Medieval Men: Male Friendship and Desire in Early Medieval English Literature* (Oxford: Oxford University Press, 2009), 100.
30. See John Boswell, *Christianity, Social Tolerance, and Homosexuality: Gay People in Western Europe from the Beginning of the Christian Era to the Fourteenth Century* (Chicago: University of Chicago Press, 1980); Larry Scanlon, "Unspeakable Pleasures: Alain de Lille, Sexual Regulation and the Priesthood of Genius," *Romantic Review* 86.2 (1995): 213–242; and Mark Jordan, *The Invention of Sodomy in Christian Theology* (Chicago: University of Chicago Press, 1997).
31. Clark, *Between Medieval Men*, 100–101.
32. Matthew Dickerson, *Following Gandalf: Epic Battle and Moral Victory in* The Lord of the Rings (Grand Rapids, MI: Brazos Press, 2003), 123–124.
33. Laura Garcia, "Pride and Humility in *The Hobbit*," in The Hobbit *and Philosophy*, eds. Gregory Bassham and Eric Bronson, Philosophy and Pop Culture Series, ed. William Irwin (Hoboken, N.J.: Wiley Press, 2012), 76.
34. John Treloar, "The Middle-Earth Epic and the Seven Capital Vices," *Mythlore* 16:1 (1989): 59.
35. Charles Nelson. "The Sins of Middle-earth," 87.
36. Aeon Skoble, "Virtue and Vice in *The Lord of the Rings*," in The Lord of the Rings *and Philosophy*, edited by Bassham and Bronson, vol. 5 of Pop Culture and Philosophy Series, ed. William Irwin (Chicago: Open Court, 2003), 118.
37. Alain de Lille, *De Planctu Naturae*, Meter 7, 68.
38. Alain de Lille, *De Planctu Naturae*, Meter 7, 66.
39. J. R. R. Tolkien, *The Return of the King*, 2nd ed. (Boston: Houghton Mifflin, 1987), VI, vi, 261–262.
40. Tolkien, *The Return of the King*, VI, vi, 261.
41. Alain de Lille, *De Planctu Naturae*, Prose 8, 83.

42. Alain interestingly points out that water is frequently used to punish the proud. "Let water break the pride of Lyaeus" (Meter 8, 75).
43. Alain de Lille, *De Planctu Naturae*, Prose 7, 69.
44. John Rateliff, *The History of* The Hobbit, vol. 2 (Boston: Houghton Mifflin, 2007), 565.
45. Tolkien, *The Fellowship of the Ring*, I, ii, 57.
46. Tolkien, *The Fellowship of the Ring*, II, ii, 272.
47. Tolkien, *The Two Towers*, III, x, 186.
48. Alain de Lille, *De Planctu Naturae*, Prose 3, 26.
49. Alain de Lille, *De Planctu Naturae*, Prose 4, 37.
50. Alain de Lille, *De Planctu Naturae*, Prose 3, 26.
51. "Pasiphae also driven by the madness of inordinate lust in the form of a cow corruptly celebrated her bestial nuptials with a brute animal, and concluding with a vile error, ends by the miscreated enormity of the bullock" (Minotaur). Alain de Lille, *De Planctu Naturae*, Prose 4, 37.
52. Alain de Lille, *De Planctu Naturae*, Prose 5, 55.
53. Alain de Lille, *De Planctu Naturae*, Prose 6, 60.
54. Alain de Lille, *De Planctu Naturae*, Prose 6, 65.
55. Alain de Lille, *De Planctu Naturae*, Prose 3, 26. Alain evokes a common grammatical trope to speak of such things: mankind "commits monstrous acts in its union of genders and perverts the roles of love by a practice of extreme and abnormal irregularity" (Prose 4, 36).
56. Nelson, Charles. "The Sins of Middle-earth," 92. Jes Battis argues that "[t]here is an undercurrent of eroticism that tinges many of the pivotal scenes within *The Lord of the Rings*, and that eroticism does not always conform to heteronormative models of sexual expression (and sexual difference)." "Gazing Upon Sauron: Hobbits, Elves, and the Queering of the Postcolonial Optic," *Modern Fiction Studies* 50.4 (2004): 14, note 2.
57. Rohy argues that the degree of sentimentalized love between Sam and Frodo is built almost to a climax and never allowed release or expression. Readers glimpse this "longing of desire" and match it perhaps with their own "longing for desire" since the only desire permitted expression seemingly surrounds Sauron's Ring. Valerie Rohy, "On Fairy Stories," *Modern Fiction Studies* 50.4 (2004): 927–948.
58. Gergely Nagy, "The 'Lost' Subject of Middle-earth: The Constitution of the Subject in the Figure of Gollum in *The Lord of the Rings*," *Tolkien Studies* 3 (2006): 67. Nagy goes on to discuss the aspect of sublimation and suppression of unwanted desires: "As seen in Gollum's case, the normal desires of the subject's functioning are turned inside out, as it were, by the Ring. Desire, as we have known since Plato's *Symposium*, is essentially a *lack*: it is a tension resulting in an action, aimed at something the subject does not possess, but which is sensed as needed, either physically

(like food or sleep) or sublimated into symbolic actions toward symbolic objects. These objects are signs that stand in for suppressed objects of desire, objects which for some reason cannot be desired consciously by the subject without too much tension" (66).

59. Jane Chance, The Lord of the Rings*: Mythology of Power*, rev. ed. (Lexington, KY: University of Kentucky Press, 2001), 30.
60. Tolkien, *The Fellowship of the Ring*, II, ii, 273.
61. Chance, *Mythology of Power*, 79.
62. "Saruman corrupted the reasoning powers," says Tolkien regarding Saruman's voice. *Letters*, 277.
63. Alain de Lille, *De Planctu Naturae*, Prose 4, 87.
64. Ibid.
65. Chance, *Mythology of Power*, 29. Randel Helms, *Tolkien's World* (Boston: Houghton Mifflin, 1974), 91.
66. Frantzen, *Before the Closet*, 136.
67. Chance, "'In the Company of Orcs': Peter Jackson's Queer Tolkien," in *Queer Movie Medievalisms*, ed. Kathleen Coyne Kelly and Tison Pugh (London, England: Ashgate, 2009), 91.
68. In his *Homosexual Desire* (1972), Guy Hocquenghem writes of the centrality of sublimation in western capitalist communities and calls for a sexual communism revolving around pleasure of the anus, the most private (and privatized) part of the body and psyche. The hobbits display the sublimated "anality" Hocguenghem describes. *Homosexual Desire* (Durham and London: Duke University Press, 1993).
69. Chance, *Tolkien, Self and Other*: "This Queer Creature" (New York: Palgrave, 2016), 229.
70. Alain de Lille, *De Planctu Naturae*, Prose 9, 94.
71. Tolkien, *The Two Towers*, III, v, 118–119.
72. "dwimor," *Bosworth-Toller Anglo-Saxon Dictionary Online*, accessed July 2, 2016, http://www.bosworthtoller.com/043123.
73. In her work on the Genius figure, Jane Chance provides this clear description: "he censures homosexuality, that unnatural vice, but he also censures the seven deadly sins, and excommunicates from the realm of nature all who have succumbed to such sin." *The Genius Figure in Antiquity and the Middle Ages* (New York and London: Columbia University Press, 1975), 2. My reading suggests a comparison not a direct borrowing.
74. Tolkien, *The Two Towers*, III, v, 124.
75. Tolkien, *The Return of the King*, VI, viii 285.
76. Chance, *Mythology of Power*, 74.
77. Tolkien, *The Return of the King*, VI, viii, 286.
78. Tolkien, *Two Towers*, IV, viii, 322.
79. Alexander Doty argues that "queer reception" cannot be relegated to mere "alternative readings" and subtext. Queer agency emerges

from personal interpretive strategies. *Making Things Perfectly Queer: Interpreting Mass Culture* (Minneapolis: University of Minnesota Press, 1993). Working with critical fantasy theory, Elizabeth Cowie locates an agency within a subject who can imagine her/himself within scenes of desire. *Representing the Woman: Cinema and Psychoanalysis* (Minneapolis: University of Minnesota Press, 1997).

80. Tolkien, *The Two Towers*, III, iv, 77.
81. Tolkien, *The Return of the King*, VI, ix, 302.
82. Chance, *Tolkien's Art*, 166.
83. I am in no way arguing for allegory here, only suggesting that these correspondences offer new insights into the characters.
84. Tolkien, *The Return of the King*, VI, vi, 261.
85. "And the two angels came to Sodom in the evening, and Lot was sitting in the gate of the city *Douay-Rheims Bible*, *Genesis* 19: 1 (London: Catholic Truth Society, 1956). The men of Sodom in their pride and lust failed to be hospitable; they attacked Lot and his angelic guests, and for this, the city was destroyed. See Clark, *Between Medieval Men*, 68–70 for more on the connections between Sodom and inhospitality.
86. Tolkien, *The Fellowship of the Ring*, II, ii, 272.
87. Tolkien, *The Two Towers*, III, x, 183.
88. Alain de Lille, *De Planctu Naturae*, Prose 1, 11. The Latin reads "Vestris vero, ex serica lana contexta, multifario protecta colore, puellae pepli serviebat in nusum, quam discolorando colorans temporum alteritas multiplici colore faciem alterabat" (Wright, *De Planctu*, 437).
89. Tolkien, *The Fellowship of the Ring*, II, ii, 272.
90. Alain de Lille, *De Planctu Naturae*, Prose 5, 156.
91. James J. Sheridan, trans., *The Plaint of Nature* (Toronto: Pontifical Institute of Mediæval Studies, 1980), 164.
92. Tolkien, *The Two Towers*, III, x, 189.
93. In the scene, Gandalf makes rather Shakespearean allusions to Saruman deserving stripes (whips) for his behaving as a fool. In the London dialect of that period, the two words "voice" and "vice" were homophones much like "loins" and "lines."
94. See Kit Williamson, "Gay Men Should Be Ashamed of Slut-Shaming," *The Advocate*. November 3, 2015, accessed July 21, 2016. http://www.advocate.com/commentary/2015/11/03/gay-men-should-be-ashamed-slut-shaming.
95. Jane Chance, "Tolkien and the Other: Race and Gender in Middle-earth," in *Tolkien's Modern Middle Ages*, edited by Jane Chance and Alfred K. Siewers (New York: Palgrave Macmillan, 2005), 171–186.
96. Chance, *The Mythology of Power*, 78.

Bibliography

Alain de Lille. *De Planctu Naturae*. In *The Anglo-Latin Satirical Poets and Epigrammatists of the Twelfth Century*, edited by Thomas Wright. 2 vols., 429–522. Rerum Britannicarum Medii Aevi Scriptores 59. London: Longman, 1872.

———. *The Complaint of Nature*. Translated by Douglas M. Moffat. Yale Studies in English 36. New York: Henry Holt and Co., 1908.

———. *The Plaint of Nature*. Translated by James J. Sheridan. Toronto: Pontifical Institute of Mediæval Studies, 1980.

Battis, Jes. "Gazing Upon Sauron: Hobbits, Elves, and the Queering of the Postcolonial Optic." *Modern Fiction Studies* 50.4 (2004): 908–926.

Birns, Nicholas. "The Stones and the Book: Tolkien, Mesopotamia, and Biblical Mythopoeia." In *Tolkien and the Study of His Sources: Critical Essays*, ed. Jason Fisher, 45–68. Jefferson, NC: McFarland, 2011.

Boswell, John. *Christianity, Social Tolerance, and Homosexuality: Gay People in Western Europe from the Beginning of the Christian Era to the Fourteenth Century*. Chicago: University of Chicago Press, 1980.

Bosworth-Toller Anglo-Saxon Dictionary Online. "Dwimor." Accessed July 2, 2016. http://www.bosworthtoller.com/043123.

Carpenter, Humphrey. *J. R. R. Tolkien: A Biography*. New York: HarperCollins, 1978.

Calcidius. *Commentary on Plato's* Timaeus. Translated by John Magee (Boston: Harvard University Press, 2016.

Chance, Jane. *The Genius Figure in Antiquity and the Middle Ages*. New York and London: Columbia University Press, 1975.

———. "'In the Company of Orcs': Peter Jackson's Queer Tolkien." In *Queer Movie Medievalisms*, ed. Kathleen Coyne Kelly and Tison Pugh, 79–96. London, England: Ashgate, 2009.

———. *The Lord of the Rings: Mythology of Power*. Rev. ed. Lexington, KY: University of Kentucky Press, 2001.

———. *Tolkien's Art: A Mythology for England*. Rev. ed. Lexington, KY: University of Kentucky Press, 2001.

———. *Tolkien, Self and Other: "This Queer Creature."* New York: Palgrave, 2016.

———. "Tough Love: Teaching the New Medievalisms." Studies in Medievalism 18. Defining Medievalism(s) II, ed. Karl Fugelso, 76–98. Cambridge: D. S. Brewer, 2009.

Chaucer, Geoffrey. The Parliament of Fowls. *The Riverside Chaucer*. Ed. Larry Benson. 3rd ed. Oxford: Oxford University Press, 2008.

Clark, David. *Between Medieval Men: Male Friendship and Desire in Early Medieval English Literature*. Oxford: Oxford University Press, 2009.

Cowie, Elizabeth. *Representing the Woman: Cinema and Psychoanalysis*. Minneapolis: University of Minnesota Press, 1997.

Dickerson, Matthew. *Following Gandalf: Epic Battle and Moral Victory in* The Lord of the Rings. Grand Rapids, MI: Brazos Press, 2003.

Doty, Alexander. *Making Things Perfectly Queer: Interpreting Mass Culture*. Minneapolis: University of Minnesota Press, 1993.

Economou, George D. "The Character Genius in Alain de Lille, Jean de Meun, and John Gower." *Chaucer Review* 4.3 (1970): 203–210.

———. *The Goddess Natura in Medieval Literature*. Cambridge, MA: Harvard University Press, 1972.

Fisher, Jason, ed. *Tolkien and the Study of His Sources: Critical Essays*. Jefferson, NC: McFarland, 2011.

Flieger, Verlyn and T.A. Shippey. "Allegory versus Bounce: Tolkien's Smith of Wootton Major." *Journal of the Fantastic in the Arts* 12.2 (46) (2001): 186–200.

Frantzen, Allen. *Before the Closet: Same-sex Love from* Beowulf *to* Angels in America. Chicago and London: University of Chicago Press, 1998.

Garcia, Laura. "Pride and Humility in *The Hobbit*." In The Hobbit *and Philosophy*, edited by Gregory Bassham and Eric Bronson. Philosophy and Pop Culture Series, ed. William Irwin, 74–89. Hoboken, N.J.: Wiley Press, 2012.

Green, Richard Hamilton. "Alan of Lille's *De Planctu Naturae*." *Speculum* 31 (1956): 649–674.

Helms, Randel. *Tolkien's World*. Boston: Houghton Mifflin, 1974.

Hocquenghem, Guy. *Homosexual Desire*. Durham and London: Duke University Press, 1993.

Jordan, Mark. *The Invention of Sodomy in Christian Theology*. Chicago: University of Chicago Press, 1997.

Lewis, C. S. *The Allegory of Love*. New York: Oxford University Press, 1958.

Macrobius (Ambrosius Theodosius). *Commentary on the Dream of Scipio*. Translated by William Harris Vol. 48 of Records of Civilization: Sources and Studies. New York: Columbia University Press, 1990.

Nagy, Gergely. "The 'Lost' Subject of Middle-Earth: The Constitution of the Subject in the Figure of Gollum in *The Lord of the Rings*." *Tolkien Studies* 3 (2006): 57–79.

Nelson, Charles. "The Sins of Middle-earth: Tolkien's Use of Allegory." In *J. R. R. Tolkien and His Literary Resonances*, ed. George Clark and Daniel Timmons, 83–94. Westport, CT and London: Greenwood Press, 2000.

Rateliff, John. *The History of* The Hobbit. 2 Vols. Boston: Houghton Mifflin, 2007.

Rohy, Valerie. "On Fairy Stories." *Modern Fiction Studies* 50.4 (2004): 927–948.

Rubin, Gayle. "Thinking Sex: Notes for a Radical Theory of the Politics of Sexuality." In *Pleasure and Danger: Exploring Female Sexuality*, ed. Carole S. Vance, 3–44. Boston: Routledge and Kegan Paul, 1984.

Scanlon, Larry. "Unspeakable Pleasures: Alain de Lille, Sexual Regulation and the Priesthood of Genius." *Romantic Review* 86.2 (1995): 213–242.

Shippey, Tom. *The Road to Middle-earth*. Boston: Houghton Mifflin, 2003.

Skoble, Aeon J. "Virtue and Vice in *The Lord of the Rings*." In The Lord of the Rings *and Philosophy*, edited by Bassham and Bronson. Vol. 5 of Pop Culture and Philosophy Series, ed. William Irwin, 110–119. Chicago: Open Court, 2003.

Tolkien, J. R. R. *The Fellowship of the Ring*. 2nd ed. Boston: Houghton Mifflin, 1987.

———. *Letters of J. R. R. Tolkien*. Edited by Humphrey Carpenter. Boston: Houghton Mifflin, 2000.

———. *The Return of the King*. 2nd ed. Boston: Houghton Mifflin, 1987.

———. *The Silmarillion*. Boston: Houghton Mifflin, 1977.

———. *The Two Towers*. 2nd ed. Boston: Houghton Mifflin, 1987.

———. *Unfinished Tales*. Boston: Houghton Mifflin, 1980.

Treloar, John. "The Middle-earth Epic and the Seven Capital Vices." *Mythlore* 16.1 (1989): 37–42.

Warner, Michael. *The Trouble with Normal: Sex, Politics, and the Ethics of Queer Life*. New York: Free Press, 1999.

Williamson, Kit. "Gay Men Should Be Ashamed of Slut-Shaming." *The Advocate*, November 3rd, 2015. Accessed July 21st, 2016. http://www.advocate.com/commentary/2015/11/03/gay-men-should-be-ashamed-slut-shaming.

CHAPTER 8

Cruising Faery: Queer Desire in Giles, Niggle, and Smith

Stephen Yandell

Avoid the fairies!—it's a warning that would sound as natural coming from a medieval farmer pointing to a forest as from modern schoolboys choosing teams for dodgeball. Admittedly, "fairies" has changed in meaning over time. In the late nineteenth century, it expanded to include effeminate, presumably homosexual men.[1] However, the threat to mainstream society embodied by the term has remained largely the same: Fairies are the dainty, unnatural creatures whose marginalization by respectable people is entirely warranted.

Yet for some, Faery—that land on the periphery where fairies dwell—represents something different. J. R. R. Tolkien, the outspoken champion of Faery, found the presentation of fairies as small and frail misleading, and he used both his fiction and scholarly works to counter the popular perception. The fairies' Otherworld is a "perilous land," he reminds us in "On Fairy-stories,"[2] and its danger lies on multiple fronts. We should be wary not simply of the strength and beauty of Faery's creatures but of the overwhelming passion they generate. The primary risk of fairies for a human is their ability "to play on the desires of his body and his heart."[3]

S. Yandell (✉)
Xavier University, Cincinnati, OH, USA

C. Vaccaro and Y. Kisor (eds.), *Tolkien and Alterity*, The New Middle Ages, DOI 10.1007/978-3-319-61018-4_8

Readers of Tolkien's legendarium know well what the desire for Faery looks like. *The Lord of the Rings* is filled with longing (for home, individuals, and the past, for example), but few moments generate as much poignancy as when the unquenchable yearning for Elvenhome (or Aman, the Undying Lands) reveals itself. Bilbo and Frodo are driven by a deep desire to explore the world beyond Hobbiton and to seek something neither can fully name. This longing for the borders both defines their characters and moves forward the action of *The Hobbit* and *The Lord of the Rings*; it also earns them the label "queer" from the locals.[4]

Tolkien begins hinting at the source of Frodo's desire during his second night in Tom Bombadil's house: "Frodo heard a sweet singing running in his mind: a song that seemed to come like a pale light behind a grey rain-curtain… until at last it was rolled back, and a far green country opened before him under a swift sunrise."[5] Frodo glimpses Middle-earth's Faery in this moment, and by the novel's end, we see how heavily the need for comfort in the Otherworld weighs on him, whether or not the value of a trip to the Undying Lands is something he can even articulate. His longing approaches fulfillment when, after departing the Grey Havens, Frodo's ship "went out into the High Sea and passed on into the West, until at last on a night of rain Frodo smelled a sweet fragrance on the air and heard the sound of singing that came over the water…. The grey rain-curtain turned all to silver glass and was rolled back, and he beheld white shores and beyond them a far green country under a swift sunrise."[6]

A longing for Faery generally (one shared by Tolkien's fellow Inklings[7]) and for Valinor specifically, punctuates some of the most significant moments in *The Lord of The Rings.* Galadriel's warning to Legolas of seagulls, for example, is rooted in Faery's pull—a desire for the West that she knows from experience cannot be quenched once raised;[8] and the depth and immediacy of Legolas's reaction proves her right: "The Sea! Alas! I have not yet beheld it. But deep in the hearts of all my kindred lies the sea-longing…. No peace shall I have again under beech or under elm."[9] Legolas's longing is for the Sea, ostensibly, but in actuality is also for Elvenhome, to where the Sea leads. All of Middle-earth with its extensive coastline ultimately establishes for Tolkien a sequence of signification that points metonymically and relentlessly to Faery.

Tolkien's passion for his earliest subcreative work, his *Silmarillion* myths, also undergirds many of these moments, sometimes revealing a whole chain of signification that points to Aman. When Beregond of

Minas Tirith looks for imagery to describe the hope he feels so deeply inside, he invokes *Silmarillion*-inspired Faery space: "Though all things must come utterly to an end in time, Gondor shall not perish yet.... Hope and memory shall live still in some hidden valley where the grass is green."[10] Readers later recognize this reference to a specific slope on Mount Mindolluin where Aragorn finds a seedling of the White Tree;[11] however, like other glimpses of Valinor offered through Frodo and Legolas, the line of white trees ultimately points back to Faery—to the primeval vale that once nurtured the source of the line of trees, Telperion.[12]

This same desire for Faery undergirds three shorter, more often overlooked works by J. R. R. Tolkien, *Farmer Giles of Ham*, *Leaf by Niggle*, and *Smith of Wootton Major*. Spanning almost thirty years of Tolkien's writing, these tales offer varied depictions of the supernatural Otherworld. The mythic borderlands of the Little Kingdom, for example, are a source of fantastic creatures that stumble into Ham, and after trekking to those margins with his magic sword, Farmer Giles stumbles into the role of hero. The painter Niggle finds a different success after traveling to a purgatorial country where his unappreciated art is fully realized, and like Giles, he is reluctant to start a journey with unclear goals. Equally unsure in his abilities, Smith learns as a boy he has been marked with a fay star that grants him access to Faery, a land for which he deeply yearns. His desire for relationships in both Wootton Major and the Otherworld leaves him conflicted, however, and ultimately offers him no clear resolution.

The three tales offer themes and styles that are clearly different, but at the center of each one, Tolkien highlights humanity's relationship to Faery. This is a criterion he also identified as crucial for any author tackling the Otherworld. Rather than concentrate on fairy creatures or the land itself, "good" storytellers know to take up "the *aventures* of men in the Perilous Realm or upon its shadowy marches."[13] *Giles*, *Niggle*, and *Smith* each opens with its titular protagonist settled into an imagined version of England,[14] but readers see immediately that none of the men fits neatly within his domestic box nor lives a particularly happy life. The same mismatch between mainstream society and a Faery-inclined protagonist ends up driving each narrative's *aventure*.

The term "fairies," a code for queers, has been equally powerful in dividing modern outcasts from the mainstream, and numerous queer scholars have explored the connection. Film theorist Richard Dyer ties fairies to the uncategorizable queer figure in film. It is hard to "believe" in any of them, he laments, because of their elusive nature.[15] In trying to identify the space in which fairies, outsiders, and homosexuals come together, one finds a usefully broad definition from Alexander Doty; he proposes that queer is "a quality related to any expression that can be marked as contra-, non-, or anti-straight…. It also includes all other potential (and potentially unclassifiable) non-straight positions."[16] Doty allows for a wide range of queer pleasures to be taken from texts, regardless of their surface narratives. Equally usefully, Doty points to the inherent label-smashing quality of queerness: its presence allows us to "challenge and break apart conventional categories."[17] Poet Judy Grahn points to her own mid-twentieth-century upbringing to reveal a modern fairy-queer connection: when "those of us who secretly knew our queer state never, under any circumstance, wore green on Thursday" lest the label of fairy might out them.[18]

Giles, Niggle, and Smith, I argue, embody a range of non-straight positions while negotiating their outsider status within society. Each finds it necessary to keep parts of his life hidden, maintaining a public front that obscures various secrets: the source of Giles' dragon-fighting prowess, for example, the artistic passion inside Niggle, and Smith's longings for Faery. Secrecy is a key feature of the queer; according to Eve Kosofsky Sedgwick: "a lot of the energy of attention and demarcation that has swirled around issues of homosexuality … has been impelled by the distinctively indicative relationship of homosexuality to wider mappings of secrecy and disclosure, and of the private and the public, that were and are critically problematic for the gender, sexual, and economic structures of the heterosexist culture at large."[19] In *Covert Operations*, Karma Lochrie expands on this premise while exploring the queer implications of secrecy; she reminds us that creating secrets, keeping secrets, and being a secret oneself are all acts inherently tied to power.[20]

Together, the themes of marginalized individuals, mainstream conformity, and hidden lives in the three tales make them rife for queer analysis, but Tolkien's foray into queer territory pushes deeper than this. He adopts queer imagery at key moments in *Giles*, *Niggle*, and *Smith* in order to highlight the world/Otherworld distinction on which his narratives depend. He aligns fairies and queers in subtle ways to make use of a discourse that was not only firmly in place within the literary traditions he invokes, but was also highly effective at articulating the tensions between a marginalized, passion-driven individual and his mainstream surroundings—a relationship Tolkien himself had to negotiate throughout his life.

Fortunately, several decades of scholarship have provided the three tales with a wealth of critical attention. Tom Shippey's *J. R. R. Tolkien: Author of the Century* has helped to build a broad audience for Tolkien's non-Middle-earth works; Shippey reveals the narratives' numerous connections with Tolkien's broader thematic and etymological interests. Similarly, Wayne Hammond and Christina Scull's fiftieth anniversary edition of *Farmer Giles of Ham* offers new access to the long-overlooked work, and Verlyn Flieger's extended edition of *Smith of Wootton Major* skillfully sets Tolkien's last fictional work amid the critical sources it had long required. Particularly important to the current study is a recent precedent of reading Tolkien through a queer lens; Jane Chance has been chiefly responsible for offering the most insightful queer readings of Middle-earth and championing the call for ongoing research. As a result, this study seeks to build on both of these scholarly platforms which, to now, have generated only a small overlap.

Tolkien's admiration for the outsider is one that undergirds most of Tolkien's writings according to Chance. Her scholarship has proven particularly foundational in this regard, pointing to a range of personal identifications that caused Tolkien to side with marginalized individuals. These include "his own otherness in England as a southern African Catholic orphan with ties to the similarly marginalized western Midlands cities of Birmingham and Sheffield. An orphan like Frodo, he can also be described as an exile much of his life."[21] Tolkien's career as an educated white male teaching at Oxford University certainly placed him in multiple privileged positions, but as Chance notes, his love of languages separated him from his colleagues in literary studies.[22] Tolkien's love of pre-modern texts also pitted him against modernist scholars. He had to defend the erroneous notion that before Chaucer all English poetry was "dumb and barbaric," for example. He reminded others that Chaucer was actually "in the middle of a 1200 year literary tradition for England, not the beginning."[23] Much of Tolkien's scholarly career was built on explicating the margins of his already marginalized fields of medieval literature and language. He published a 1962 Early English Text Society edition of the obscure *Ancrene Wisse*, defended *Beowulf*'s artistry in the 1936 lecture "Beowulf: The Monsters and the Critics," and turned to underappreciated differences in regional dialects within the *Canterbury Tales* for his 1934 essay "Chaucer as a Philologist."

Chance rightly concludes that "Tolkien's very creation of the Hobbits as a species reflects his own sense of himself as displaced, marginal, exiled, queer, and different from other species and individuals."[24] Tolkien's Middle-earth writings as a whole appear to be a queer project, consistently challenging "segregation of the Other, and isolation of those who are different, whether by race, nationality, culture, class, age, or gender."[25] In "Tolkien and the Other," Chance argues that Tolkien is inherently interested in people on the edges—those who come to the margins for all sorts of reasons. Even as epic battles are taking place in the novel, "Tolkien seems more interested in those who come to the battle, if at all, in ways and forms and for reasons that differ from those in the conventional epic-romance."[26] Tolkien's interest in the disenfranchised grew from his own upbringing, and his scholarship reveals a specific political bent: He is "supremely conscious of precisely those individuals or groups or races who might be considered marginal within a Fascist system of exclusion, that is, who exist on the peripheries of society, often in exile, or as outcasts."[27]

Chance's Foucauldian reading of the queer proves crucial in considering these short stories in the ways I suggest. By championing Queer's connections to identity politics and institutional oppression, Chance builds her foundation for "Tolkien and the Other" on Michel Foucault's understanding that "'technologies of sex' were designed to preserve and foster a productive and procreative population (or workforce) that met the needs of a developing capitalist system."[28] One of Chance's greatest strengths in reading Tolkien, however, lies in her questioning some of the fundamentals of Foucault's identity politics, challenging the uniformity of separate identity groups, and breaking apart an exclusive Foucauldian focus on male homosexuality.

Valerie Rohy follows similar tactics in connecting desire in *The Lord of the Rings* specifically to queerness. One might deny that any sex appears in Tolkien's work, but such a claim says more about what the denier calls sex than anything else, Rohy argues.[29] Her own reading of the novel, coupled with a larger body of scholarship, allows her to conclude that sexuality not only exists in the book, it "also asks that we recognize much of it as queer."[30] Rohy reminds us that all the romantic entanglements introduced in the novel point ultimately to "all marriage and no plot."[31] Sam and Rosie's relationship, for example, is "compressed into the few remaining pages after her very late introduction."[32] The same solemnity that colors *The Lord of the Rings* when characters are drawn to

Faery is matched in tenderness only by those moments shared by the two male Hobbit protagonists. Rohy points to Sam and Frodo's relationship as central to the novel's larger trend of "lack and incompletion mark[ing] all love in *The Lord of the Rings*, not least same-sex relations. If heterosexuality is finished but never started, homosexuality is started but never finished.... [Homosexuality] becomes an emblem of desire's endlessly postponed possibility."[33] What is particularly crucial to this study, however, is that for Tolkien, queer desire inevitably shifts into the realm of Faery. As she notes, "One narrative path... may close with Sam's return to the Shire... but another moves beyond the novel's formal limits, into the appendices and into the West."[34] At the end of the second appendix, we are given the briefest information about Sam's reunion with Frodo,[35] which Rohy finds telling: "The brief and clumsy line omits as much as it tells: Sam's passage to Valinor is little more that a rumor, and Tolkien leaves unnamed the friend he must meet there."[36] Chance and Rohy thus offer an invaluable foundation on which to make sense of Faery in Tolkien's short fiction.

Farmer Giles of Ham

Although J. R. R Tolkien's ties to fairy tales were built in his childhood,[37] *The Hobbit*'s 1937 publication and subsequent success proved a key moment in cementing the link in the public's eye. Whether fairly or not, the book's genre as children's literature had a large part to do with this. *The Hobbit* was soon followed by the composition of *Farmer Giles of Ham*, which received a warm reception at its first public reading in February 1938 to Worcester College's Lovelace Society. Tolkien had been asked to provide an academic essay on fairy stories, but having not completed it, he chose to offer this short, comic tale, originally named "The Legend of Worming Hall."[38] The event helped reinforce the public's perception of fairies, children's literature, and the fantastic as synonymous categories—and added Tolkien to the mix.

Tolkien expanded *Giles* immediately in 1938, but it reached publication only eleven years later. The tale's "lighthearted" tone separated it from most of Tolkien's writings, which also contributed to its long-delayed release.[39] Publishers Allen & Unwin felt *Giles*'s short length made the work unpublishable unless it was combined with similar texts, but Tolkien had written nothing else quite like it; no story balanced broad and erudite humor in nearly the same way. Starting in December

1937, Tolkien had also begun his twelve-year journey of composing *The Lord of the Rings*, originally conceived as a simple sequel to *The Hobbit*. During these years, he found it increasingly difficult to keep any new works separate from his deepest passion, the tales that would eventually be published as *The Silmarillion*. In his *Letters*, Tolkien reveals the conflict he felt over the strength that the passion held over him: The story of Elves and Elvenhome "has refused to be suppressed. It has bubbled up, infiltrated, and probably spoiled everything (that even remotely approached 'Faery') which I have tried to write since. It was kept out of *Farmer Giles* with an effort, but stopped the continuation [of sequels]."[40]

In *Giles*, queer elements bubble up in similar ways. Secret passions all seem to point to the folly of locating any definitive boundaries between the mainstream world of Ham and the mythic lands on the borders. These queer aspects emerge initially in a shifting space of faux medievalism. The tale announces part of its queerness immediately through a faux manuscript history outlined in the mock-scholarly foreword. It then goes on to describe a medieval setting that includes a number of anachronistic elements—like the inclusion of the blunderbuss firearm which creates a temporal rift in Tolkien's imagined alternate version of medieval England, buffered by no attempt to apologize or explain. In one letter, a reader of Tolkien received an assurance that in the days of Giles, "there can have been nothing in the least like a fire-arm";[41] however, in the tale itself, the discordance is an embedded feature of the world.

Farmer Giles's medieval setting also allows Tolkien to place word origins as a central concern while simultaneously challenging the rigidness of words. Much of the tale's playfulness, in fact, grows out of its etymological premise of explaining the origin of "Thames" through the word "tame."[42] Real and imagined folly become blurred for readers in the story's etymological moments as Tolkien both celebrates and ridicules the public's fondness of (and gullibility for) folk etymologies. Tolkien the linguist also understood very well the reason an "h" had been added to the name "Thames," though not made explicit in the tale. "Thames" had been spelled and pronounced with a simple "t" throughout the Anglo-Saxon and Middle-English periods; "th" was indeed a folly. In the seventeenth century, the name was falsely believed to have a Greek origin, and scholars felt it ought to match the "th" counterparts used on the continent.[43] In telling us that "Thame with an *h* is a folly without warrant," Tolkien is right on several levels; the H is a folly among everyday English users, just as his own explanation linking the word to the taming of a dragon is a folly. This same grand explanation thus performs an imaginary access to one reality while constructing its own folly. In much the same way, all of Little Kingdom is slowly revealed to be a mock version of medieval England, posing itself with comical desperation to be taken as a normal, natural, and real Middle Ages. The queerness of the project proves to be only barely below the surface at any moment of the narrative.

Indeterminacy in both history and language sets the stage for a world where Giles has to negotiate a range of shifting boundaries. Several of these binary divisions are named immediately to highlight Ham's fluid categories. For example, "sober annals" are contrasted with "popular lays."[44] However, neither proves so different from the other under scrutiny, despite the tale's insistence otherwise. Similarly, the world of *Giles* also undergoes "swift alternations of war and peace, of mirth and woe," while talking dogs and idiotic rulers challenge neat divisions between human and animal, court and country.[45] The conflict that takes place in the grey areas between the ordinary world of Ham and the extraordinary margins is fundamental to the tale, according to Tom Shippey. He highlights the distinction not merely between real life and "old, heroic songs," but also between public and private identity.[46]

Giles's home is a fallen world marked not merely by instability and unfixed boundaries, but also by queerness. As the tale reminds us, the primary division of Britain into three lands was the result of an ancient familial division. Founder Brutus's three sons, Locrin, Camber, and Albanac, ruled over separate territories, which "was only the first of many shifting divisions.... [It was] a time of unsettled frontiers."[47] The town's name of Ham cannot help but invoke the queerest version of a three-part family division, that of Noah's sons. According to the Genesis narrative, Noah's three sons divided the world's population by founding the continents of Europe (by Japheth), Asia (Shem), and Africa (Ham). Genesis 9 explains Ham was cursed for having approached his drunk, naked father and covering him: "When Noah awoke from his wine and found out what his youngest son had done to him, he said, 'Cursed be Canaan! The lowest of slaves will he be to his brothers.'"[48] For centuries, the narrative was used to justify the marginalization of Africans as inherently cursed, and the incestuous, homosexual overtones forever linked Ham with an irredeemable queerness.

Tolkien's change of title from "The Legend of Worming Hall" to "Farmer Giles of Ham" reveals a shift in interest toward his protagonist. Readers should admire immediately the ways in which Giles does not fit into mainstream society; he is cleverer than his fellow townsfolk, less jealous, and less vindictive. He represents authenticity in a region steeped in inauthenticity. By the end, Giles holds the credentials for tackling a real dragon, which sets him apart from the realm's knights and kings, men who had relied "for many years now" on the Royal Cook making "a marvelous confection, a Mock Dragon's Tail" for the King's Christmas Feast.[49]

Giles's queerness is not easy to read on the surface, though. His adherence to certain traditionally masculine traits is never questioned; he very much looks the part of a rugged farmer. While reviewing proposed illustrations by Milein Cosman for *Giles*, Tolkien complained about their inability to capture Giles's full masculine display, insisting the farmer should be depicted as "a large blusterer bigger than his fellows."[50] Giles's marriage to his wife, Agatha, also appears quite traditional on the surface; their sexual relations were real enough to produce a son who could have carried a proposed sequel.[51]

However, attempts to pin down Giles's traditional masculinity must also be filtered through a recognition that the multiple phalluses he wields all have more control over him than he has of them. Perhaps the most identifying sign by which Giles is marked is the belt and long sword sent as a gift by the king. The sword Caudimordax, also called Tailbiter, once belonged to Bellomarius, "the greatest of all the dragon-slayers of the realm."[52] We learn that it has magic properties that both point to and stand in for the bravery of its owner: It "will not stay sheathed, if a dragon is within five miles; and without a doubt in a brave man's hands no dragon can resist it."[53] The tale hinges on Giles's need to defend a fairly singular view of maleness, his own strength as dragon-slayer, but readers simultaneously find gender roles becoming fluid as the tale continues. Although the Little Kingdom appears to be populated almost entirely by men, its giants, dragons, kings, and farmers all represent non-straight versions of masculinity. All of the men prove inadequate by the end. Giles' self-presentation depends on the defense of his own heroism, for example, but his success also requires keeping the fundamental source of this dragon-taming prowess a secret.

The anachronicity of the blunderbuss helps to reveal ruptures in English history generally, but it also highlights its peculiarity as a phallus, since its features invoke both masculine and feminine imagery. In addition to functioning as "a short gun with a large bore," Giles's blunderbuss is non-standard as a launcher of projectiles: It "had a wide mouth that opened like a horn, and it did not fire balls or slugs, but anything that he could spare to stuff in."[54] The long, masculine shaft and open, feminine mouth of the weapon are brought together in Giles' hands, signaling yet another unfixed position that Giles (and readers) must negotiate going forward.

The wide mouth of the blunderbuss calls to mind not simply female anatomy, but also Giles's wife Agatha. She is drawn in the medieval tradition of exasperating wives, much like Noah's wife in the Wakefield cycle play who is defined most prominently by her harping, dangerous, open mouth.[55] In one of the few instances in which Agatha is given lines, she simply barks commands, emasculating her husband: "Get back to bed and don't be a fool!" At this same moment of brandishing her queer masculinity, Agatha also reminds Giles of his need to perform the role of husband: "Be bold and quick!"[56] Once armed with a barely functioning phallus, Giles must turn to an eclectic mix of both domestic and industrial arsenal to load it: "he stuffed old nails and bits of wire, pieces of broken pot, bones and stones and other rubbish."[57]

Giles's wife may make very little appearance in the tale, and we witness no display of affection from Giles to her, but she at least helps maintain a public display of heteronormativity. Nevertheless, her presence does not make him any less queer a figure. As Alexander Doty reminds us in *Making Things Perfectly Queer*, concrete images of straightness have little to do with the presence of a queer subtext: "I've got news for straight culture: your readings of texts are usually 'alternative' ones for me, and they often seem like desperate attempts to deny the queerness that is so clearly a part of mass culture. The day someone can establish without a doubt that… representations of men and women getting married… undeniably depict 'straightness,' is the day someone can say no lesbian or gay has ever been married."[58]

The female for whom Giles actually holds the greatest fondness is Galathea, "the farmer's favourite cow" and the first victim of the giant Garm's foray into Ham.[59] Galathea's classical name alludes to several queer relationships,[60] much like the wide range of boundary-crossing couples that fill Tolkien's Middle-earth corpus. As Jane Chance has noted, such couples include Thingol and Melian, Beren and Lúthien, and Arargorn and Arwen.[61] Central to Chance's analysis is the role these intermarriages play, representing ideal unions for Tolkien.[62] Queer intimacy appears in other relationships as well, including ones held up as admirable models such as Legolas and Gimli's as well as Galadriel and Gimli's, both of which champion passion above "naturalness."

Leaf by Niggle

Tolkien continued his challenge of naturalness immediately after completing *Farmer Giles of Ham*. Between 1938 and 1939, in the midst of struggling to advance his *Hobbit* sequel beyond the opening chapters, Tolkien composed *Leaf by Niggle*, eventually publishing the piece in the *Dublin Review*'s January 1945 issue. The tale is unique among Tolkien's writings for many reasons, but perhaps most notably for having been produced in practically one sitting. This new defense of a marginalized protagonist appeared almost fully formed to Tolkien, as he explained to Stanley Unwin: It was "the only thing I have ever done which cost me absolutely no pains at all. Usually I compose only with great difficulty and endless rewriting. I woke up one morning… with that odd thing virtually complete in my head. It took only a few hours to get down.… I am not aware of ever 'thinking' of the story or composing in the ordinary sense."[63] Its unique creation might also explain why Tolkien employed allegory in the tale, at least partially, despite famously despising allegory "in all its manifestations."[64] Paramount to the project was being true to a vision that seems to have bubbled up from his subconscious.

Leaf by Niggle's protagonist is as out of place in mainstream society as Giles. The unmarried Niggle lives alone on the margins of town[65] and spends as much time as he can painting. He is reluctant to talk about his art with others (few even know it exists) and resents any tasks that get in the way. Niggle's marginalization is only intensified by his habit of obsessing over the details in his art, which leads to a manic work environment. The character of Tompkins, meanwhile, provides the primary voice of mainstream society in the tale; he finds Niggle "a silly little man… no use to Society at all."[66] As in *Giles*, we find Tolkien championing individuals who pursue non-standard passions and stand up to worldly contempt.

In its presentation of "niggling," *Leaf by Niggle* also provides us with one of the most insightful glimpses into Tolkien's own marginalized struggles as a writer. Richard Purtill finds the tale highly autobiographical, but prefers the term "applicable" over "allegorical."[67] Tolkien described the tale as both "purgatorial"[68] and "mythical,"[69] but otherwise hoped it could speak for itself. Many scholars have pointed to ways in which the tale points to Tolkien's own anxieties about not having the time, or possibly the skill, to perfect the artistic segments over which he had been poring for years. What Niggle finds when traveling to the

Otherworld, however, is a space mediated by an artistic and spiritual purgatory. Here, Niggle's artistic vision can be fully realized, something Tolkien never had the pleasure of seeing. *Leaf by Niggle*'s purgatorial margins offer a space, as in *Giles*, where partial, incomplete individuals discover pieces that had been missing in their mainstream lives. The queerness of the project rests alongside what Tolkien ultimately posits as a divine proposition. Both the source of artistic desire and the methods necessary for fulfilling it belong to a Christian God, and only by responding to the call is humanity able to join an act that fulfills its highest calling, subcreation.[70]

Before being published, *Leaf by Niggle* also underwent a significant name change like *Giles*. In shifting its title from a key object in the tale, in this case "The Tree," to a central character,[71] Tolkien signals to readers where his focus will lie: squarely on the protagonist, whose relationship to the Otherworld drives every central theme. Niggle thus emerges in clear contrast to a mainstream society that is not merely unaware of the kinds of work being done on the queer margins, but fundamentally unprepared to appreciate its value. The tree and Niggle are both odd according to the narrator, but it is the painter on whom our attention is ultimately fixed: "The Tree, at any rate, was curious. Quite unique in its way. So was Niggle; though he was also a very ordinary and rather silly little man.... When [his neighbor Parish] looked at Niggle's pictures (which was seldom) he saw only green and grey patches and black lines, which seemed to him nonsensical."[72]

Women are largely absent in this tale, which reflects a large part of Tolkien's own experience with creativity. As we saw with Giles, whose relationship with almost every other male took precedence over that with his wife, the primacy of male relationships in these short stories mimics Tolkien's reliance on the male friendships that surrounded him through his years of reading, writing, and thinking with all-male groups. Tolkien was part of several all-male reading and writing groups, including the T.C.B.S. (Tea Club, Barrovian Society) while at King Edward's School in Birmingham, the *Kolbitar* which he founded at Oxford for reading Icelandic sagas, and from the early 1930s through 1949, the Inklings with fellow authors C.S. Lewis, Owen Barfield, and Charles Williams among others.[73]

As Brenda Partridge notes in "No Sex Please—We're Hobbits," Tolkien's creative life was in many ways indebted to the series of secret societies to which he belonged, each defined by its male-only companionship. He excluded his wife from these groups and was jealous when the intimacy they afforded got threatened. She argues that Tolkien creates in *The Lord of the Rings* "a very exclusive male world. …The interaction between the male characters and the female is for the most part stilted and distant. The relationships between the males on the other hand is often intensely close and supportive."[74] She claims that the best of Tolkien's works inevitably depict a bunch of boys who love each other's company and are not quite sure what to do with the small number of women who appear.

In *Women Among the Inklings*, Candice Fredrick and Sam McBride work to explain the misogynistic traits they identify among the Inklings. The members' "theistic worldview and their preference for a culture of the past… separated the Inklings from the progressive Oxford mainstream… Equally noteworthy is the group's gender exclusivity, which they shared with the greater Oxford community, yet which for the Inklings was itself linked to their appreciation of earlier Christian-dominated culture."[75] The authors also identify the divide as one that goes back to Tolkien's early life, when his academic endeavors were placed in opposition to the romantic ties he held to his future wife Edith. Between the ages of 18 and 21, Tolkien stayed away from Edith, despite his love, and devoted himself to his studies. The result, according to Fredrick and McBride, was Tolkien holding "his relationship with Edith as an idealized fantasy while enjoying immensely the actual male relationships available at King Edward's school. Thus, even romance had the effect of emphasizing the importance and pleasure of male camaraderie."[76]

Others have formed similar conclusions about an inherent queerness to the Inklings's gatherings. As a student of C. S. Lewis, Derek Brewer observed that the Inklings were a group that "depend[ed] on a profound sense of masculine comradeship, engendered in worlds in which women could not by definition in those days enter: the fighting services, Oxford and Cambridge colleges…"[77] In studying male-dominated writerly communities, Diana Pavlac Glyer is less harsh in her judgment though, acknowledging that "single-sex groups were a long established fact of Oxford life."[78] She points to Karen Burke Lefevre, however, in the lament she makes in *Invention as a Social Act* that the underpinning ideologies to such organizations were inevitably circular: If society believes women cannot contribute to creative and scholarly works, they are barred from the professional organizations, which in turn prevents them from ever developing the skills.[79]

Niggle's oddness is painted in increasingly queer terms as *Leaf by Niggle* continues, and the queerness is brandished as a strength. Niggle not only stands successfully against mainstream pressures to conform, but he also ultimately fulfills his artistic calling by setting up a domesticated life with his neighbor, Parish, in the new Fairy space. First, Niggle comes to realize the importance of the relationship with his neighbor: "what I need is Parish";[80] and their intimacy grows after Parish joins him: "they walked about together, arm in arm. Without talking, Niggle and Parish agreed exactly where to make the small house and garden, which seemed to be required.... They went on living and working together: I do not know how long."[81]

Here, creative works are accomplished not simply with the absence of women (or lack of heteronormativity), but through the active construction of a domestic life established between two men. Niggle and Parish's male-only household in the afterlife proves more generative than anything either had experienced while alive. In fact, the art they jointly create becomes an artistic legacy, clearly suggesting to readers an alternative form of progeny; just as their domestic relationship begins to fuel greater generativity, their roles emerge as an alternative Adam and Eve populating a paradisal Otherworld. As the tale closes, we learn that Parish's marriage does prevent him from moving forward with Niggle; Parish chooses to wait for his wife.[82] As Niggle continues to travel deeper into the Otherworld, readers understand that the separation neither precludes a later reunion nor negates the depth of the queer foundation already laid down.

Smith of Wootton Major

Tolkien's composition of *Smith of Wootton Major* came several decades after the completion of *Leaf by Niggle*, largely between 1965 and 1966, and it was first published in *Redbook*'s November 1967 issue. The thirty-year interim between *Niggle* and *Smith* is marked most notably by the publication of *The Lord of the Rings* in 1954 and 1955, the highlight of Tolkien's writing successes. Originally titled "The Great Cake,"[83] *Smith of Wootton Major* allowed Tolkien to reflect on his own relationship to Faery in the wake of public success. The tale began as one component piece for an introduction Tolkien was asked to provide in 1964 for a new edition of George MacDonald's *The Golden Key*.[84] Tolkien's preference for bringing alive the desires of Faery in fiction rather than dissecting the pieces though an academic essay is something he had revealed years earlier when offering *Giles* to the Lovelace Society. Narrativizing the desires of Faery—a translation of the form we might call "faerying" the text, and a skill at which Tolkien excelled—allowed Tolkien to offer, as Verlyn Flieger explains, "the uncommunicable experience of Faërie, about what it is like to find it and what it is like to give it up and go on."[85] *Smith of Wootton Major* also stands out among Tolkien's fiction for having been composed almost entirely on the typewriter, a rare practice for the author, and for being the last prose fiction he wrote.[86] Like *Giles* and *Niggle*, *Smith* defies easy categorization or straightforward interpretation; as Roger Lancelyn Green quipped, "to seek for the meaning is to cut open the ball in search of its bounce."[87]

This somber, complex tale warrants close scrutiny, though, despite a risk of any analytical castration Green suggests. Verlyn Flieger stands out as a lead defender of *Smith of Wootton Major*'s complexity.[88] She argues that we capture only part of its spirit when scholars such as Paul Kocher liken it to Prospero's voicing of a farewell speech for his author Shakespeare,[89] or Humphrey Carpenter posing the tale as an exploration of Tolkien's "anxiety over the future."[90] While the tale is as highly personal as *Niggle* and as unique in tone as *Giles*, reading *Smith* through a queer lens reveals Tolkien's personal ambivalence to negotiating difficult loyalties; movement between Wootton Major and Faery requires balancing a mainstream world of prosaic duties (and, admittedly, domestic happiness) with a marginalized realm where the deepest passions lie.

Perhaps most explicitly of the three tales, *Smith of Wooton Major* casts its closeted protagonist "Other" as queer. Smith's desires to enter Faery are rooted deep inside him, for example, arising after he has swallowed a fay star. From the age of ten onward (suggesting a kind of sexual awakening), he finds himself increasingly uncomfortable in mainstream society. Faery represents both excitement and danger and is quickly fetishized by Smith, an outsider who seeks escape. Alongside Smith, readers come to understand "that the marvels of Faery cannot be approached without danger."[91]

The character of Nokes serves as the clearest representation of mainstream society in *Smith*, and according to Tom Shippey, this Master Cook stands in for "many of the things which Tolkien most disliked.... Those 'professional persons' who 'suppose their [own] dullness and ignorance to be a human norm.'"[92] In Tolkien's own explanatory essay on the tale, published in Flieger's Extended Edition, Tolkien makes clear that Nokes best articulates mainstream society's positions; he displays the "vulgarization of Wootton" and "clearly represents an attitude fast spreading in the village and growing in weight."[93] Nokes typifies what it means to live both geographically and mythically as far as possible from the faery forest; he is eager not simply to demean anything related to Faery as simpleminded, but to shun any form of alterity.

The swallowed star that both permits passage into the Perilous Realm and protects its owner invokes another queer marker of outsidedness. Like Cain, from whom the line of Fairies springs,[94] Smith is marked on his forehead. Medieval depictions of Cain often included a visible sign on the forehead or a pair of horns.[95] Like Smith's star, the horns were believed to have served multiple functions: marking Cain as an outsider worthy of banishment to the borderlands while simultaneously providing him the necessary protection to survive there. Smith's act of swallowing the star is further queered by suggesting that in this penetration, the boy has participated in an alternative form of impregnation. Similarly, his eventual passing of the star to a Faery-traveling successor invokes images of alternative, non-heteronormative reproduction and a queer progeny.

Verlyn Flieger sees the interaction between world and Otherworld articulated particularly clearly in *Smith*, but also used differently than we have seen in Tolkien's earlier writings: "The point of fusion between Faery and the outside world is, as in all of Tolkien's fiction, but most successfully in *Smith*, that wandering figure, be he Cook, seafarer, or hobbit, in whom and by whom Faery and human time and space are made to touch. *Smith* thus represents the culmination of a major shift over the years in Tolkien's concept of that world and suggests that he had come to a newer view of Faery as being—at least to some extent—on a two-way street."[96] *Smith* champions an aspect of the outsider Tolkien largely ignores elsewhere: Smith must come to terms with eventually being cut off from Faery; he "comes finally to give [his passage to Faery] up of free will—albeit reluctantly—and returns to ordinary life and love."[97]

In an essay addressing the background of *Smith of Wootton Major*, Tolkien offers a fuller picture of the actions taken by Smith's Grandfather Rider. Although the expanded details of Rider's movement between Faery and the normal world hardly enter the published story, they reveal the complexities that undergird humanity's struggle with forbidden passion. Tolkien reveals that the Elves of Faery probably arranged for Rider to find them initially, and that "it would have been possible for Elves in disguise to go about the villages unrecognized—especially as 'riders' and 'travellers' and itinerant workfolk."[98] The image Tolkien creates is of a kind of closeted class of fairies circulating among the mainstream, unbeknownst to "normal" society. Rider's backstory also reinforces the importance of queer desire in the tale: "in his youthful journeys Rider was attracted by the Forest. At some time, probably about the time when he became eighteen, he ventured into it, and came 'by accident' upon one of the 'entrances' to Faery."[99] By discovering his desire to explore the margins at age of eighteen, Rider follows a pattern similar to Smith's story; however, his tale points less to a burgeoning sexuality at the onset of puberty than to a coming-out revelation the protagonist must wrestle with as adulthood arrives.

We learn through Rider more of the ways in which humanity's connection to Faery is problematic, especially in terms of intimate relationships. Rider cannot travel to Faery while he is married, for example. We are told that Rider could have made brief visits to Faery when he was still an apprentice, but once he became Master Cook, he "was too much under observation" to slip away.[100] Rider feels tortured as he gets older since his deep desires cannot be reconciled with daily life, forcing him to endure an intense "deprivation."[101] Ultimately, Tolkien's description of Rider's life in the mainstream aligns very closely with a coming-out narrative: "After 18 years he could stand it no longer without a break."[102] Later after Rider's wife has died, we find he has achieved a new level of peace, not simply because his responsibilities to domestic life had decreased and he had arranged for an apprentice to take over, but because he was finally being regularly "refreshed by his visit to Faery."[103]

Perhaps, the queerest part of Grandfather Rider's story is his bringing back a young apprentice (fifteen years old by appearance) to the village to work with him. Anxieties of pederasty grow immediately from the implications that sit just below the surface: "No doubt it was at first rather to his surprise, even dismay, when Alf insisted on appearing in Wootton as a young boy."[104] Tolkien clearly recognizes the awkwardness of having a grown man return with "this 'boy' [of whom] Rider was plainly very fond. They were on intimate and confidential terms."[105] He explains that Rider probably had to come up with a story of the boy being from nearby Walton so that his fellow townsfolk would assume the boy came from his wife's family.[106] The complexities of Rider's story perhaps played a role in keeping Tolkien's extensive notes on the story relegated to a minimal backstory for the published work, but the risk of queerness being made visible was almost certainly a factor.

By the end of the tale, we see Smith's relationship to the two worlds moving toward reconciliation, specifically in the form of mediation. After speaking to the Queen of Faery, Smith "seemed to be both in the World and in Faery, and also outside them and surveying them, so that he was at once in bereavement, and in ownership, and in peace."[107] Faery, we are reminded, is not simply marginal, but also a middle space. Here, more than in *Giles* or *Niggle*, Tolkien is able to show what he means when he claims "The road to fairyland is not the road to Heaven; nor even to Hell."[108] Smith's Faery stands for an indeterminacy which the protagonist must simply come to accept. We are reminded in Tolkien's "Suggestions for the ending of the story" that movement between the world and Otherworld happens in both directions: the Fairy King as apprentice was himself "on an 'adventure' or mission in the mortal world" and presumably gains some pleasure by circulating among humans.[109] Together, *Smith*'s narrative points reveal a much greater concern at the end of Tolkien's life of coming to peace with a life firmly planted in the mainstream world, accompanied endlessly by an insatiable longing for Faery.

The tale's ending, with Smith giving up the star, highlights a conflict that Tolkien himself was learning to negotiate in a post-*Lord-of-the-Rings* world. *Smith* was written at a time when Tolkien's long-hidden, marginalized passions had become increasingly exposed to the public. Tolkien held various secrets, and over time his passions were not only revealed, they also dominated mainstream culture. He kept his passions hidden from most people to avoid being ridiculed, such as his love of writing the *Silmarillion* myths, which he called "my absurd private hobbies."[110] However, this was also a huge source of conflict in both his private and professional life, because "of course, my only real desire is to publish 'The Silmarillion.'"[111]

Creating languages was an equally secret passion of Tolkien, and as with his *Silmarillion* writings, he learned to become transparent about it over time. His essay "A Secret Vice" celebrates the privacy of his passion but simultaneously serves as a public revelation. In the essay, he explains his internalized discomfort with finding others of the same creative persuasion. He describes the shocking moment, for example, when he overheard a fellow language-creation enthusiast "out" himself, all through a simple, unguarded reference to an imagined "accusative case." Tolkien responded to the comment with both fascination and trepidation (rooted, at some level, with a kind of self-loathing), but ultimately identifies this kindred spirit as simply a "queer creature," implicating himself in the queerness through the judgment.[112] Similarly in *Smith,* we find the protagonist struggling to learn how to be enriched by his interactions with Faery (relishing the time when he can live out his passions) while also getting used to leaving the marginalized world (recognizing that such folks are, ultimately, "queer"). Flieger argues that the central point of the story, as Tolkien continued to revise it, came to be "more about Smith's acceptance of the fact that at the end he must give up the star, and with it his entrée to Faery, so that the torch may pass."[113]

Fame and an accompanying increased public profile took its toll on Tolkien's life in a variety of ways. In 1945, he accepted the Merton Chair of English Language and Literature, which gave him responsibility for Middle English to 1500 C.E.,[114] and in 1959, five years after *The Lord of the Rings* had come out, Tolkien retired at the age of 67. In 1968, he moved with Edith to Bournemouth to help make his wife's life easier in a number of ways; she was suffering from severe arthritis, and Tolkien now had to deal with growing public recognition and assertive interruptions from admirers.[115] As Tolkien conceded in 1968, "I am now leaving Oxford and going to live on the south coast…. For my own protection I shall remove my address from all books of reference or other lists."[116]

Tolkien's love for the world and love for the Otherworld remained, as for Smith, in irreconcilable conflict. In his "Suggestions for the ending of the story," Tolkien muses on the ways in which the passions of Faery move in both directions between the human and Faery world: "The relationship must therefore be one of love: the Elven Folk… have an ultimate kinship with Men and have a permanent love for them in general."[117] A love that crosses worlds and unites men—that holds men in relationships both within the world and in the Otherworld—is thoroughly queer in its transgressiveness.

Verlyn Flieger points to the same essay to argue that for Tolkien, love serves as the primary defining feature of the Otherworld. As Tolkien explains, "Faery represents at its weakest a breaking out (at least in mind) from the iron ring of the familiar, still more from the adamantine ring of belief that is known, possessed, controlled, and so (ultimately) all that is worth being considered—a constant awareness of a world beyond these rings. More strongly it represents love: that is, a love and respect for all things, 'inanimate' and 'animate,' an unpossessive love of them as 'other.'"[118] Tolkien's words certainly support Flieger's reading of *Smith,* and one cannot help but see equally potent implications for the marginal Otherworlds in his other tales.

Flieger points to another moment in *Smith* as particularly poignant for Tolkien's message: A Birch tree serves as a guardian of Faery. Over his evolving drafts, Tolkien increased the degree of harshness in the Birch's treatment of Smith. Only in the last version, for example, does the tree say "Go away from here!" and "You do not belong here!" The final version of the scene is, as Flieger notes, "more intense, more sharply focused, and considerably more ominous," and Tolkien's outsidedness to Faery seems to "have intensified as well."[119] Flieger's chief interest in the scene, without labeling it queer herself, is in its ultimate unresolvedness: "The scene both invites and defeats attempts to interpret it.… It demands attention but it defies exegesis."[120] From an author who strove for such high levels of consistency in his Middle-earth corpus, this may seem unthinkable, but for an author contemplating his own movement within unfixed, shifting queer spaces, this seems a natural inclusion for a late-career piece of fiction. Flieger points to this as one of the text's great strengths, in fact: "to say Tolkien's vision was not perfect does not limit his work; rather, it sets it free. It is not a closed system. It is both inconsistent and incomplete."[121]

The value of the transgressive, the oppositional, and the queer thus emerges as a central theme in all three works and allows Tolkien to use the texts in powerful ways. As with *Smith*'s closing ambiguity, one leaves *Giles* celebrating the folly of signs in the same ways in which the short story opened. Giles is both a dragon-taming hero and a sword-wielding fraud simultaneously. The degree to which the dragon has been tamed remains questionable, as much as the entire etymological premise of the tale. We are reminded in all three tales that the marginalized world is not simply titillating, but also incredibly dangerous. The joy that comes to Niggle as he finds fulfillment in art is accompanied by real pain. The tension of negotiating a queer and mainstream world takes a toll on all three characters, but in Tolkien's presentation, it also seems an inevitable step in doing creative work. Smith's melancholic star seems to represent, as we see in many of Tolkien's works, the inability of characters to achieve their desires fully; yet it is because of the tension that creative work is accomplished.

David Halperin identifies several benefits that come from this oppositional nature of queerness: "Resistance to normativity is not purely negative or reactive or destructive; it is also positive and dynamic and creative. It is by resisting the discursive and institutional practices which, in their scattered and diffuse functioning, contribute to the operation of heteronormativity that queer identities can open a social space for… the development of new cultural forms."[122] Resistance to the mainstream, embodied by the simple existence of Faery, is a transgressive move that allows us to call into question the naturalness and desirability of what mainstream society labels normal.

One finds that the physical movement of Giles, Niggle, and Smith through their respective Faery Otherworlds also reinforces the tales' shared, conflicted concerns with marginalization. The details of queer cruising may shock (perhaps intentionally) mainstream society, but the term is useful for considering the implications of queer desire. In a queer lexicon, "cruising" is not simply travel, but moving through a space specifically to pursue sexual pleasure; it is driven by passion and punctuated by intimate encounters. Cruising spaces are typically located on society's margins—out of the way, not well traveled, and often hidden from the mainstream.[123] Much of Giles's, Niggle's, and Smith's travels in the Otherworld are inevitably forms of cruising; they pursue forms of pleasure tied to non-straight character traits, follow desires that grow from internal conflicts, and respond actively to the ways in which their desires place them at odds with mainstream society. None of the tales is interested simply in having characters travel back and forth to the Otherworld; rather, their *aventures* grow precisely from the pursuit of passions that originate in the marginal realms, a place where the protagonists are no longer misunderstood and that allows them to make self-discoveries. By the end of each narrative, the queer implications remain only barely, if at all, below the surface.

In employing a queer discourse, then, Tolkien is able to challenge perhaps the most damning charge against Faery (and against his own life's passions)—its authenticity. Facing the charges of counterfeit (that Faery is a delusional escape or a copy of the "real" world), or the criticism of imitation (queers merely play at mock versions of "real" gender or "real" marriage),[124] the queer, odd, and marginalized find a champion in Tolkien for Faery as supremely authentic. As he explains in "On Fairy-stories," fairy tales are not only *not* falsehoods, they are also perhaps unparalleled bearers of truth: Fantasy "certainly does not destroy or even insult Reason; and it does not either blunt the appetite for, nor obscure the perception of, scientific verity. On the contrary. The keener and the clearer is the reason, the better fantasy will it make."[125] Rather than seeing Faery as shadowed mimicry, audiences leave these three tales understanding that Faery holds up a shining model to follow. Without lecturing his readers about the value of fairies, Tolkien employs narrative to challenge the world-Otherworld divide. Only the least reflective members of mainstream society choose to avoid fairies, we learn; the wisest understand that fairies are the figures one ought to pursue with passion.

Notes

1. The *Oxford English Dictionary* identifies three primary lexical spheres for the noun "fairy": an enchantment (or illusion), the race of supernatural creatures (or individual members) who wield enchantments, and the land in which such creatures reside. The creatures vary in description, but include "tiny, delicate" individuals as well as ones "having human form." All forms provide their earliest written evidence in the fourteenth century, coming into Middle English from Anglo-Norman and Old French (in more than forty variants: *faierie*, *fairi*, *farye*, *fayeryie*, *fayerye*, for example). We find the term in *Sir Orfeo*, Chaucer's *Wife of Bath's Tale*, and Gower's *Confessio Amantis.* Latin *Fata* (the Fates, plural of *fatum*—that which is ordained) appears to have entered Old French in the twelfth century as *fae* and began circulating in English as both *fate* and *fairy*. As a reference to effeminate and/or homosexual men, *fairy* is first noted in 1895 (*American Journal of Psychology* 7: 216: "the peculiar societies of inverts… where men adopt the ladies' evening dress"), and gained familiarity throughout the twentieth century. Used adjectivally, *fairy* pointed to fairy-like qualities generally in the sixteenth century, and at the same time became increasingly linked to *elfe*: Guilpin's *Skialetheia* (c. 1598) refers to "this fayery elfe," and Shakespeare's *A Midsummer Night's Dream* (c. 1600) invokes "Euery Elfe and Fairy spright." The term shifted especially toward "small, delicate, or finely formed" creatures in the late seventeenth century, and its derogatory usage for effeminacy grew from 1925 throughout the twentieth century.
2. J. R. R. Tolkien, *Tolkien On Fairy-stories*, Expanded Edition, with Commentary and Notes, eds. Verlyn Flieger and Douglas A. Anderson (London: HarperCollins, 2008), 27.
3. Tolkien, *On Fairy-stories*, 31.
4. J. R. R. Tolkien, *The Fellowship of the Ring*, 2nd ed. (Boston: Houghton Mifflin, 1987), I, i, 32.
5. Ibid., I, viii, 146.
6. J. R. R. Tolkien, *The Return of the Ring*, 2nd ed. (Boston: Houghton Mifflin, 1987), VI, ix, 310.
7. A longing for Faery was shared by C. S. Lewis especially. Like the passion that drew Tolkien to an unattainable West, feelings of intense desire that mixed joy, longing, and pain overwhelmed Lewis at significant moments in his life. Lewis credits his Christian conversion to the

passion, which he assigned to a divine source, and he spent much of his career explicating the phenomenon as *sehnsucht* (German for "longing"), most notably in his autobiographical *Surprised by Joy*. The same Faery-like longing plays a role in most of Lewis's fiction, especially his Narnia tales. In *The Voyage of the Dawn Treader*, for example, Lucy Pevensie reads a powerful narrative in the Magician's house (a spell "for the refreshment of the spirit") whose plot she can barely remember: "She was living in the story as if it were real…. 'Oh dear, it's all fading away…. It was about a cup and a sword and a tree and a green hill'": C. S. Lewis, *The Voyage of the Dawn Treader* (New York: Macmillan, 1970), 133. Numerous scholars have simply labeled the forgotten tale as a retelling of Christ's death and resurrection, including Paul A. Karkainen, *Narnia Explored* (Tarrytown, New York: F. H. Revell, 1979), 77–78. However, such a reading fundamentally misunderstands the Inklings's complicated relationship with myth, linking it not simply to Faery, but also truth and desire. True myth, the Inklings argued, comes out of Faery and attracts its audience precisely because it points to truth on many fronts. An explicit, sole Christian reading risks shutting down Lewis's experimentation with myth in his children's books, just as he felt it would have done if he had encountered it in the myths he read as a boy. Lewis's mouse character Reepicheep also experiences a longing for Faery that echoes Legolas's. Haunted by a lifelong desire instigated by a nursery verse, the mouse knows he will have reached the World's End when he finds "sweet" water: Lewis, *Dawn Treader*, 16–17. As a result, Reepicheep's time on the *Dawn Treader* is shaped chiefly by his pursuit of this personal longing. As with Legolas, water serves merely as signifier for a larger desire, Faery (which Lewis labels the Utter East or Aslan's Country) and, ultimately, what lies there—for Lewis, God. Númenor, a related version of the West in Tolkien's Middle-earth, was also borrowed by Lewis as his version of Atlantis, a source of fairy magic in *The Magician's Nephew* and *That Hideous Strength*. In his Preface to the latter, Lewis acknowledges his debt to Tolkien for the term but does not make clear that his misspelling of "Numinor" is based on not having seen the word written and incorrectly assuming that the name was rooted etymologically in "numinous" rather than Tolkien's Quenyan phrase for "west-land": C. S. Lewis, *That Hideous Strength* (New York: Macmillan, 1971), 7. Lewis admired Tolkien's skill at articulating Faery's pull so eloquently, but as Clyde S. Kilby and others have noted, Lewis's borrowings put a strain on his friendship with Tolkien, who "insisted there were unacknowledged 'echoes'" throughout Lewis's writings: Clyde S. Kilby, *Tolkien and The Silmarillion* (Wheaton, IL: Harold Shaw Publishers, 1977), 76.

8. J. R. R. Tolkien, *The Two Towers*, 2nd ed. (Boston: Houghton Mifflin, 1987), III, v, 106.
9. Tolkien, *Return of the King*, V, ix, 149.
10. Ibid., V, i, 39.
11. Ibid., VI, v, 250.
12. J. R. R. Tolkien, *The Silmarillion* (Boston: Houghton Mifflin, 1977), 38.
13. Tolkien, *On Fairy-stories*, 32.
14. Paul H. Kocher, *Master of Middle-earth: The Fiction of J. R. R. Tolkien* (Boston: Houghton Mifflin, 1972), 17–18.
15. Richard Dyer, "Believing in Fairies: The Author and The Homosexual," in *Inside/Out: Lesbian Theories, Gay Theories*, ed. Diana Fuss (New York: Routledge, 1991), 187.
16. Alexander Doty, *Making Things Perfectly Queer: Interpreting Mass Culture* (Minneapolis: University of Minneapolis Press, 1993), xv–xvi.
17. Ibid., xv.
18. Judy Grahn, *Another Mother Tongue: Gay Words, Gay Worlds*, Updated and Expanded Edition (Boston: Beacon Press, 1984), 77.
19. Eve Sedgwick, *Epistemology of the Closet* (Berkeley: University of California Press, 1990), 71.
20. Karma Lochrie, *Covert Operations: The Medieval Uses of Secrecy* (Philadelphia: University of Pennsylvania Press, 1999), 9.
21. Jane Chance, "Tolkien and the Other: Race and Gender in Middle-Earth," in *Tolkien's Modern Middle Ages*, eds. Jane Chance and Alfred K. Siewers (New York: Palgrave Macmillan, 2009), 177.
22. Ibid.
23. J. R. R. Tolkien, *The Letters of J. R. R. Tolkien*, ed. Humphrey Carpenter (Boston: Houghton Mifflin, 2000), 39.
24. Chance, "Tolkien and the Other," 177.
25. Ibid., 172.
26. Ibid.
27. Ibid.
28. Tamsin Spargo, *Foucault and Queer Theory* (New York: Totem, 2000), 18.
29. Valerie Rohy, "On Fairy Stories," *Modern Fiction Studies* 50.4 (2004): 929.
30. Ibid., 928.
31. Ibid., 927.
32. Ibid.
33. Ibid., 930.
34. Ibid., 942.
35. Tolkien, *Return of the King*, Appendix B, 378.

36. Rohy, "On Fairy Stories," 943.
37. Humphrey Carpenter, *Tolkien: A Biography* (Boston: Houghton Mifflin, 1977), 22–23.
38. Ibid., 165–166.
39. Tolkien, *Letters*, 42.
40. Ibid., 136.
41. Ibid., 133.
42. *Farmer Giles of Ham* offers a comic, medieval explanation for the name of Worminghall, an east Oxfordshire village that Tolkien and his family visited by car as the children were growing up. In offering the tale to the public, Tolkien also worried whether "this local family game played in the country just round us is more than silly": Tolkien, *Letters*, 43. The tamed dragon at the end of the tale is ultimately held up as the source of the name of the town (and river) Thame; as the narrator explains, "Ham… became known by [Tame], which it retains to this day; for Thame with an *h* is a folly without warrant": Tolkien, *Giles*, 76.
43. C. T. Onions, ed., *The Oxford Dictionary of English Etymology* (Oxford: Clarendon Press, 1978), 914.
44. J. R. R. Tolkien, *Farmer Giles of Ham: 50th Anniversary Edition*, eds. Christina Scull and Wayne G. Hammond (Boston: Houghton Mifflin, 1999), 7.
45. Ibid.
46. Tom Shippey, *J. R. R. Tolkien: Author of the Century* (Boston: Houghton Mifflin, 2001), 291.
47. Tolkien, *Giles*, 7.
48. Genesis 9:24–25, New International Version.
49. Tolkien, *Giles*, 22.
50. Tolkien, *Letters*, 131.
51. Ibid., 43.
52. Tolkien, *Giles*, 33.
53. Ibid., 34.
54. Ibid., 15.
55. David Bevington, *Medieval Drama* (Boston: Houghton Mifflin, 1975), 290.
56. Tolkien, *Giles*, 14.
57. Ibid., 15.
58. Doty, *Perfectly Queer*, xii.
59. Tolkien, *Giles*, 13.
60. Giles' cow's name appears to be rooted in the Greek *galatea* ("milk white") for her color. This milk cow invokes at least three different female figures in Greek mythology, and all of them introduce queer edges to the tale, while reminding readers what is at stake in the division

between the mainstream world and marginal Otherworld. In Book X of Ovid's *Metamorphoses*, we are introduced to perhaps the most well known Galatea, the female statue brought to life by Aphrodite after the confirmed bachelor Pygmalion falls in love with his non-human creation and pleads to the goddess for help. The transformation allows Ovid (and subsequently Tolkien) to challenge what it means to be female and human, while at the same time, blurring the boundaries between art and life, creative and romantic passion. Later in Book XIII, Ovid also describes Galatea, a nereid daughter of the ocean who loves the river spirit Acis, a freshwater naiad. Their joining invokes a similarly unnatural, boundary-crossing relationship, complicated further by Galatea's lineage through the Titan Nereus and Acis's lineage through Faunus, a forest god. The lovers are queered additionally by their placement in a love triangle with the Cyclops Polyphemus who loves Galatea alongside Acis, whom he eventually kills. Finally, Antonius Liberalis describes a third Galatea in his own *Metamorphoses.* Galatea is the mother of Leucippus, whom she dresses as a boy to trick her husband into loving the child, and who is ultimately transformed into a boy by the goddess Leto. We cannot know, of course, whether Tolkien intended any of these explicit associations with his reference, but the name is too clearly tied to queer transgressions of boundaries not to reinforce the odd middle space into which he has cast his central character.

61. Chance, "Tolkien and the Other," 182.
62. Ibid.
63. Tolkien, *Letters*, 113.
64. Tolkien, *Fellowship of the Ring* , Foreword, 7.
65. J. R. R. Tolkien, *Tree and Leaf* (London: HarperCollins, 2001), 96.
66. Ibid., 116.
67. Richard L. Purtill, *J. R. R. Tolkien: Myth, Morality, and Religion* (San Francisco: Harper & Row, 1984), 17.
68. Tolkien, *Letters*, 195.
69. Ibid., 320.
70. Tolkien, *On Fairy-stories*, 42.
71. Tolkien, *Letters*, 257.
72. Tolkien, *Tree and Leaf*, 96–97.
73. Michael D. C. Drout, ed., *J. R. R. Tolkien Encyclopedia: Scholarship and Critical Assessment* (New York: Routledge, 2007), 495.
74. Brenda Partridge, "No Sex Please—We're Hobbits: The Construction of Female Sexuality in The Lord of the Rings," in *J. R. R. Tolkien: This Far Land*, ed. Robert Giddings (Totowa: Vision Press, 1984), 183.

75. Candice Fredrick and Sam McBride, *Women Among the Inklings: Gender, C. S. Lewis, J. R. R. Tolkien, and Charles Williams* (Westport: Greenwood Press, 2001), 7.
76. Ibid., 11.
77. Derek Brewer, "The Tutor: A Portrait," in *C. S. Lewis at the Breakfast Table and Other Reminiscences*, ed. James T. Como (New York: Macmillan, 1979), 64–65.
78. Diana Pavlac Glyer, *The Company They Keep: C. S. Lewis and J. R. R. Tolkien as Writers in Community* (Kent: Kent State University Press, 2007), 23.
79. Ibid., 72.
80. Tolkien, *Tree and Leaf*, 111.
81. Ibid., 112–113.
82. Ibid., 114.
83. Verlyn Flieger, ed., *Smith of Wootton Major: Extended Edition* (London: HarperCollins, 2005), 62.
84. Carpenter, *Biography*, 242–243.
85. Verlyn Flieger, *A Question of Time: J. R. R. Tolkien's Road to Faërie* (Kent: The Kent State University Press, 1997), 229.
86. Carpenter, *Biography*, 243.
87. Tolkien, *Letters*, 388.
88. Flieger, *Smith*, 65.
89. Paul H. Kocher, *Master of Middle-earth: The Fiction of J. R. R. Tolkien* (Boston: Houghton Mifflin, 1972), 203.
90. Carpenter, *Biography*, 242.
91. J. R. R. Tolkien, *Smith of Wootton Major* (Boston: Houghton Mifflin, 1978), 27.
92. Shippey, *Author*, 299.
93. Flieger, *Smith*, 93.
94. Tolkien, *On Fairy-stories*, 34.
95. Ruth Mellinkoff, *The Mark of Cain* (Berkeley: University of California Press, 1981), 29, 36.
96. Flieger, *Question*, 239.
97. Ibid., 229.
98. Flieger, *Smith*, 94–95.
99. Ibid., 94.
100. Ibid., 96.
101. Ibid.
102. Ibid., 98–99.
103. Ibid., 99.
104. Ibid., 96.
105. Ibid., 91.

106. Ibid., 98.
107. Tolkien, *Smith*, 41.
108. Tolkien, *On Fairy-stories*, 28.
109. Flieger, *Smith*, 81.
110. Tolkien, *Letters*, 137.
111. Ibid., 113.
112. J. R. R. Tolkien, "A Secret Vice," in *The Monsters and the Critics and Other Essays*, ed. Christopher Tolkien (Boston; Houghton Mifflin, 1984), 199. For further analysis of Tolkien's secret obsession with language, see J. R. R. Tolkien, *A Secret Vice: Tolkien on Invented Languages*, eds. Dimitra Fimi and Andrew Higgins (London: HarperCollins, 2016).
113. Flieger, *Question*, 230.
114. Drout, *Encyclopedia*, 494.
115. Ibid., 498.
116. Tolkien, *Letters*, 390.
117. Flieger, *Smith*, 93.
118. Ibid., 101.
119. Flieger, *Question*, 245.
120. Ibid.
121. Ibid., 253.
122. David Halperin, *St. Foucault: Towards a Gay Hagiography* (New York: Oxford University Press, 1997), 66–67.
123. Steve Hogan and Lee Hudson, *Completely Queer: The Gay and Lesbian Encyclopedia* (New York: Henry Holt and Co., 1999), 160.
124. Riki Wilchins, *Queer Theory, Gender Theory: An Instant Primer* (New York: Alyson Books, 2004) 134.
125. Tolkien, *On Fairy-stories*, 65.

Bibliography

Bevington, David. *Medieval Drama*. Boston: Houghton Mifflin, 1975.

Brewer, Derek. "The Tutor: A Portrait." In *C. S. Lewis at the Breakfast Table and Other Reminiscences*, edited by James T. Como, 41–67. New York: Macmillan, 1979.

Carpenter, Humphrey. *Tolkien: A Biography*. Boston: Houghton Mifflin, 1977.

Chance, Jane. "Tolkien and the Other: Race and Gender in Middle-Earth." In *Tolkien's Modern Middle Ages*, edited by Jane Chance and Alfred K. Siewers, 171–186. New York: Palgrave Macmillan, 2009.

Doty, Alexander. *Making Things Perfectly Queer: Interpreting Mass Culture*. Minneapolis: University of Minneapolis Press, 1993.

Drout, Michael D. C., ed. *J.R.R. Tolkien Encyclopedia: Scholarship and Critical Assessment*. New York: Routledge, 2007.

Dyer, Richard. "Believing in Fairies: The Author and The Homosexual." In *Inside/Out: Lesbian Theories, Gay Theories*, edited by Diana Fuss, 185–201. New York: Routledge, 1991.

Flieger, Verlyn. *A Question of Time: J. R. R. Tolkien's Road to Faërie*. Kent: The Kent State University Press, 1997.

———, ed. *Smith of Wootton Major: Extended Edition*. By J. R. R. Tolkien. London: HarperCollins, 2005.

Fredrick, Candice, and Sam McBride. *Women Among the Inklings: Gender, C. S. Lewis, J. R. R. Tolkien, and Charles Williams*. Westport: Greenwood Press, 2001.

Glyer, Diana Pavlac. *The Company They Keep: C. S. Lewis and J. R. R. Tolkien as Writers in Community*. Kent: Kent State University Press, 2007.

Grahn, Judy. *Another Mother Tongue: Gay Words, Gay Worlds*. Undated and Expanded Edition. Boston: Beacon Press, 1984.

Halperin, David. *St. Foucault: Towards a Gay Hagiography*. New York: Oxford University Press, 1997.

Hogan, Steve, and Lee Hudson. *Completely Queer: The Gay and Lesbian Encyclopedia*. New York: Henry Holt and Co., 1999.

Karkainen, Paul A. *Narnia Explored*. Tarrytown, New York: F. H. Revell, 1979.

Kilby, Clyde S. *Tolkien and The Silmarillion*. Wheaton, IL: Harold Shaw Publishers, 1977.

Kocher, Paul H. *Master of Middle-earth: The Fiction of J. R. R. Tolkien*. Boston: Houghton Mifflin, 1972.

Lewis. C. S. *Surprised by Joy*. New York: Harcourt, Brace, Jovanovich, 1966.

———. *The Magician's Nephew*. New York: Macmillan, 1970.

———. *The Voyage of the Dawn Treader*. New York: Macmillan, 1970.

———. *That Hideous Strength*. New York: Macmillan, 1971.

Lochrie, Karma. *Covert Operations: The Medieval Uses of Secrecy*. Philadelphia: University of Pennsylvania Press, 1999.

Mellinkoff, Ruth. *The Mark of Cain*. Berkeley: University of California Press, 1981.

OED Online. "fairy, n. and adj." June 2016. Oxford University Press. Accessed July 13, 2016. http://www.oed.com/view/Entry/67741?redirectedFrom=fairy.

Onions, C. T., ed. *The Oxford Dictionary of English Etymology*. Oxford: Clarendon Press, 1978.

Partridge, Brenda. "No Sex Please—We're Hobbits: The Construction of Female Sexuality in The Lord of the Rings." In *J. R. R. Tolkien: This Far Land*, edited by Robert Giddings, 179–197. Totowa: Vision Press, 1984.

Purtill, Richard L. *J. R. R. Tolkien: Myth, Morality, and Religion*. San Francisco: Harper & Row, 1984.

Rohy, Valerie. "On Fairy Stories." *Modern Fiction Studies* 50.4 (2004): 927–948.

Sedgwick, Eve Kosofsky. *Epistemology of the Closet*. Berkeley: University of California Press, 1990.

Shippey, Tom. *J. R. R. Tolkien: Author of the Century*. Boston: Houghton Mifflin, 2001.

Spargo, Tamsin. *Foucault and Queer Theory*. New York: Totem, 2000.

Tolkien, J. R. R. *The Silmarillion*. Boston: Houghton Mifflin, 1977.

———. *Smith of Wootton Major*. Boston: Houghton Mifflin, 1978.

———. "A Secret Vice." In *The Monsters and the Critics and Other Essays*, edited by Christopher Tolkien, 198–223. Boston; Houghton Mifflin, 1984.

———. *The Fellowship of the Ring*. 2nd ed. Boston: Houghton Mifflin, 1987.

———. *The Return of the King*. 2nd ed. Boston: Houghton Mifflin, 1987.

———. *The Two Towers*. 2nd ed. Boston: Houghton Mifflin, 1987.

———. *Farmer Giles of Ham: 50th Anniversary Edition*, edited by Christina Scull and Wayne G. Hammond. Boston: Houghton Mifflin, 1999.

———. *The Letters of J. R. R. Tolkien*. Edited by Humphrey Carpenter. Boston: Houghton Mifflin, 2000.

———. *Tree and Leaf*. London: HarperCollins, 2001.

———. *Tolkien On Fairy-stories: Expanded Edition, with Commentary and Notes*. Edited by Verlyn Flieger and Douglas A. Anderson. London: HarperCollins, 2008.

———. *A Secret Vice: Tolkien on Invented Languages*. Edited by Dimitra Fimi and Andrew Higgins. London: HarperCollins, 2016.

Wilchins, Riki. *Queer Theory, Gender Theory: An Instant Primer*. New York: Alyson Books, 2004.

PART IV

Language

CHAPTER 9

Language and Alterity in Tolkien and Lévinas

Deidre Dawson

In her essay "Tolkien and the Other: Race and Gender in Middle-earth," from her book *Tolkien's Modern Middle Ages*, Jane Chance reminds us that Tolkien was born in southern Africa,[1] transplanted to England at the age of three, orphaned of both father and mother by the age of twelve, ostracized and marginalized by his mother's family because of her conversion to Catholicism, isolated in academia because of his specialization in Old and Middle English, and denigrated by his peers because he wrote works of fiction instead of focusing exclusively on scholarly works. Even his foreign-sounding surname, of German derivation, set Tolkien uncomfortably apart from his peers during England's two wars with Germany. It is little wonder, Chance notes, that Tolkien chose "the little guy," "the ignominious exile," and characters of mixed race as heroes or rather anti-heroes, in his epic *The Lord of the Rings*. That the cast of characters will be diverse and unusual is established in the first page of the first chapter, "A Long-Expected Party," in a discussion of Bilbo Baggins between Sam Gamgee's father the Gaffer and the miller, Mr. Sandyman, who complains of Bilbo, "He's often away from home. And

D. Dawson (✉)
Michigan State University, East Lansing, MI, USA

C. Vaccaro and Y. Kisor (eds.), *Tolkien and Alterity*, The New Middle Ages, DOI 10.1007/978-3-319-61018-4_9

look at the outlandish folk that visit him: dwarves coming at night, and the old conjuror, Gandalf, and all. You can say what you like, Gaffer, but Bag End's a queer place, and its folk are queerer."[2] In Chance's analysis, these marginal figures appealed to Tolkien's "own sense of himself as displaced, marginal, exiled, queer, and different from other species and individuals."[3] Chance makes a compelling argument that Tolkien's concept of otherness was heavily influenced by the various forms of marginalization that he endured and the same can certainly be said of the philosopher Emmanuel Lévinas, whose direct experience with the most extreme form of hatred of the Other[4]—genocide—left an indelible mark on his thought. Born in 1905 into a Jewish community in Kovno, Lithuania, by the age of 10 Lévinas and his family were forced to flee as refugees when the Germans occupied their homeland during World War I, and eventually settled in the Ukraine. The Lévinases were able to return to Kovno after the war, but Emmanuel soon left to pursue studies in Strasbourg and Freiberg, because of his interest in the German phenomenologist philosophers Husserl and Heidegger. Lévinas became a French citizen in 1930 and distanced himself from Heidegger when the latter embraced National Socialism in 1932; Lévinas understood that certain elements of Heidegger's philosophy provided an ontological foundation for the Nazi project to promote a monolithic, homogenous Aryan nation which would have no tolerance for otherness. Years later, in *Totality and Infinity*, he analyzed Heidegger's philosophy thus: "Heideggerian ontology, which subordinates the relationship with the Other to the relation with Being in general, remains under obedience to the anonymous, and leads inevitably to another power, to imperialist domination, to tyranny."[5] During World War II, owing to his extraordinary linguistic skills, Lévinas was drafted as a German and Russian interpreter for the French Army. He was taken prisoner by the Germans in 1940 but spared from being sent to a concentration camp because he was an officer. Instead, he was sent to do heavy labor in a work camp, where he and the other Jewish officers were segregated from the rest of the prisoners. During this time, his wife and daughter were hidden by French friends, but all the rest of his immediate family—his mother-in-law, parents, and siblings—and many of his extended family as well, were murdered by the Nazis. After the war, Lévinas remained in France, where he resided for the rest of his life, holding many prestigious university positions.

The suffering and deep personal losses that Lévinas endured at the hands of a regime driven by a fascist and racist ideology led him to devote his philosophical writings to the argument that one's relationship to the Other, and not one's relationship to the Self, is the foundation on which all philosophy must be based. Lévinas is often credited with being the originator of the concept of alterity, and his major works in this area include *Time and the Other* [*Le temps et l'autre*,1947], *Totality and Infinity* [*Totalité et Infini*, 1961], *Humanism of the Other* [*Humanisme de l'autre homme*, 1972], *Otherwise than Being* [*Autrement qu'être*, 1974], *Entre Nous: On thinking-of the-Other* [*Entre nous: Essais sur le penser-à- l'autre*, 1991], and *Alterity and Transcendance* [*Altérité et Transcendance*, 1995]. Lévinas's thinking departs from the ideas of other continental philosophers in that it does not begin by focusing on the nature of Being or the Self, but rather takes as its point of departure recognition of and respect for the Other: "Instead of the thinking 'I' epitomized in 'I think, therefore I am' — the phrase with which René Descartes launched much of modern philosophy — Dr. Lévinas began with an ethical 'I.' For him, even the self is possible only with its recognition of 'the Other,' a recognition that carries responsibility toward what is irreducibly different."[6] *The Stanford Encyclopedia of Philosophy* states that Lévinas's philosophy is "neither traditional logic nor metaphysics… It is an interpretive, phenomenological description of the rise and repetition of the face-to-face encounter, or the intersubjective relation at its precognitive core; viz., being called by another and responding to the other."[7] In *Humanism of the Other*, Lévinas explains that our first contact with this otherness is through language: "…the phenomenon that is the apparition of the Other is also face…the face speaks. The manifestation of the face is the first discourse. Speaking is first and foremost this way of coming from behind one's appearance, behind one's form; an opening in the opening."[8] Lévinas's theory of the essential link between alterity and language is also developed in *Totality and Infinity*: "…the *relation* between the same and the other—is language. For language accomplishes a relation such that the terms are not limitrophe within this relation, such that the other, despite the relationship with the same, remains transcendent to the same. The relation between the same and the other, metaphysics, is primarily enacted as conversation…"[9] It is thus through language that the Other expresses himself as *absolutely other*: "Absolute difference… is established only by language. Language establishes a relationship between terms that breaks up the unity of a genus. The terms, the interlocutors, absolve themselves from the relation, or remain absolute within the relationship."[10]

Tolkien also viewed language as crucial to defining and maintaining difference. Writing as a philologist rather than a philosopher, he explains, "For though cultural and other traditions may accompany a difference of language, they are chiefly maintained and preserved by language. Language is the prime differentiator of peoples—not of 'races,' whatever that much-misused word may mean in the long-blended history of western Europe."[11] In his famous letter to the German publisher Rütten and Loenig Verlag, drafted on July 25, 1938 in response to inquiries about whether he had Aryan origins, Tolkien used his expertise on Indo-European languages to expose the pernicious motives behind the publisher's question: "I regret that I am not clear as to what you intend by *arisch*. I am not of *Aryan* extraction: that is Indo-iranian; as far as I am aware none of my ancestors spoke Hindustani, Persian, Gypsy, or any related dialects. But if I am to understand that you are inquiring whether I am of *Jewish* origin, I can only reply that I regret that I have *no* ancestors of that gifted people."[12] In a similar manner to Lévinas's concept of language as the primary manifestation of absolute otherness between individuals, Tolkien sees languages as the distinguishing factor among peoples; it is language which makes each people unique, and which defines their otherness in relation to other peoples. The diversity of languages conceived by Tolkien for the beings who populate his legendarium is impressive. As Jonathan Edwards points out in his essay "The Anthropology of Arda: Creation, Theology, and the Race of Men," in another volume edited by Jane Chance, *Tolkien the Medievalist*, the linguistic landscape of Middle-earth is anything but anthropocentric: "J. R. R. Tolkien's works of fiction…display a great deal of sensitivity to these [linguistic] issues, revealing a remarkable capacity for decentering the anthropological perspective—the perspective of race Tolkien describes as 'Men'—in a culturally complex imagined world…that includes other kinds of people. Men are not the only race in Tolkien's imaginary world, and they are not the most important."[13] Were he alive today, Tolkien would no doubt be distressed by the phenomenon of "linguicide,"[14] the extinction, sometimes though violent means (environmental destruction, cultural or political coercion) of many of the world's languages,[15] for he delighted in the otherness of languages; the "strange" Welsh writing on the side of a truck, the "intoxicating" effect of Finnish grammar.[16] In a letter written to his son Christopher Tolkien dated December 9, 1943, Tolkien expressed disapproval of the idea that English was becoming what we call today a "global language": "Col. Knox says 1/8 of the world's population speaks 'English', and that is the biggest language group. If true, damn shame—say I. May the curse of Babel strike all their tongues till they can only say 'baa baa'. ...I think I shall have to refuse to speak anything but Old Mercian."[17] In both his scholarly work and the way he defined himself, Tolkien embraced alterity and linguistic and cultural diversity. In the opening remarks of his essay "English and Welsh," which he gave at Oxford on October 21, 1955 as the first of the O'Donnell Trust lectures, Tolkien described himself first from the point of view of another culture, as "a Saxon in Welsh terms," and then from the perspective of his own culture: "one of the English of Mercia." Even as an Englishman, Tolkien is "other": he is not like all English, he is "of Mercia."[18] Throughout his writings, Tolkien emphasized the importance of language to the identity of both peoples and individuals: "...language—and more so as expression than as communication—is a natural product of our humanity. But it is also therefore a product of our individuality."[19]

Like Tolkien, Lévinas had knowledge of many languages, both modern and ancient, including Latin, Greek, and Hebrew, so it is not surprising to find in the works of both men a reflection on the primacy of language in our interactions with the Other. One aspect of Lévinas's philosophy that has the greatest implications for Tolkien's work is the idea that although we are incapable of fully comprehending the Other—we would literally have to be in that Other's body to do so—we have a responsibility for the Other which compels us to respond to him or her with respect. Philosopher Simon Critchley views this notion of acceptance and responsibility for the incomprehensible Other as Lévinas's most important contribution to philosophy: "... the relation to the other cannot be reduced to comprehension, and... this relationship is ethical...That is to say, there is something about the other person, a dimension of separateness, interiority, secrecy or what Lévinas calls 'alterity' that escapes my comprehension" and yet "demands acknowledgement."[20] Not just acknowledgment, but in Lévinas's own words, empathy and love: "Our relationship with him [the Other] consists certainly in wanting to comprehend him, but this relationships is beyond comprehension. Not just because the knowledge of the Other demands, outside of curiosity, empathy or love, which are ways of being distinct from impassive contemplation. But because, in our relationship with the Other, the way he affects us does not originate in a concept. He is a being, and counts as such."[21]

We establish an ethical rapport with the Other through language. The act of speaking, which Lévinas calls *le dire* (saying) transcends both the person who is speaking, *le signifiant* (the signifier) and the content of speech, *le signifié* (the signified, or the said), because any act of saying requires a recognition of and an engagement with the Other. Summarizing Lévinas's philosophy of language, linguist August Ponzo writes, "[It is] to speak in order to say to the Other that one is listening to him; to express only that: I am speaking to you, I am listening to you, I want to exist for you: this is the presupposition of all communication."[22] The connection that Lévinas recognized—and as I argue, Tolkien's work illustrates—between saying or speaking and our ethical relationship with the Other has been referred to as *semioethics* by Professor Ponzo and Professor Susan Petrilli from the Department of Linguistic Practices and Text Analysis at Bari University, Italy. Ponzo describes semioethics as "the attitude of semiotics conscious of its responsibility toward life on this planet…and consequently of the 'intercorporal' connection between all living beings…"[23] In Lévinas's own words, from his work *Otherwise than Being*, "…saying states and thematizes the said, but signifies it to the other, a neighbor, with a signification that has to be distinguished from that borne by words in the said. This signification to the other occurs in proximity. Proximity is quite distinct from every other relationship, and has to be conceived as *a responsibility for the other* [my italics]; it might be called humanity, or subjectivity, or self. Beings and entities weigh heavily by virtue of the saying that gives them light. Nothing is more grave … than responsibility for the other, and saying…has a gravity more grave than its being or not being."[24]

Jane Chance argues that Tolkien's experience of being labeled as "other" led him to explore through his creative work, "how the construction of alterity—when stereotyped as pejorative—can be halted."[25] Therefore, if we are to speak of alterity in Tolkien's work, I would argue that it is not the pejorative kind, which as Chance stresses, Tolkien's work rejects—but rather the Lévinasian concept of alterity, which carries an imperative to embrace and be responsible for the Other, an imperative, as Lévinas explains in *Alterity and Transcendance*, "…to go toward the other where he is truly other in the radical contradiction of their alterity, that place from which, for an insufficiently mature soul, hatred flows naturally…"[26] In the chapter "The Mirror of Galadriel" from *The Fellowship of the Ring*, we find a striking contrast between hatred and fear of the Other versus love and acceptance of the Other. The verbal exchange between Gimli, Celeborn, and Galadriel after the Company has been led blindfolded into the Elven realm of Lothlòrien illustrates the "gravity" and significance of *saying* in Lévinasian terms. It is important to recall that the reason the Company is blindfolded is because of a prejudicial rule which prohibits Dwarves from entering Lothlòrien. Frodo points out that Elrond himself chose Gimli the dwarf as a member of the Fellowship which would accompany him on his task and is able to obtain a compromise: Gimli may enter only if he is blindfolded. In his wisdom, Aragorn requires the other members of the Company to also be blindfolded, to reduce somewhat the sting of this negative "othering" of Gimli. The blindfolds are not removed until the Company has been led to Galadriel and Celeborn, who question them about their journey, and inquire about Gandalf. Aragorn assumes the task of recounting the Fellowship's treacherous trek through the mines of Moria and Gandalf's battle with the Balrog, with some help from Legolas. Gimli, with "dread…in his eyes," speaks last, "in a low voice": "Indeed I saw upon the bridge that which haunts our darkest dreams, I saw Durin's Bane."[27] In this act of *saying*, Gimli, who knows he is not welcome, has shown his face, has revealed his fear, and has exposed himself as the Other to a powerful leader of Elves, traditional enemies of his kind.

But Celeborn does not answer the call of his neighbor who is Other, he does not respond to the fact that the *absolutely other* Gimli, through his courageous act of speaking, or *saying*, is asking for acknowledgment and acceptance. Celeborn instead reacts negatively both to the *signifier* Gimli and to the *signified*, the message Gimli conveys. He blames the arousal of the Balrog on the Dwarves' greed and Gandalf's folly and regrets letting the Company enter his domain: "But had I known that the Dwarves had stirred up this evil in Moria again, I would have forbidden you to pass the northern borders, you and all that went with you." Galadriel responds "gravely" to Celeborn, urging him to acknowledge the tragic situation of Gimli: "If our folk had been exiled long and far from Lothlórien, who of the Galadhrim, even Celeborn the Wise, would pass nigh and would not wish to look upon their ancient home, though it had been an abode of dragons?"[28] Galadriel then addresses Gimli directly. The following passage is, in my view, one of the most important in *The Lord of the Rings* for how it illustrates the power of language to express acceptance and love of the Other:

> Dark is the water of Kheled-zâram, and cold are the springs of Kibilnâla, and fair were the many-pillared halls of Khazad-dûm in Elder Days before the fall of mighty kings beneath the stone.' She looked upon Gimli, who sat glowering and sad, and she smiled. And the Dwarf, hearing the names given to him in his own ancient tongue, looked up and met her eyes; and it seemed to him that he looked suddenly into the heart of an enemy and saw there love and understanding. Wonder came into his face, and then he smiled in answer. He rose clumsily and bowed in dwarf-fashion, saying, 'Yet more fair is the living land of Lórien, and the Lady Galadriel is above all the jewels that lie beneath the earth.[29]

The content—the *signified*—of Galadriel's words is important, but above all it is the act of *saying*, of facing Gimli and uttering the names of the ancient Dwarf landmarks, that erases generations of enmity between Elves and Dwarves. In a Lévinasian analysis, by engaging Gimli as Other, Galadriel enters into an ethical bond with him. Gimli in turn answers her call and accepts his "enemy" in spite of her Otherness, through his *saying* of her name—Galadriel—and the name of the Elvish homeland Lórien. Through this face-to-face exchange, each interlocutor acknowledges and assumes responsibility for the Other, *as Other*, and Tolkien reinforces the importance of this moment by having Gimli and Galadriel each speak in the other's language. Later, when the Company is about to leave Lórien and Gimli is asked what gift he would like from Galadriel, he initially responds, "None, Lady…It is enough for me to have seen the Lady of the Galadhrim, and to have *heard her gentle words* [my italics]."[30]

Lévinas makes clear that our responsibility for the Other does not end in the act of saying, through which we recognize the humanity of the Other—the act of saying is just the beginning of the ethical relationship with him or her. In *Otherwise than Being* he writes: "To maintain that the relationship with the neighbour, incontestably set up in saying, is a responsibility for the neighbour, [and] that saying is to respond to another, is to find no longer any limit or measure for this responsibility…." In pure saying, "there is an abandon of the sovereign and active subjectivity…"[31] The ethical relationship into which Galadriel enters with Gimli through answering his call is in effect without limits, for Gimli eventually finds the courage to express to Galadriel his desire for a strand of her golden hair, which he pledges to treasure "in memory of our first meeting."[32] Gimli's acceptance of Galadriel's gift is a tangible manifestation of his acceptance of *his* responsibility toward *her*;

he not only will cherish her memory, he will defend Galadriel against accusations of sorcery and evil-doing, even risking his life when he later angrily reprimands Éomer for characterizing her as a "net-weaver or sorcerer."[33] Éomer's negative "othering" of Galadriel is based on hearsay and prejudice, in contrast to the face-to-face encounter between Galadriel and Gimli.

Even more significantly, Galadriel's words to Gimli also bring about a dramatic change in the relationship between Legolas and Gimli, who have previously only tolerated each other with suspicion and contempt because of the resentment that Elves and Dwarves harbor toward each other. After hearing Galadriel's "gentle words" to Gimli, Legolas no longer keeps his distance from the Dwarf, but on the contrary desires his presence: "Often he took Gimli with him when he went abroad in the land, and the others wondered at this change."[34] Perhaps the experience of sharing the prejudicial treatment that is imposed on Gimli—the blindfold—makes clear to Legolas the ethical imperative of taking responsibility for the Other, precisely because he is Other: "all relation toward the other is a relation to a being to whom I have obligations," wrote Lévinas.[35] Throughout the rest of the quest, Gimli and Legolas accept responsibility for each other, to the point of becoming nearly inseparable. In Appendix A, it is stated that Gimli "was named Elf-friend because of the great love that grew between him and Legolas, son of Thranduil, and his reverence for the Lady Galadriel."[36] This great love and friendship is remarkable not just because historically Elves and Dwarves have a past fraught with conflict, but because everything about these two peoples seems to be polar opposites: their habitats and habits, likes and dislikes, skills and natural talents, physical characteristics, and languages make them irreducibly other. They illustrate Lévinas' s concept of alterity which, as philosopher Brian Treanor explains, "seeks to preserve the otherness of the other and to respect the difference that distinguishes that other from the self. …in order to encounter the other as other, we must encounter the other on her terms rather than ours."[37] We see this in Legolas's pledge to visit the Glittering Caves with Gimli, in spite of Elves' abhorrence for underground caverns, and in Gimli's reciprocal promise to visit the Forest of Fangorn with Legolas; each accepts the other on his own terms.

In *The Lord of the Rings*, there are other examples of the Lévinasian ethics of alterity—the establishment, through language, of an ethical relationship between beings who are irreducibly other, such as the encounter between Treebeard and Merry and Pippin. Treebeard illustrates Lévinas's statement "Speaking is first and foremost this way of coming from behind one's appearance, behind one's form; an opening in the opening," when he first speaks to the Hobbits before picking them up "to have a look at [their] faces." Treebeard acknowledges the Hobbits' presence in his forest by repeating what he has heard them say: "Almost felt like you liked the Forest! That's good! That's uncommonly kind of you," and he reveals that it was the sound of the Hobbits' speech, their voices, which drew him toward them: " …if I had seen you before I heard your voices—I liked them: nice little voices; they reminded me of something I cannot remember—if I had seen you before I heard your voices, I should have just trodden on you, taking you for little Orcs, and found out my mistake later."[38] As Jane Chance notes in her essay, Treebeard's isolationism and self-absorption have led him to ignore the needs of others, even the trees which the Ents are supposed to protect, and which are being devastated by Saruman: "So preoccupied with his own point of view, Treebeard has to learn how to understand others—including younger members of his own species and even the insignificant Hobbits—in order to rectify the situation."[39] Merry and Pippin's sharing of their names and then their story with Treebeard is a sign of openness and trust toward the Other on their part; Treebeard is taken aback by this, objecting "I am honored by your confidence, but you should not be too free all at once."[40] Still, according to Chance, "… despite Treebeard's insensitivity, he is no tyrant"; his "self-centeredness has not resulted in totalitarian domination over or manipulation of others."[41] In fact, it is he who, in Lévinasian terms, first showed his face by speaking to the Hobbits, holding them up close and declaring, "Turn round and let me have a look at your faces." In peering into Merry and Pippin's faces, Treebeard is revealing his face too, and "they found that they were looking at a most extraordinary face."[42] Lévinas claimed "… the Other not only comes to us from a context but signifies by itself, without … mediation … the phenomenon that is the apparition of the Other is also face…the face speaks. The manifestation of the face is the first discourse," and this is certainly true of this first encounter between the Hobbits and Treebeard. Before they reveal their names, before they explain how they came to be there, before Treebeard tells them anything about who or what he is, they manifest their faces to each other through speech. And again, as in the case with Gimli and Galadriel, the responsibility for the Other does not end here, in this encounter, but is only a beginning…Treebeard takes responsibility for Merry and Pippin, providing them with nourishment, protection, and rest, and they in turn share all of their knowledge of events brewing in Middle-earth with him.

For both Tolkien and Lévinas, then, our relationship with the Other is necessarily an ethical relationship. In his essay "Philosophy and the Idea of Infinity," Lévinas writes: "Here is established a relationship not with a very great resistance but with the absolutely other, with the resistance that has no resistance, with ethical resistance…We call the face the epiphany of what can thus present itself directly and therefore also exteriorly to an I…the epiphany of a face is wholly language." The resistance referred to here is the resistance of "the gaze which forbids my conquest" to "the imperialism of the same and the I."[43] Drawing in particular upon this essay, Joseph Tadie has illustrated that the character of Gandalf as he appears in *The Hobbit* embodies Lévinas's "imperative of an-Other" expressed through the face-to-face encounter and through language. In his first meeting with this strange Other, the intensity of the gaze of the peculiar, bearded old man who has wandered up to his doorstep unsettles Bilbo Baggins and elicits a response from him: "Gandalf's face commanded Bilbo."[44] Thus compelled to acknowledge Gandalf's presence, Bilbo wishes him a good morning but is hardly prepared for the "marvelously complicated linguistic interchange" that ensues when Gandalf responds with an "ethically evocative interrogation" through which he questions Bilbo as to what he really *means* by wishing him a good morning.[45] As Tadie demonstrates in his close reading of this exchange, Bilbo falls back on conventional hobbit customs such as offering to share a pipe with the stranger in an attempt to avoid having to engage with him about the real purpose of his visit, specifically, to wrest Bilbo from his comfortable, Self-centered existence which has hitherto been resistant to the call of Others: "The natural hobbit tendencies toward hospitality, contentment, and generosity are not the stuff of which either ethical discourse or virtue is made…" Ethical discourse will make steep demands that run contrary to the "natural" or "inherited hobbit approach to relations with others…"[46] It will take some time before Bilbo is able to overcome his "concupiscent self-indulgence,"[47] and take full responsibility for others through revealing himself honestly to them. Tadie suggests that it is not until many years later at the Council of Elrond that Bilbo allows an "ethical opening" by verbally admitting his theft of the Ring from Gollum. In Tadie's analysis, Bilbo's growth as a character is emblematic of both Tolkien's and Lévinas's belief that there can exist no fully realized Self without the Other: "…those who wish to secure release from bondage to self-aggrandizing power, self-important wisdom, or constraining custom must recognize, accept, and embrace their own weakness and limitation by implicating themselves in a linguistically-grounded adventure with odd-seeming others."[48]

But this relationship with the Other, while it carries obligations, should not be experienced as an onerous duty to be performed. On the contrary, for Lévinas, we are naturally drawn to that which is other; we desire the Other. This desire is not a craving to satisfy a need, or a yearning to selfishly seek in the Other fulfillment of something that is lacking in oneself. In *Totality and Infinity* Lévinas writes:

> The term of this movement, the elsewhere or the other, is called *other* in an eminent sense. No journey, no change of climate or of scenery could satisfy the desire bent toward it. The other metaphysically desired is not 'other' like the bread I eat, the land in which I dwell, the landscape I contemplate, like, sometimes, myself for myself, this 'I,' that 'other.' I can 'feed' on these realities and to a very great extent satisfy myself, as though I had simply been lacking them. Their *alterity* is thereby reabsorbed into my own identity as a thinker or possessor. The metaphysical desire tends toward *something else entirely*, toward the *absolutely other*.[49]

We have seen above that Lévinas's concept of proximity, of seeing the Other as our neighbor, encourages us to draw closer to the Other, even as we acknowledge his absolute otherness. Throughout the *The Lord of the Rings*, as Chance illustrates in "Tolkien and the Other," qualities of "acceptance and understanding," and the virtues of "forgiveness of and love for those who are different" are taught by mentor figures, such as Gandalf, Aragorn, and Galadriel, and learned by the hobbits and other characters as they encounter loss, hardships, stigmatization, and discrimination throughout their journey.[50] This ethos of "love for those who are different" is prevalent even in the complex and diverse family trees of Arwen and Aragorn, which as Chance notes contain intermarriages between different peoples at nearly every generation, going back all the way to the marriage of Melian, one of the quasi-divine Maia, with Thingol, one of the Eldar. "But Lúthien's ancestry, before Aragorn's, is even more symbolically important in the uniting of different species: Lúthien's mother was Melian the Maia (servant to the Valar) and her father, Thingol (or Elwë), the Elf brother of Olwë."[51] The great love between the immortal Lúthien and the mortal man Beren was the story most dear to Tolkien's heart, as it reflected his own obstacle-ridden courtship of his wife Edith. "After Edith's death more than fifty years later he wrote to his son Christopher, explaining why he wished to include the name 'Lúthien' on her tombstone: 'She was (and knew she was) my Lúthien.'"[52] Religious and class differences, forced separation, his guardian's ban of all communication with Edith and even her engagement to another man only strengthened the young Tolkien's resolve to marry his first and only love, and their union lasted fifty-five years. Beren and Lúthien face far more formidable challenges, with Beren being sent to a near-certain death by Thingol, who opposes what he considers to be a serious misalliance between a mere mortal and his Elf/Maia daughter. Lúthien escapes from a tower where she has been imprisoned by her father and aids her lover in his quest through courage and "by her arts and love."[53] When Beren is finally slain, Lúthien's grief is so great that Mandos, keeper of the Houses of the Dead, agrees to bring Beren back to life, if Lúthien will give up her immortality to live a mortal life with him.

Arwen makes the same choice, against the stern opposition of her father Elrond, so that she can wed Aragorn. In these unions between mortals and immortals—beings who are radically other—the immortal partner gives up the defining characteristic of her identity, the essence of her Self, her immortality, in order to join her fate with an Other who is doomed to die. One might almost be tempted to read these stories as cautionary tales against marrying outside of one's clan, culture or family if it were not for the fact that these lovers as Others, through their courage to transgress cultural boundaries and the legacy that their examples leave on their communities, reach a level of transcendence that goes beyond their individual desire. It is as if the greater the suffering, the longer the waiting, and the more numerous the obstacles, the greater the desire to sacrifice the Self entirely to the Other, even though total union with the Other is remote, if not impossible. Lévinas explains in *Totality and Infinity*, "It is a generosity nourished by the Desired, and thus a relationship that is not the disappearance of distance, not a bringing together, or—to circumscribe more closely the essence of generosity and of goodness—a relationship whose positivity comes from remoteness, from separation, for it nourishes itself, one might say, with its hunger."[54] Beren and Lúthien's desire endows them with immense generosity and bravery, which ultimately enables them to defy Sauron and recover from Morgoth the stolen Silmaril, the loss of which had caused great grief in Valinor. Arwen and Aragorn's situation perhaps best illustrates "a relationship that is not the disappearance of distance, not a bringing together… a relationship whose positivity comes from remoteness, from separation," for not only does Arwen endure a long separation from Aragorn before their eventual reunion in Gondor at the end of the War of the Ring, she must bid a bitter, eternal farewell to her people when she marries Aragorn, and she fades away with grief when her mortal husband eventually dies. Their marriage is brief (by Elf standards) but happy and serves as an exemplar of peace and cultural tolerance among the peoples of Middle-earth after the fall of Sauron. As Hope Rogers points out in her article "No Triumph without Loss: Problems of Intercultural Marriage in Tolkien's Works," the numerous intercultural alliances in Tolkien's legendarium involve both joy and sacrifice for the individuals involved, yet overall, the embracing of difference leads to the greater good: "Intercultural marriage's strength as a form of interaction thus results not only from the peaceful and fruitful nature of the relationships themselves, but also because it is tied to the acceptance of all difference."[55]

In his book *Aspects of Alterity: Lévinas, Marcel and the Contemporary Debate*, Brian Treanor states: "When otherness is thought in absolute, all-or-nothing terms, it encourages us to think of preserving the otherness of the other as a primary goal. On this reading, the proper response to otherness is not to question the other—for if otherness is absolute, understanding the other is out of the question—but to maintain distance and to respect the difference of the other."[56] Thus, while Lévinas's concept of proximity, of seeing the Other as our neighbor, also encourages us to draw closer to and even desire the Other, we must be careful that our desire to understand and know the Other does not transgress on his autonomy; we must know when to let the Other be: "To understand a person, is first and foremost to speak to him. To acknowledge the existence of the Other through letting him be, is to have already accepted this existence, to have taken it into account."[57] Both Lévinas's and Tolkien's ethics demand that we respect Others for their otherness and that we treat them justly, even if our encounter with them does not result in a close relationship such as the friendship between Legolas and Gimli or the love between Beren and Lúthien. Perhaps the most striking example of respect for radical alterity is manifested in Aragorn's response to the Woses, the Wild Men of the Woods, a people who have lived in their wooded mountains in quasi-seclusion for many years and are considered primitive by the other peoples of Middle-earth. In "Tolkien's Wild Men: From Medieval to Modern," from Jane Chance's book *Tolkien the Medievalist*, Verlyn Flieger describes the character of the Wild Man in Western literature as the quintessential Other: "The Wild Man is the archetypal outsider, the prowler on the borderlands between the wild and tame, exiled either by his fellow men or by his own misanthropy."[58] As he does with the other peoples of his legendarium, Tolkien emphasizes the Woses' unique otherness not only with physical descriptions, but also through language. Part I of Appendix F of *The Lord of The Rings*, "The Language and Peoples of the Third Age," offers this short but highly significant description of the language used by the Woses: "Wholly *alien* [my italics] was the speech of the Wild Men of Drúadan Forest."[59] Tolkien's efforts to underscore the alien nature of the Woses through their language have been viewed by some critics as awkward; Flieger finds that when the leader of the Wild Men, Ghân-buri-ghân, speaks, "his dialogue sounds like that of a Hollywood Tarzan."[60] Still, Tolkien gives a voice and assigns an important role to these "noble savages,"... "whose primitiveness" Dmitra Fimi observes, "is respected rather than despised."[61] When they make their first appearance in the narrative, however, in "The Ride of the Rohirrim," Chapter V of *The Two Towers*, the Woses are not treated respectfully by the Riders, who view them as little better than animals, "wild and wary as the beasts."[62] Ghân-buri-ghân meets with King Théoden and Éomer and warns them that Sauron's forces have set fire to the stronghold of Mundburg and are advancing on Gondor. Éomer fails to recognize that Ghân-buri-ghân's *saying* is a genuine offer of help, a reaching out to the Other. Éomer refuses to engage with Ghân-buri-ghân. He interrupts and questions the leader of the Woses with suspicion, prompting Ghân-buri-ghân to declare defensively "Wild men are wild, free, but not children," and even forcing him to demand to be heard: "Let Ghân-buri-ghân finish!"[63] King Théoden finally accepts Ghân-buri-ghân's offer to guide the Rohirrim through the Wild Men's territory so that they can avoid encountering Orc armies on their way to the final confrontation with Sauron's forces. The King of Rohan offers the Woses a "rich reward" for their aid, to which Ghân-buri-ghân replies. "...if you live after the Darkness, then leave Wild Men alone in the woods and do not hunt them like beasts anymore."[64] King Théoden perishes in the Battle of the Pelennor Fields, but his agreement with Ghân-buri-ghân is not forgotten. After the defeat of Sauron, as Aragorn and his queen

Arwen, accompanied by Galadriel, Elrond, the Company, and representatives of many of the peoples of Middle-earth ride out of Gondor, they hear drums coming from the woods under the mountain Amon Dîn, and Aragorn declares, "Behold, the King Elessar is come! The forest of Drúadan he gives to Ghân-buri-ghân and to his folk, to be their own forever, and hereafter let no man enter it without their leave!"[65] Aragorn thus expresses his gratitude to the Woses for helping assure his victory, but he understands that these are not folks who wish to be assimilated in any way into his or anyone else's realm. What the Woses most value is their freedom and autonomy. Through his declaration and his remaining at a distance, Aragorn acknowledges their right to be Other and to remain undisturbed in their Mountains, and this is a just reward for their help.

It has been said that Emmanuel Lévinas started a "philosophical revolution" with the publication of *Totality and Infinity*, "turning twenty-five hundred years of philosophy on its head" with his "astounding claim that philosophy is not about ontology—the nature of Being, but about ethics in our relationship with the Other."[66] Ethics, not ontology, is first philosophy, according to Lévinas. How does this relate to Tolkien? The presence of many of Lévinas's ethical principles in *The Lord of the Rings* indicates that Tolkien's fiction was on the cutting edge of philosophical inquiry. Well before the publication of Lévinas's major works, Tolkien had begun exploring similar themes related to language as the primal and primordial expression of our relationship with the Other, and with the world in general. Lévinas's philosophy and Tolkien's creative work both upheld the rights of the individual Other in the face of dogmatism and totalitarianism. Just as the greatest gift of the Elves, according to Treebeard, was teaching the trees and other beings to speak, so the greatest gift an individual can give her neighbor, the Other, is through *saying*, the act of acknowledging the Other through speech. Speech which is not meant to dominate or assimilate, but which signifies acceptance of a different voice from our own.

Notes

1. Tolkien was born on January 3, 1892 in Bloemfontein, capital of the Orange Free State, which was an independent Boer republic until 1900.
2. J.R.R. Tolkien, *The Fellowship of the Ring*, 2nd ed. (Boston: Houghton Mifflin, 1987), I, i, 32.

3. Jane Chance, "Tolkien and the Other: Race and Gender in Middle-earth," in *Tolkien's Modern Middle Ages*, eds. Jane Chance and Alfred K. Siewers (New York: Palgrave Macmillan, 2005), 177.
4. The words *autrui* and *l'autre* and sometimes *l'autre homme* are used in Lévinas's original French texts to designate the Other. Some of the English translations of Lévinas used in this essay capitalize "Other," and some use only lower case letters, as in "the other." In my own prose, I capitalize Other when it is a noun and use lower case most of the time when it is an adjective or verb. A word about gender is also in order: French is a gendered language, and both *autrui* and *l'autre* are masculine nouns requiring masculine pronouns (*il, le, lui, celui,* etc.). In Lévinas's text, as in French in general, *autrui* and *l'autre* are universal terms designating people of both sexes. Lévinas's philosophy concerns the ethical treatment of human beings in general, without gender distinctions, and so in my own prose I chose to primarily use the masculine pronoun, both to avoid introducing the question of gender where there is none, and for the sake of consistency, since all of the English translations of Lévinas cited here also use the masculine pronoun.
5. Lévinas, *Totality and Infinity*, trans. Alphonso Lingis (Pittsburgh: Dusquesne University Press, 1969), 46–47.
6. Peter Steinfels, "Emmanuel Lévinas, 90, French Ethical Philosopher," *New York Times*, December 27, 1995, accessed April 29, 2013, http://www.nytimes.com/1995/12/27/world/emmanuel-Lévinas-90-french-ethical-philosopher.
7. *Stanford Encyclopedia of Philosophy*, "Emmanuel Lévinas," first published July 23, 2006, revised Aug 3, 2011, accessed April 29, 2013, http://plato.stanford.edu/entries/Lévinas/.
8. Emmanuel Lévinas, *Humanism of the Other*, trans. Nidra Poller (Urbana and Chicago: University of Illinois Press, 2003), 31.
9. Lévinas, *Humanism*, 39.
10. Lévinas, *Humanism*, 195.
11. Tolkien, "English and Welsh," *The Monsters and the Critics* (London: Harper Collins, 2006), 166.
12. J.R.R. Tolkien, *The Letters of J. R. R. Tolkien*, ed. Humphrey Carpenter (Boston: Houghton Mifflin, 2000), 37, italics original.
13. Jonathan Edwards, "The Anthropology of Arda: Creation, Theology, and the Race of Men," in *Tolkien the Medievalist*, ed. Jane Chance (New York: Routledge, 2003), 197.
14. For a thorough discussion of the many causes of language death, see Daniel Nettle and Suzanne Romaine, *Vanishing Voices: The Extinction of the World's Languages* (New York: Oxford University Press, 2002), 4–6, and Claude Hagège, *On the Death and Life of Languages*, trans. Jody Gladding (New Haven and London: Yale University Press, 2009), 119–120.

15. The *Enduring Voices* project estimates that languages are dying out at the rate of roughly fourteen a month. See "Disappearing Languages, Enduring Voices- Documenting the World's Endangered Languages," National Geographic Mission Program and Living Tongues Institute for Endangered Languages, accessed April 30, 2013. http://travel.nationalgeographic.com/travel/enduring-voices/.
16. Of Welsh, Tolkien wrote, "I heard it coming out of the west. It struck me in the names on coal trucks and drawing nearer, it flickered past on station-signs, a flash of strange spelling and a hint of a language old and yet alive…" "English and Welsh," 192. In a letter to W.H. Auden written on June 7, 1955, Tolkien described his discovery of a Finnish grammar in the Exeter College library: "It was like discovering a complete wine-cellar filled with bottles of an amazing wine of a kind and flavor never tasted before. It quite intoxicated me…" *Letters*, 214.
17. Tolkien, *Letters*, 65.
18. Tolkien, "English and Welsh," 162.
19. Tolkien, "English and Welsh," 190.
20. Simon Critchley and Robert Bernasconi, *The Cambridge Companion to Lévinas* (Cambridge: Cambridge University Press, 2002), 25–26.
21. "Notre rapport avec lui consiste certainment à vouloir le comprendre, mais ce rapport déborde la compréhension. Non seulement parce que la connaissance d'autrui exige, en dehors de la curiosité, aussi de la sympathie ou de l'amour, manières d'être distinctes de la compréhension impassible. Mais parce que, dans notre rapport avec autrui, celui-ci ne nous affecte pas à partir d'un concept. Il est étant et compte comme tel." Emmanuel Lévinas, *Entre nous: Essais sur le penser-à-l'autre* (Paris: Librairie Générale Française [Livre de Poche] 1991), 17. My translation.
22. Augusto Ponzo, "Corps, langage et altérité chez Emmanuel Lévinas," in *Semiotica* 148 1/4 (2004): 124.
23. Ponzo, "Corps, langage et altérité,"139.
24. Emmanuel Lévinas, *Otherwise than Being*, trans. Alphonso Lingis (Pittsburgh: Duquesne University Press, 1998), 46.
25. Chance, "Tolkien and the Other,"180.
26. Emmanuel Lévinas, *Alterity and Transcendance* (New York: Columbia University Press,1999), 88.
27. Tolkien, *The Fellowship of the Ring*, II, vii, 371.
28. Ibid.
29. Ibid.
30. Ibid., II, viii, 392.
31. Lévinas, *Otherwise than Being*, 47. "The act of saying will turn out to have been introduced here from the start as the supreme passivity of exposure to another, which is responsibility for the free initiatives of the other."

32. Tolkien, *The Fellowship of the Ring*, III, vii, 392.
33. Tolkien, *The Two Towers*, 2nd ed. (Boston: Houghton-Mifflin, 1987), III, ii, 35.
34. Tolkien, *The Fellowship of the Ring*, II, vii, 374.
35. Lévinas, *Alterity and Transcendence*, 101.
36. J. R. R. Tolkien, *The Return of the King*, 2nd ed. (Boston: Houghton-Mifflin, 1987), Appendix A, 360.
37. Brian Treanor, *Aspects of Alterity: Lévinas, Marcel and the Contemporary Debate* (New York: Fordham University Press, 2006), 5.
38. Tolkien *The Two Towers*, III, iv, 66–67.
39. Chance, "Tolkien and the Other," 181.
40. Tolkien *The Two Towers*, III, iv, 68.
41. Chance, "Tolkien and the Other," 180.
42. Tolkien, *The Two Towers*, III, iv, 66.
43. Emmanuel Lévinas, *Collected Philosophical Papers*, trans. Alphonso Lingis (Pittsburgh: Duquesne University Press, 1998), 55; cited in Joseph Tadie, "'That the World Not Be Usurped': Emmanuel Lévinas and J.R.R. Tolkien on Serving Others as Release from Bondage," in *Tolkien Among the Moderns*, ed. Ralph C. Wood (Notre Dame, Indiana: Notre Dame University Press 2015), 229.
44. Tadie, 228.
45. Ibid., 229.
46. Ibid., 230.
47. Ibid., 231.
48. Ibid., 236.
49. Lévinas, *Totality and Infinity*, 33.
50. Chance, "Tolkien and the Other," 181.
51. Chance, "Tolkien and the Other," 183.
52. Humphrey Carpenter, *J.R.R. Tolkien: A Biography* (Boston: Houghton Mifflin, 2000), 105.
53. J.R.R. Tolkien, *The Silmarillion* (Boston: Houghton Mifflin, 1977), 178.
54. *Totality and Infinity*, 34.
55. Hope Rogers, "No Triumph without Loss: Problems of Intercultural Marriage in Tolkien's Works," *Tolkien Studies* 10 (2013): 74.
56. Treanor, *Aspects of Alterity*, 8.
57. Lévinas, *Entre nous, 17.* "Comprendre une personne, c'est déjà lui parler. Poser l'existence d'autrui en la laissant être, c'est déjà avoir accepté cette existence, avoir tenu compte d'elle."
58. Verlyn Flieger, "Tolkien's Wild Men: From Medieval to Modern," in *Tolkien the Medievalist*, ed. Jane Chance (New York: Routledge, 2003), 95.
59. Tolkien, *The Return of the King,* Appendix F, 407.

60. Flieger, "Tolkien's Wild Men," 100.
61. Dmitra Fimi, *Tolkien, Race and Cultural History: From Fairies to Hobbits* (New York: Palgrave Macmillan, 2009), 151.
62. Tolkien, *The Return of the King*, V, v, 105.
63. Ibid.,V, v, 106.
64. Ibid.,V, v, 107.
65. Ibid.,VI, vi, 254.
66. Treanor, *Aspects of Alterity*, 4.

Bibliography

Carpenter, Humphrey. *J.R.R. Tolkien: A Biography*. Boston: Houghton Mifflin, 2000.

Chance, Jane. "Tolkien and the Other: Race and Gender in Middle-earth." In *Tolkien's Modern Middle Ages,* edited by Jane Chance and Alfred K. Siewers, 171–188. New York: Palgrave Macmillan, 2005.

Critchley, Simon and Robert Bernasconi. *The Cambridge Companion to Lévinas*. Cambridge: Cambridge University Press, 2002.

Edwards, Jonathan. "The Anthropology of Arda: Creation, Theology, and the Race of Men." In *Tolkien the Medievalist*, edited by Jane Chance, 194–224. New York: Routledge, 2003.

Fimi, Dmitra. *Tolkien, Race and Cultural History: From Fairies to Hobbits*. New York: Palgrave Macmillan, 2009.

Flieger, Verlyn. "Tolkien's Wild Men: From Medieval to Modern." In *Tolkien the Medievalist*, edited by Jane Chance, 95–105. New York: Routledge, 2003.

Hagège, Clause. *On the Death and Life of Languages*. Translated by Jody Gladding. New Haven and London: Yale University Press, 2009.

Lévinas, Emmanuel. *Alterity and Transcendance*. Translated by Michael B. Smith. New York: Columbia University Press, 1999.

-----. *Collected Philosophical Papers*. Translated by Alphonso Lingis. Pittsburgh: Duquesne University Press, 1998.

-----. *Entre nous: Essais sur le penser-à-l'autre*. Paris: Librairie Générale Française [Livre de -Poche] 1991.

-----. *Humanism of the Other*. Translated by Nidra Poller. Urbana and Chicago: University of Illinois Press, 2003.

-----. *Otherwise than Being*. Translated by Alphonso Lingis. Pittsburgh: Duquesne University Press, 1998.

-----. *Totality and Infinity*. Translated by Alphonso Lingis. Pittsburgh: Dusquesne University Press, 1969.

Nettle, Daniel and Suzanne Romaine. *Vanishing Voices: The Extinction of the World's Languages*. New York: Oxford University Press, 2002.

National Geographic Mission Program and Living Tongues Institute for Endangered Languages. "Disappearing Languages, Enduring Voices-Documenting the World's Endangered Languages." Accessed April 30, 2013. http://travel.nationalgeographic.com/travel/enduring-voices/.

Ponzo, Augusto. "Corps, langage et altérité chez Emmanuel Lévinas." in *Semiotica* 148-1/4 (2004): 137–151.

Rogers, Hope. "No Triumph without Loss: Problems of Intercultural Marriage in Tolkien's Works." *Tolkien Studies* 10 (2013): 69–87.

Stanford Encyclopedia of Philosophy. "Emmanuel Lévinas." First published July 23, 2006. Revised Aug 3, 2011. Accessed April 29, 2013. http://plato.stanford.edu/entries/Lévinas/.

Steinfels, Peter. "Emmanuel Lévinas, 90, French Ethical Philosopher." *New York Times*, December 27, 1995. Accessed April 29, 2013. http://www.nytimes.com/1995/12/27/world/emmanuel-Lévinas-90-french-ethical-philosopher.

Tadie, Joseph. "'That the World Not Be Usurped': Emmanuel Lévinas and J. R. R. Tolkien on Serving Others as Release from Bondage." In *Tolkien Among the Moderns*, edited by Ralph C. Wood, 219–246. Notre Dame, Indiana: Notre Dame University Press, 2015.

Tolkien, J. R. R. "English and Welsh." In *The Monsters and the Critics*, 162–197. London: Harper Collins, 2006.

-----. *The Fellowship of the Ring*. 2nd ed. Boston: Houghton Mifflin, 1987.

-----. *The Letters of J.R.R. Tolkien*. Edited by Humphrey Carpenter. Boston: Houghton Mifflin, 2000.

-----. *The Return of the King*. 2nd ed. Boston: Houghton Mifflin, 1987.

-----. *The Silmarillion*. Boston: Houghton Mifflin, 1977.

-----. *The Two Towers*. 2nd ed. Boston: Houghton Mifflin, 1987.

Treanor, Brian. *Aspects of Alterity: Lévinas, Marcel and the Contemporary Debate*. New York: Fordham University Press, 2006.

[illegible] Institute for [illegible] Languages [illegible] Languages [illegible] Enduring Voices [illegible] Accessed [illegible] 30, 2013. [illegible]

[illegible] 158–168.

[illegible] Bakhtin [illegible] 2013: 69–87.

[illegible] First published [illegible] Accessed April 29, 2013. [illegible]

[illegible] New York [illegible] Accessed April 29, 2013. [illegible] philosophe [illegible]

[illegible] Notre Dame, Indiana: [illegible] Press [illegible]

[illegible] 1972 [illegible]

[illegible] English [illegible] Humphrey [illegible] Boston [illegible]

[illegible] Dublin [illegible]

[illegible]

[illegible] Contemporary [illegible] New York: [illegible]

CHAPTER 10

The Orcs and the Others: Familiarity as Estrangement in *The Lord of the Rings*

Verlyn Flieger

The Problem

How to make the already strange even stranger. This was the problem Tolkien faced in *The Lord of the Rings* when he brought his monstrous Orcs on stage not just as masses in an army, as at Helm's Deep, but as individual players in the drama with lines of their own. As might be expected, he solved the problem linguistically by reversing the norms, juxtaposing incompatibilities of sight and sound, and having his most grotesque, monstrous, and exaggerated characters speak language more typical of fans at a football match than monsters in a secondary world fantasy. To propose as an alienating factor, language which in its proper context is familiar seems not just a far-fetched, but a contradictory approach to alterity. Nevertheless, I will argue that it is just such alienation that readers of *The Lord of the Rings* experience when they encounter the speech of Tolkien's Orcs. The technique works. The more we recognize the Orcs by their speech as familiar types the more they stand out as aliens among, and other than, the peoples of Middle-earth.

V. Flieger (✉)
University of Maryland, College Park, MD, USA

C. Vaccaro and Y. Kisor (eds.), *Tolkien and Alterity*, The New Middle Ages, DOI 10.1007/978-3-319-61018-4_10

Tolkien gave his Orcs four scenes and a wealth of character portrayal starting in Book 3, Chapter 3 of *The Two Towers*, "The Uruk-hai"; continuing at the end of Book 4, Chapter 10 of *The Two Towers*, "The Choices of Master Samwise," and again in Book 6, Chapters 1 and 2 of *The Return of the King*, "The Tower of Cirith Ungol" and "The Land of Shadow." In the vivid dialogue of these scenes Uglûk, Grishnakh, Shagrat, Gorbag, Snaga, and the anonymous Soldier and Tracker Orcs come to embody and exemplify what makes the Orcs among the most memorable of Tolkien's characters.

The question of racism is pertinent here, although it bears only tangentially on my main argument, which hinges on incongruity.[1] Orcs have long been targeted as a species of "other" in *The Lord of the Rings*, their slant eyes and dark-to-sallow complexions invoking familiar Western-inspired racial stereotypes. In addition to his fictional descriptions of them, Tolkien said, in a long commentary on the proposed screenplay of *The Lord of the Rings*, that he meant them to be "corruptions of the human form … in fact degraded and repulsive versions of the (to Europeans) least lovely Mongol-types."[2] Allowing him *degraded*, *repulsive*, and *(to Europeans)* as mitigating modifiers, it is still difficult not to see in this reference to the conventional nineteenth-century European projections of the racially suspect East. Arguments rage pro and con, and it is not my intention here to enter the debate, except to say that in the above instance he was objecting to a screen treatment which had endowed the Orcs with beaks and feathers. Nevertheless, as Tolkien himself described them in the book, Orcs appear to be the objects of distinct racial bias.

The Solution

Racism notwithstanding, my purpose in discussing Orcs and alterity is to explore what happens (to the reader) when estranging characteristics are accompanied by language that is at once familiar and out of place. When this happens, alterity doubles back upon itself and the result is radical estrangement through the incongruity of unexpected familiarities. Recognizable speech patterns and diction conventionally associated with familiar, even stereotypical character types (lower-class, uneducated) fall strangely on the ear when put in the mouths of equally stereotypical monsters, and we realize with surprise that Orcs actually talk as much or more like real people than do the rest of the species that inhabit Middle-earth. After all the fantasy the reader has encountered in a pseudo-medieval world peopled by Wizards, Elves, Dwarves, Dragons, and Hobbits—a world whose story settings include sentient forests and malevolent mountains and whose plot hinges on a ring of power and invisibility—the Orcs' speech is so colloquially modern that it is jarring and is therefore counter, original, spare, and arrestingly strange in this fantastic world.

Tolkien's term for this estrangement (borrowed from Chesterton) is *Mooreeffoc* ("Coffee-room viewed from the inside through a glass door") or Chestertonian Fantasy. The word was used by Chesterton "to denote the queerness of things that have become trite when they are seen suddenly from a new angle."[3] In an unfamiliar setting and context, the known becomes strange. This deliberate mismatch of appearance and language divides the Orcs not just from the reader but from their own identity as monsters. Their appearance is estranging. Their language is familiar, even trite, that of bullies in the locker room or at the bus stop, petty and petty-minded individuals isolated from the society against which they stand out so clearly. Erupting into the secondary world Tolkien called Faërie, the primary triteness of Orc street slang acts as *Mooreeffoc*, illustrating the queerness of monstrosity when seen suddenly from a new angle. To paraphrase Marianne Moore's call for "imaginary toads in real gardens"[4], it makes Orcs into real toads in an imaginary garden.

Setting aside for the moment Tolkien's invented languages (though they will reappear shortly), in the conventional English of the narrative, each of the species of Middle-earth can be recognized by speech, from Ted Sandyman at his most patronizingly ironic to Treebeard at his most mellifluous to Aragorn at his most declamatory. Tolkien might easily say, as fellow-writer Mark Twain said of the dialects in *Huckleberry Finn*, that "[t]he shadings have not been done in a haphazard fashion, or by guesswork; but painstakingly, and with the trustworthy guidance and support of personal familiarity with these several forms of speech."[5] The narrative first introduces readers to the standard but relaxed English diction and usage of the middle-class Hobbits (both in Hobbiton and Bree), informal but governed by the conventions of written English orthography in which what is elided in actual speech is spelled out on the page. Of Bilbo's wealth: "It will have to be paid for … . It isn't natural, and trouble will come of it."[6] There are few contractions; characters tend to say "will not" instead of "won't," "does not" instead of "doesn't," "do not" instead of "don't." From the top of the scale, the somewhat poeticized cry of Frodo, "O Gandalf, best of friends, what am I do to?"[7] to the hurried, breathless, run-on syntax of Barliman Butterbur to the lower end of the scale with Sméagol's "Give us that, my love" and "I wants it,"[8] decorum, the fitting of the word to the speaker, is preserved. The slightly stilted English spoken by Gildor and his Elves—"Hail, Frodo!," "You do not know whither we are going," "Ask no more of me"[9]—presages the plain but correct speech of Strider, as well as the more formal English used by Gandalf and Saruman, and the multiple debaters at the Council of Elrond. At the very end of *The Fellowship of the Ring* and the beginning of Book 3 of *The Two Towers*, we are given the very formal, archaic and heroic inverted syntax of Aragorn, Éomer, and Theoden as well as the wheedling, whiney but correct diction of Wormtongue. Having read *The Fellowship of the Ring*, the reader has become accustomed to such nuances in tone and diction.

Sight and Sound

Tolkien's invented languages enhance this experience. "*A Elbereth Gilthoniel/silivren penna míriel*" sings a voice at Rivendell as Frodo and Bilbo leave the Hall of Fire. The song is described as "clear jewels of blended word and melody."[10] Frodo has already heard the song, at his meeting with Gildor in the Woody End; while he hears it in Elvish, his thought reshapes it into English as "*Gilthoniel! O Elbereth!/Clear are thy eyes and bright thy breath!*,"[11] and the English translation does its best to match the Elven sound and appearance. This and other examples of Sindarin/English in the text invite the reader to expect sound matched not just to sense but to the outward appearance of the speaker. Elves' language matches their beauty, both in Sindarin and Common Speech. Likewise, we would expect Orcs' language to match Orc ugliness, and so it does, but only halfway. Physically Orcs are "yellow-fanged,"[12] "very broad," with "clawlike" hands,"[13] "rending nails,"[14] and legs "made of wire and horn."[15] These dehumanizing phrases compound Orcs' otherness, creating the image of a creature out of a bestiary.

Actual Orcish Black Speech is a good fit with Orcish appearance. It also is dehumanizing, harsh and ugly in both explicit appearance and implicit sound, as the examples in the book will show. There's the Ring verse: *Ash nazg durbatulûk, ash nazg gimbatul,/Ash nazg thrakatulûk agh burzum-ishi krimpatul.*[16] There are a few scattered words: *gâsh* "fire," *sharkû* "old man," *snaga* "slave" and *Uruk*, Orcish for "Orc," which fit the Orcs in both appearance and (presumed) sound. So far, so good. The monsters have a monstrous language. The Black Speech and the Orcs' appearance together have what Tolkien calls the "inner consistency of reality."[17] The clashing consonants, gutturals, and dark vowels of Black Speech in the Ring inscription fit the Orcs' physical appearance just as the lyrical, melodious Elven language Sindarin fits the described beauty of Elves in Middle-earth.

It is just here, however, that Tolkien uses the familiar as double estrangement, for most of the Orc dialogue is not in Black Speech but in English of the most colloquial kind. The subsequent encounter with the actual barrack-room lingo of the Orcs in English creates culture shock for the hobbits (Pippin thinks it is "hideous") and dissonance for the reader, who experiences the confusion of meeting the familiar in an unfamiliar context. Tolkien uses several devices by which to enable such experience. In the first Orc-conversation in "The Uruk-hai," the Orcs are presented as using a kind of lingua franca called "Common Speech" or "ordinary language" because they are from different tribes and cannot "understand each other's Orc-speech."[18] At the Tower of Cirith Ungol, the Ring enables Sam to understand the Orcs' language and we are given a "translation" of the actual Orc conversation, presumably conducted in Black Speech, into Sam's Common Speech and the reader's native English. By the time, Frodo and Sam are caught by the Durthang Orcs in Mordor this rationale has been abandoned, and Orc speech is rendered in English with no pretense at translation or enhanced hearing.

This is less carelessness on Tolkien's part than expediency. Appendix F of *The Return of the King*, "Orcs and Black Speech," notes that while the Ring inscription "was in the ancient Black Speech," the curse of the Mordor Orc and of Grishnákh was "in the more debased form used by the soldiers of the Dark Tower."[19] In other words, army slang, a patois far easier for Tolkien to reproduce in English than to try to invent in Black Speech. The one example in actual Orcish of what Tolkien called the "debased form" is the curse of the "yellow-fanged guard" (the Mordor Orc) against Uglúk: *Uglúk u bagronk sha pushdug Saruman-glob búbhosh skai.*[20] This is translated by Tolkien in a draft of "The Appendix on Languages" in *The Peoples of Middle-earth* as "*Uglúk to the cesspool, sha! the dungfilth; the great Saruman-fool, skai!*"[21] Carl Hostetter offers a variant translation as "*Uglúk to the dung-pit with stinking Saruman-filth— pig-guts, gah!*"[22]

The curse is effective in the Black Speech, but both translations fall strangely on the ear in the "debased form," the Common Speech translation. Tolkien was probably wise not to include translation in the text, for it makes the strange both too strange and too familiar. He comes perilously close to tipping the balance as it is. Pippin's interior monologue at the opening of Chap. 3, reported by the narrator, has him hearing the Orcs' "abominable tongue," which when translated into the Common Speech of the narrative becomes in Pippin's mind "almost as hideous as [the Orc's] own language" (*TT* III iii 48). Hideous and abominable it may be in both languages, but in the "translation" into the Common Speech of the debased form, the "hideous" is immediately recognizable as slang, a mode that distinguishes it from the Ring verse as well as from the conventionally poetic English of the Elbereth hymn, with its "thy" direct address and syntactic inversion. Elven Common Speech harmonizes with Elves' appearance, where Orcish Debased Common Speech clashes with the fantasy of their nature as monsters. It is as if in the middle of *Beowulf* Grendel were to start talking like a rapper.

Much of this debased speech involves name-calling of one kind or another. While Orcs regularly curse one another as well as everybody else, and call each other names ("snotty," "sneakthief," "slugs"), as much as they do Eomer and his Rohirrim ("cursed Whiteskins"), and their abuse is not couched in the language of fantasy but in the earthy realism of barnyard and gutter. Not just Merry and Pippin, and Frodo and Sam, but Snaga, Shagrat, Uglúk and Grishnákh are regularly cursed and name-called, the last four by each other. *Snaga*, which means "slave" in the Black Speech, may in fact be a contemptuous epithet and not a proper name, or—even more typically Orcish—a contemptuous epithet turned into a proper name.

Orcs' debased barrack-room vocabulary—*swine*, *guts*, *sties*, *maggots*, *slugs*, *dung*, *swag*, *dunghill rat*—chimes discordantly within its fantasy setting. Where the narrator refers to Sauron synecdochically as *the Eye*, or the *Hand*, or metonymically as the *Tower*, within the story proper it is the Orcs, whose formal name for Barad-Dûr is *Lugbúrz* (probably meaning "Dark Tower" but listen to the effect of those gutturals and the buzz of that voiced fricative), who more richly than the other inhabitants of Middle-earth use figures of speech. They refer to Sauron and/or the Nazgûl not just as the Great Eye, but more familiarly as the Big Bosses, the Top Ones, High Up, He, Himself, Number One, a kind of definition by omission and/or circumlocution. Shelob is "Her Ladyship." Torture is "fun." Nobody else in the book talks this way.

"Personal Familiarity"

Where did a middle-class, university-educated educated inventor of languages find the "debased," low-class street-slang he gave the Orcs, for he surely did not invent it as he did Black Speech? One possible answer is from books, for several dictionaries on such language were accessible to him, though it is not known if any was part of his personal library.[23] The earliest are *A New Dictionary of the Terms Ancient and Modern of the Canting Crew, in its Several Tribes of Gypsies, Beggars, Thieves, Cheats, &c.* by one B.E. (gent.), published in 1698 by W. Hawes, P. Gilbourne, and W. Davis, and James Francis Grose's *A Classical Dictionary of the Vulgar Tongue*, published in 1785 by S. Hooper, which lists many of the same terms but expands the list. Grose's book was eventually superseded by John Camden Hotten's Slang Dictionary in 1859. In 1889, two multivolume slang dictionaries went on sale: *A Dictionary of Slang, Jargon and Cant* by Albert Barrere and Charles Leland, and *Slang and its Analogues* by John Farmer and W.E. Henley; the latter first published in a formidable seven volumes, later abridged to a single volume and released in 1905 as *A Dictionary of Slang and Colloquial English.* This book provided the major portion of Eric Partridge's *Dictionary of Slang and Unconventional English* (1938). Given Tolkien's interest in language and languages, and his training in the history of their development, it seems reasonable that he might have availed himself of the opportunity to consult any one or several of these dictionaries, all of which fall comfortably within or before the time frame of his composition.

But there is no proof. Moreover, he need not have relied on such academic sources, for he had a more personal and immediate one ready to hand. I suggest that here, as in so many instances, Tolkien could have been drawing on direct experience. Much has been made (not least by Tolkien himself) of his admiration for and sense of debt to the ordinary, working-class soldiers he met during his service in France in World War I. Sam, particularly, has been singled out at the prototypical batman, the personal servant attached to an officer in the English army.[24] As a batman, Sam is portrayed as talking in a manner low-class but respectful—"Mr. Frodo, sir," "Mr. Pippin." Little has been said about the fact that since there is a range of behavior among and within all social classes, and Tolkien would certainly also have heard from his fellow-soldiers less savory material in vocabulary and manner of speech, reflective of a different stratum of society and a different attitude toward authority.

Mark Twain's phrase, "personal familiarity" with the dialects used is apposite, and it is not unreasonable to imagine that Tolkien was drawing on a similar personal familiarity with the words and expressions he put into the mouths of his Orcs. In his landmark study, *Tolkien and the Great War*, John Garth observes that "English received an enormous jolt of electricity from … the experiences of the Great War. Old words received new meanings; new words were coined; foreign phrases were bastardized."[25] Immersed as he was in army life, says Garth, "Tolkien was surrounded by wordsmiths … soldiers' slang, which spanned death, drink, food, women, weapons, the battlefield, and the warring nations, grew out of irony and contempt for what was intolerable; it was a crude and unlovely as camp life itself." A recent newspaper article on World War I concurred, describing World War I soldiers' slang as, a "privileging of the ordinary soldier's perspective … a suspicion of authority and a tendency to mock those who wield it … a taste for absurdity, sarcasm and black humor."[26]

Christopher Tolkien, though he does not refer specifically to Orc speech, has noted that the initial drafting of the chapter in Book 3 called "The Uruk-hai" which gives the first close-up account of the Orcs was "astonishingly close to the final form" in *The Two Towers* as published.[27] While Christopher is primarily referring to plot, the ease with which this chapter seems to have unfolded suggests that Tolkien had the personal familiarity of his army experience and was making good use of his well-known ear for language to create (in the most blatant example in the book) a species through its diction, through what the readers "hear" as well as what they "see."

Words in Their Mouths

The obvious question is why Tolkien picked this particular kind of language for his Orcs, and I suggest that the answer is because it was the most jarring kind of language he had at his command. We can be sure his choice was not random. The Orcs are portrayed as talking in a manner even lower-class than Sam, and anything but respectful. Their speech is "vulgar" in both the literal and colloquial senses of the word, impolite, abusive, and liberally peppered with gutter-slang. Slang it may be, but as with other examples of colloquial "folk" language, it is also precise, grammatical, rich in metaphor, and vivid in imagery. Examination of the language of Uglúk, Grishnákh, Shagrat, Gorbag, Snaga, and the unnamed but sharply delineated Soldier and Tracker who follow Frodo, Sam, and Gollum as they approach Mt. Doom, will show the skill with which Tolkien puts words in their mouths—street-slang, thieves' cant, gutter lingo—to otherize his Orcs and distance them from the rest of his two-legged creatures.

Here are examples. First, "absurdity, sarcasm and black humor":

Grishnákh: to Merry & Pippin:

> "Enjoying your nice rest? Or not? A little awkwardly placed perhaps, swords and whips on one side, and nasty spears on the other."[28]

> "What do you think you've been kept alive for? My dear little fellows, please believe me when I say that it was not out of kindness: that's not even one of Uglúk's faults."[29]

We get the message. It's Grishnákh who's "enjoying" the hobbits' exhaustion and discomfort, which is anything but a "nice rest." To be "awkwardly placed" better describes a social situation than whips and swords and spears, which are more than "awkward," they are physical, threatening, and dangerous. Spears are not "nasty," implying a psychological attitude, they are impersonal, lethal, killing tools. The hobbits have not been kept alive out of kindness but out of policy, implying that death would be preferable; moreover, in a reversal of the norm, kindness is a character flaw beyond even the capacity of the obviously flawed Uglúk. Grishnákh is not a student of rhetoric, but he's a whiz at absurdity, sarcasm, and black humor.

Next, figures of speech:

Grishnákh to Pippin:	"Lie quiet or I'll tickle you with this."[30]
Grishnákh to MerryMerry:	"Untie your legs? I'll untie every string in your bodies."[31]
Shagrat to Frodo:	"Keep your trap shut, see!"[32]
Soldier Orc:	"I'll stick you if you don't shut it down"[33]
Gorbag to Shagrat:	"She's [Shelob] sat on a nail, and we shan't cry about that"[34]

Gorbag to Shagrat:	"Who's stuck a pin into Her Ladyship?"[35]
Shagrat to Snaga:	"I'll put red maggot-holes in your belly"[36]

And diction:

Grishnákh to Merry and Pippin:	"Curse you, you filthy little vermin!"[37]
	"I'll cut you both to quivering shreds"[38]
Shagrat to Snaga:	"Curse you, Snaga, you little maggot!"[39]
	"I'll squeeze your eyes out"[40]
Shagrat to Snaga:	"I'll eat you"[41]
Snaga to Shagrat:	"I'll put an arrow in your guts"[42]

And insult:

Soldier Orc:	"I reckon eyes are better than your snotty noses."[43]
Tracker Orc:	"Garn!" "Nar!"
	"You cursed peaching sneakthief!"[44]

It is clear from this and other dialogue that while all the Orcs use abusive slang, they do not all use it in the same way. Grishnákh's silky menace is quite different from the coarse bluster of Shagrat or the schoolboy venom of the Soldier and Tracker. His voice is described as "softer than the others, but more evil"[45] and his elaborate sarcasm—"nice rest," "dear little fellows," "My dear tender little fools," "my little ones," "I'll tickle you," "quivering shreds"—has the effect of making him more dangerous by understatement. His language is proper English, but its very correctness implies a subtext of threat.

In this variegated litany of Orc abuse, from the aforementioned *maggot* and *guts* to the explicitness of *snotty noses* and *filthy vermin*, the Tracker Orc's vocabulary is particularly worth attention. Both his expletives, *garn!* (also used by Shagrat in the Tower) and *nar!*, are typical Cockney mispronunciations of standard English "Go on!" and "No." Henry Higgins' judgment of Eliza Doolittle in *My Fair Lady* that "It's *aow* and *garn* that keep her in her place"[46] says all that is needed about the separation of classes by diction and accent in Higgins' and by extension Tolkien's England. In addition, the word *peaching* with which Tolkien modifies *sneakthief* is a particularly nice touch. The Soldier Orc has threatened to report the Tracker to the Nazgûl, which provokes the Tracker to accuse him of "peaching," a term which could have come straight out of the dictionary of Grose, who lists it as "to impeach." To *peach* is London thieves cant; it means "to accuse, inform against, rat on." Compare *impeachment* (accusation, formal charge), as of a sitting president in American politics (Johnson, Clinton).

A major character in John Gay's *The Beggar's Opera*, set in the criminal underworld of eighteenth-century London, is type-named Mr. Peachum (Peach'em), an informer, fence, and receiver of stolen goods. In this world, for all its theatricality, Orcs would be at home. Orcish diction and usage when speaking among themselves, and to a lesser extent when speaking to non-Orcs (cf. Grishnakh to Pippin), marks them clearly as not just lower-class and ill-educated, but part of a criminal underworld right out of *Oliver Twist*, a seedy Underworld that sets them off from the magic of the Otherworld of Middle-earth. In a way, Orc dialogue is refreshing (once you get used to the fact that it's coming from monsters), and it can be a relief to read/hear colloquial modern English amid all the "whither" and "hither" and "heed" and "deem" and "Hail!" and "hath." A little syntactic inversion goes a long way, and the Orcs offer a perhaps welcome break from a superabundance of medievalism.

Moreover, Orc speech alone of all the verbal patterns in Middle-earth seems to have the power to affect the speech of others. Grishnakh's behavior and mode of speech cause Pippin (and later Merry) to consciously abandon their own version of the Common Speech and enter into the Orcish mode of thought and behavior in order to bargain with him. When Grishnakh begins to paw them, Pippin infers from his physical actions what he wants. "The thought came suddenly into Pippin's mind as if caught directly from the urgent thought of his enemy,"[47] and he begins to bargain with his captor on Grishnakh's own terms and in Grishnakh's own idiom. First, and non-verbally, he imitates Gollum's guttural throat-sound *gollum, gollum*. Merry picks it up. "Now's the time to do a deal,"[48] not usual Hobbit speech to one another or to anyone else, but the right words to communicate with Grishnakh on his own terms.

Linguistic Conventions and Differentiations

It is, of course, not Merry but Tolkien who is consciously drawing on linguistic conventions, as shown by his response to an adapter preparing a script of *The Two Towers* for radio performance. To him Tolkien wrote:

> … it would probably be better to avoid certain … features of modern 'vulgar' English in representing Orcs, such as the dropping of aitches (these are, I think, *not* dropped in the text, and that is deliberate). But of course, for most people, 'accent'… is confused with impressions of different intonation, articulation, and tempo. You will, I suppose, have to use such means to make Orcs sound nasty![49]

The clear implication is that the adapter was proposing the use of dropped aitches as a way for actors to portray Orcs. As a linguistic marker, the dropped aitch has, since the time of Dickens' Artful Dodger, Bernard Shaw's Eliza Doolittle, and their Cockney (or East End London) counterparts in the British music hall, been standard shorthand for a cultural stereotype. Such pronunciation signals "lower-class," and "ill-educated," rather like the stage Irishman of the eighteenth and nineteenth centuries. Tolkien had used the dropped aitch (sparingly) for the Trolls in *The Hobbit*, but by the time of *The Lord of the Rings* he had refined his technique. Unlike the Trolls (and pursuant to Tolkien's opinion as expressed in the letter), his Orcs do not drop their aitches. Nonetheless, his comments to the adapter make it clear that their diction on the page implies the omission without the orthography and, even more than their squat, bow-legged appearance, singles Orcs out from the rest of the peoples of Middle-earth. Orcish usage as printed implies the accent, the "intonation, articulation, and tempo" to which Tolkien refers. In the same letter to the radio adapter, Tolkien went on to write, "if this 'history' were real, all users of the C[ommon] S[peech] would reveal themselves by their accent, differing in place, people, and rank, but that cannot be represented when C.S. is turned into English—and is not, I think, necessary."[50] Although he says the Common Speech would reveal its speakers by their accent, it is in fact only the Orcs whose speech does so, and the accent is only by implication. It is noteworthy that Tolkien singled out the Orcs as revealing themselves—i.e., sounding "nasty"—by their presumed accent.

In the same letter, he went on to say that he "paid great attention to such linguistic differentiation as was possible in diction, idiom, and so on." A revealing use of idiom which adds practical evidence of the importance of "shadings" was noted by David Bratman in his essay on "The Literary Value of The History of Middle-earth."[51] Bratman points out that in *The Return of the Shadow*, edited by Christopher Tolkien, the first draft of what became the "Strider" chapter in *The Fellowship of the*

Ring has Trotter (not yet Strider) say to Frodo at Bree, "I don't think somehow that you will be wanting to meet any of those Black-riders, if you can help it. They give me the creeps"[52] With fastidious distaste and a discriminating ear Bratman comments, "They give him the *creeps?* Let us be grateful that Tolkien changed Trotter's speech as well as his name."[53] Not only is Bratman right, Tolkien's own ear for "diction, idiom, and so on" allowed him to spot the discrepancy and rewrite the speech. In the published version, Strider simply says, "Do you wish them to find you? They are terrible!"[54] His face is "drawn with pain," while his hands clench the arms of his chair.[55] This physical reaction speaks more loudly than any words and outpaces "the creeps" at every step.

Not only is the linguistic change from "you will be wanting" to "do you wish?" a shift to more correct, conventional literary language, the replacement of "They give me the creeps" by "They are terrible!" is both more dramatic and more in character. Strider with the creeps sounds more like a boy in the fifth form than the shadowed, mysterious stranger who arouses Sam's legitimate suspicions, much less the returning king with a line of distinguished ancestors behind him. What Bratman did not point out, but which rounds out the notion of Tolkien's sensitivity to language and caps the example, is how Tolkien found a way to reuse the idiom when he got to *The Two Towers*, changing the speaker, the addressee, and the immediate situation, and bestowing the comment on the character most likely to use an expression like that. "Grrr!" says Gorbag, Captain of the Uruks to Shagrat, Captain of the Tower of Cirith Ungol, and one can almost hear the interjection, almost see the shudder. "Those Nazgûl give me the creeps."[56] In this context, the expression fits the character and at the same time reveals and distances him from Sam Gamgee (who is listening) as well as from the reader, by now accustomed to the usage of Tolkien's more conventionally spoken characters.

We should not only be grateful for the change, as Bratman suggests, but observant of an author's growing awareness of how word choice affects character and (in this case) creates alterity, alienating a character not just from the reader but from the other peoples of Middle-earth. A further bit of dialogue will illustrate. Not long after Gorbag has the creeps, he proposes to Shagrat, "What d'you say—if we get a chance, you and me'll slip off and set up somewhere on our own with a few trusty lads, somewhere where there's good loot nice and handy, and no big bosses." "Ah," Shagrat replies, "Like old times."[57] Not only does this establish the two Orcs as mafia-style petty criminals with a history of extortion if not worse, Gorbag's description of the "set up" offers a disturbing echo of Saruman and his parallel proposition that he and Gandalf join forces to work with Sauron, with the stated goal of ultimately overthrowing him and seizing power themselves. "Our time is at hand"... "And why not, Gandalf?"... "Why not? The Ruling Ring? If we could command that, then the Power would pass to us."[58] The estrangement we feel from the Orcs' language and behavior, the assumption that such petty villainy is outside the norm and is overturned when we recognize the kinship between Gorbag and Shagrat, Orcs of the Tower, and Saruman the White Wizard, a.k.a Sharkey, a.k.a the Chief, vandal-architect of the Shire's despoliation and its attempted ruination.

All that separates the White Wizard from the black Orcs is the way each talks, and that gap is closed in "The Scouring of the Shire" when the former head of the White Council is reduced to Sharkey. The erstwhile Saruman reveals himself as having sunk to the level of the Orcs, or—even worse—as having always been at that level, his true nature as Sharkey camouflaged behind his politician's use of a rhetoric as shifting as the colors of his white robe. While the surface of his diction is proper English—indeed rather elaborately proper—its correctness is undermined by its Orcian malice, understatement, and irony. "Worm has been very hungry lately," Saruman tells the hobbits with mock regret. He is—not very obliquely—implying that Wormtongue has not just killed but eaten Lotho, a monstrous act of cannibalism the likes of which up to now has only been attributable to Orcs. "No," Saruman says, "Worm is not really nice."[59] "Not really nice" is putting it mildly. Such understatement is worthy of Grishnakh at his best, typical of the Grishnakhian penchant for "absurdity, sarcasm and black humor." That it is now equally typical of Saruman/Sharkey who "was great once, of a noble kind"[60] but is no longer either great or noble, is revealing. It's enough to give you the creeps.

Notes

1. For fuller discussion of Tolkien and racism, see Jane Chance, "Tolkien and the Other: Race and Gender in Middle-earth," in *Tolkien's Modern Middle Ages*, ed. Jane Chance and Alfred K. Siewers, The New Middle Ages (New York: Palgrave Macmillan, 2005), 171–188. Also see Dimitra Fimi's *Tolkien, Race, and Cultural History: From Fairies to Hobbits* (London: Palgrave Macmillan, 2008); Miryam Libran-Moreno's "Byzantium, New Rome!": Goths, Langobards, and Byzantium in *The*

Lord of the Rings," in *Tolkien and the Study of his Sources*, ed. Jason Fisher (Jefferson, NC: McFarland, 2011), 84–115; and Renée Vink, "'Jewish' Dwarves: Tolkien and Anti-Semitic Stereotyping," *Tolkien Studies* 10 (2013): 123–45. Though his focus is not mine, Tom Shippey examines the six Orcish conversations in the novel, highlighting the jarring existence with their diction of a shared moral code with weight placed on cooperation, mistrust, and fear. See Shippey, "Orcs, Wraiths, Wights: Tolkien Images of Evil," in *J.R.R. Tolkien and His Literary Resonances: Views of Middle-earth*, ed. George Clark and Daniel Timmons (Westport, CT: Greenwood Press, 2000), 183–198.
2. J.R.R. Tolkien, *The Letters of J.R.R. Tolkien*, ed. Humphrey Carpenter (Boston: Houghton Mifflin Co., 1981), 274.
3. J.R.R. Tolkien, *Tolkien On Fairy-Stories*, ed. Verlyn Flieger and Douglas A. Anderson (London: Harper Collins, 2004), 68.
4. Marianne Moore, *The Complete Poems of Marianne Moore* (London: Penguin, 1994), 267.
5. Mark Twain (Samuel L. Clemens), *The Adventures of Huckleberry Finn* (New York and London: Harper & Brothers Publishers, 1899), v.
6. J.R.R. Tolkien, *The Fellowship of the Ring*, 2nd ed. (Boston: Houghton Mifflin, 1987), I, i, 29.
7. Ibid., I, ii, 68.
8. Ibid., I, ii, 62.
9. Ibid., I, iii, 89, 94.
10. Ibid., II, i, 250.
11. Ibid., I, iii, 88.
12. J.R.R. Tolkien, *The Two Towers,* 2nd ed. (Boston: Houghton Mifflin, 1987), III, iii, 48.
13. Ibid., III, iii, 50.
14. Ibid., III, iii, 51.
15. Ibid., III, iii, 55.
16. Tolkien, *The Fellowship of the Ring*, II, ii, 267.
17. Tolkien, *Tolkien On Fairy-Stories*, 59.
18. Tolkien, *The Two Towers* III, iii, 48. Tolkien got round this by way of Appendix F: "It is said that they [Orcs] had no language of their own, but took what they could of other tongues and perverted it to their own liking; yet they made only brutal jargons, scarcely sufficient for their own needs, unless it were for curses and abuse. And these creatures, being filled with malice, hating even their own kind, quickly developed as many barbarous dialects as there were groups of settlements of their race, so that their Orkish speech was of little use to them in intercourse between different tribes." J.R.R. Tolkien, *The Return of the King*, 2nd ed. (Boston: Houghton Mifflin, 1987), 409.

19. Ibid., 409–410.
20. Tolkien, *The Two Towers*, III, iii, 48.
21. J.R.R. Tolkien, *The Peoples of Middle Earth*, ed. Christopher Tolkien (Boston: Houghton Mifflin Company, 1996), 83.
22. Carl Hostetter, "Uglúk to the Dung-pit," *Vinyar Tengwar* 26 (1992): 16.
23. They need not have been. His work on the OED would have familiarized him with, and given him access to, an alphabet of dictionaries.
24. See Hooker, "Frodo's Batman," *Tolkien Studies* 1 (2004): 125–136.
25. John Garth, *Tolkien and the Great War* (London: Harper Collins, 2003), 124.
26. A.O. Scott, "A War to End All Innocence," *New York Times*, June 22, 2014, AR1.
27. J.R.R. Tolkien, *The Treason of Isengard*, ed. Christopher Tolkien (Boston: Houghton Mifflin Company, 1989), 409.
28. Tolkien, *The Two Towers*, III, iii, 58.
29. Ibid., III, iii, 59.
30. Ibid., III, iii, 48.
31. Ibid., III, iii, 59.
32. Tolkien, *The Return of the King*, VI, i, 186.
33. Ibid., VI, ii, 202.
34. Tolkien, *The Two Towers*, IV, x, 346.
35. Ibid., IV, x, 349.
36. Tolkien, *The Return of the King*, VI, i, 182.
37. Tolkien, *The Two Towers*, 59.
38. Ibid., 59.
39. Tolkien, *The Return of the King*, VI, i, 181.
40. Ibid., VI, i, 182.
41. Ibid.
42. Ibid.
43. Ibid., VI, ii, 202.
44. Ibid., VI, ii, 203.
45. Tolkien, *The Two Towers*, III, ii, 49.
46. "Why Can't the English Teach Their Children How to Speak?," Act One, *My Fair Lady*, George Bernard Shaw and Alan Jay Lerner (1963).
47. Ibid., III, ii, 58.
48. Ibid., III, ii, 59.
49. J.R.R. Tolkien, *The Letters of J.R.R. Tolkien*, ed. Humphrey Carpenter (Boston: Houghton Mifflin Co., 1981), 253–254.
50. Ibid., 253–254.
51. In *Tolkien's Legendarium: Essays on the History of Middle-earth*, ed. Verlyn Flieger and Carl Hostetter (Westport, Conn.: Greenwood Press, 2000), 87.

52. J.R.R. Tolkien, *The Return of the Shadow*, ed. Christopher Tolkien, Vol. VI of The History of Middle-earth (Boston: Houghton Mifflin Company, 1988), 153.
53. Bratman, 87.
54. Tolkien, *The Fellowship of the Ring*, I, x, 177.
55. Ibid.
56. Tolkien, *The Two Towers*, IV, x, 347.
57. Ibid.
58. Tolkien, *The Fellowship of the Ring*, II, ii, 272–273.
59. Tolkien *The Return of the King*, VI, viii, 299.
60. Ibid.

Bibliography

Barrere, Albert and Charles Leland. *Slang and Its Analogues*. London: Ballantine Press, 1889.

Bratman, David. "The Literary Value of The History of Middle-earth." In *Tolkien's Legendarium: Essays on The History of Middle-earth*, ed. Verlyn Flieger and Carl Hostetter, 69–94. Westport, CT: Greenwood Press, 2000.

Chance, Jane. "Tolkien and the Other: Race and Gender in Middle-earth." In *Tolkien's Modern Middle Ages*, ed. Jane Chance and Alfred K. Siewers, 171–188. New York: Palgrave, 2005.

E., B. (Gent). *A New Dictionary of the Terms Ancient and Modern of the Canting Crew, in its Several Tribes of Gypsies, Beggars, Thieves, Cheats, &c.* London: Hawes, Gilbourne, and Davis, 1899.

Farmer, John and W. E. Henley. *A Dictionary of Slang and Colloquial English*. London: Routledge, 1890.

Fimi, Dimitra. *Tolkien, Race and Cultural History*. London: Palgrave Macmillan, 2008.

Flieger, Verlyn and Carl Hostetter. *Tolkien's Legendarium: Essays on The History of Middle-earth*. Westport, CT: Greenwood Press, 2000.

Garth, John. *Tolkien and the Great War*. London: Harper Collins, 2003.

Gay, John. *The Beggar's Opera*. New York: Penguin Classics, 1987.

Grose, James Francis. *The Classical Dictionary of the Vulgar Tongue*. London, 1785.

Honegger, Thomas. "The Rohirrim: 'Anglo-Saxons on Horseback'?" *Tolkien and the Study of his Sources*, ed. Jason Fisher, 116–132. Jefferson, NC: McFarland, 2011.

Hooker, Mark T. "Frodo's Batman," *Tolkien Studies* 1 (2004): 125–136.

Hostetter, Carl. "Uglûk to the Dung-pit." *Vinyar Tengwar* 26 (1992), 16.

Hotton, John Camden. *Slang Dictionary*. London: 1859.

Librán-Moreno, Miryam. "'Byzantium, New Rome!' Goths, Langobards, and Byzantium in *The Lord of the Rings*." In *Tolkien and the Study of his Sources*, ed. Jason Fisher, 84–115. Jefferson, NC: McFarland, 2011.

Moore, Marianne. *The Complete Poems of Marianne Moore*. London: Penguin, 1994.

Partridge, Eric. *Dictionary of Slang and Unconventional English*. London: George Routledge & Sons, 1938.

Scott, A. O. "A War to End All Innocence." *New York Times*, June 22, 2014.

Shaw, George Bernard and Alan Jay Lerner. *My Fair Lady*. 1963.

Shippey, Tom. "Orcs, Wraiths, Wights: Tolkien's Images of Evil." In *J. R. R. Tolkien and His Literary Resonances: Views of Middle-earth*, ed. George Clark and Daniel Timmons, 183–198. Westport, CT: Greenwood Press, 2000.

Tolkien, J. R. R. *Beowulf: A Translation and Commentary Together with Sellic Spell*. Edited by Christopher Tolkien. London: HarperCollins, 2014.

———. *The Fellowship of the Ring*. 2nd ed. Boston: Houghton Mifflin Co., 1987.

———. *The Peoples of Middle-earth*. Vol. XII of The History of Middle-earth, ed. Christopher Tolkien. Boston: Houghton Mifflin Company, 1996.

———. *The Return of the King*. 2nd ed. Boston: Houghton Mifflin Co., 1987.

———. *The Return of the Shadow*, Volume VI of The History of Middle-earth, ed. Christopher Tolkien, Boston: Houghton Mifflin Company, 1988.

———. *Tolkien on Fairy-Stories*. Expanded edition with commentary and notes, ed. Verlyn Flieger and Douglas A. Anderson. London: Harper Collins, 2008.

———. *The Treason of Isengard*, Vol. VII of The History of Middle-earth, ed. Christopher Tolkien. Boston: Houghton Mifflin Company, 1989.

———. *The Two Towers*. 2nd ed. Boston: Houghton Mifflin Co., 1987.

Twain, Mark (Samuel L. Clemens). *The Adventures of Huckleberry Finn*. New York and London: Harper & Brothers Publishers, 1899.

Vink, Renée. "'Jewish' Dwarves: Tolkien and Anti-Semitic Stereotyping." *Tolkien Studies* 10 (2013): 123–145.

PART V

Identities

CHAPTER 11

Silmarils and Obsession: The Undoing of Fëanor

Melissa Ruth Arul

It is said that of all the Noldor, "fiercest burned the flame of desire for freedom and wider realms" in the heart of Fëanor.[1] Fëanor, who "became of the Noldor, then or after, the most subtle in mind and the most skilled in hand," was renowned for his creation of three incomparable jewels, the Silmarils.[2] For it was the doom of the Elves "to love the beauty of the world, to bring it to full flower with their gifts of delicacy and perfection."[3] And Art, especially Elvish Art, Tolkien explains, is supposed to be "subcreation, not domination and tyrannous reforming of Creation."[4] The Art of the Elves was to further engender beauty and creation. Yet, in creating the Silmarils, Fëanor created his downfall. His love for the jewels would soon become an obsession. The loss of them, alongside the death of his father Finwë, led to Fëanor's abjection of his kin and clan, the departure of the Noldor from Valinor, and ultimately his death. How could such Art, filled with the sacred Light of Valinor, cause such ruin? In her examination of Fëanor, Verlyn Flieger opines that while the fate of the Elves is far more complex than apparent, it was always fated that Fëanor would lose the Silmarils.[5] As a scholar and a craftsman

M.R. Arul (✉)
University of Malaya, Kuala Lumpur, Malaysia

C. Vaccaro and Y. Kisor (eds.), *Tolkien and Alterity*, The New Middle Ages, DOI 10.1007/978-3-319-61018-4_11

himself, Tolkien would have felt an affinity to Fëanor and his love for his creation. Why then such a fate for Fëanor, aside from the fact that it drives the plot? Tom Shippey points out that Fëanor was not the only "dangerous maker in Tolkien's work."[6] Aulë, creator of the Dwarves, Saruman with his use of fire and Thorin's obsession over the Arkenstone are noted as well.[7] All three suffer disastrous fates with the exception of Aulë. My essay, therefore, examines the psychological nature of Fëanor and his compulsion to view the Other as a threat, which subsequently leads to his undoing.

Julia Kristeva defines the abject as that which threatens the boundary between the Self and the Other. It is an atavistic reaction towards a threat against the borders of the Self.[8] On a psychosexual level, the abject symbolizes the moment when the Self separates itself from the mother. Fëanor's abjection of his kin began with the untimely death of his mother Míriel. She put forth all of her strength and spirit into bearing Fëanor, yet after giving life to him she found herself yearning to be freed "from the labour of living."[9] While Finwë was distressed as he thought it "an unhappy chance that the mother should depart and miss the beginning at least of the childhood days of her son," Míriel was adamant.[10] She countered Finwë saying, in what was to be prophetic words, "it is indeed unhappy… and I would weep, if I were not so weary. But hold me blameless, in this, and in all that may come after."[11]

Indeed, the cause of Fëanor's mental disintegration cannot solely be placed at the feet of Míriel. Finwë remarrying must also be taken into account. Although Fëanor expressed his disapproval with this choice, Finwë thought otherwise. His choice was an anomaly as Tolkien states that Elves marry for life, the only exception being Finwë.[12] Because of Finwë's choice, Fëanor retreated further into himself and more still at the coming of his half-brothers. Yet, as Anne Petty notes, "the histories of the elves would have not benefited from the sons of Indis …if she had not become Finwë's second wife."[13] While his half-brothers went on to become "great and glorious, and their children also," Fëanor's anger at his father's betrayal of his mother only served to further darken his spirit.[14]

For the mother and thus for Míriel having a child is an attempt to create a symbolic phallus in order to be accepted. To quote Kristeva: "[t]he difficulty a mother has in acknowledging (or being acknowledged by) the symbolic realm—in other words, the problem she has with the phallus that her father or her husband stands for—is not such as to help the future subject leave the natural mansion."[15] The attempt failed, and Míriel left the order unable to bear her identity as the mother. Fëanor became her abjection, thus inversing the process that the child experiences in order to turn to the father and gain entry into the symbolic.

Kristeva notes that the maternal figure is "the trustee of that mapping of the self's clean and proper body; it is distinguished from paternal laws within which, with the phallic phase and the acquisition of language, the destiny of man will take shape."[16] This is the pre-Oedipal stage for the child, the semiotic. In this space, the child is unable to differentiate itself from the mother's body and its surrounding. This is termed by Kristeva as *chora*. It is a space in which the child has yet to learn of guilt that is radically different from the symbolic stage where the authoritarian father resides. The child will soon learn to outgrow the semiotic to successfully enter the symbolic and thus into society. It is the parents who assume the role as "programmer" of the child's subjectivity.[17] The child is taught that the abject, as defined by society and in turn by the parents, is what it should repel from the inside and into the outside.

Míriel denied her child this process, so Fëanor effectively lost the authority needed to distinguish between clean and unclean. Fëanor was thrust into the symbolic, without having outgrown the semiotic as *he* was expelled by his mother. Míriel, in turn, became the ultimate abjection leaving behind her corpse, for "though she seemed to sleep, her spirit indeed departed from her body, and passed into silence to the halls of Mandos."[18] Indeed, it is such an anomaly that Tolkien mentions in Letter 212 that "in the Elvish legends there is record for a strange case of an Elf (Míriel, mother of Fëanor) that tried to *die*, which had disastrous results, leading to the 'Fall' of the High-Elves…Míriel wished to abandon being, and refused rebirth."[19]

Kristeva positions "the corpse, the most sickening of wastes" as the "border that has encroached upon everything. It is no longer I who expel. 'I' is expelled."[20] Míriel's very soul was expelled. She made a conscious choice to delete herself. While such a choice may not necessarily be condemned as evil, it can certainly be argued as selfish. Yet, is it not *her* life to choose as she wishes? For Catholics, as Tolkien was, the answer to such a question is clear. The *Catechism of the Catholic Church* makes the following points about suicide:

> Suicide contradicts the natural inclination of the human being to preserve and perpetuate
> his life. It is gravely contrary to the just love of self. It likewise offends love of neighbor
> because it unjustly breaks the ties of solidarity with family, nation, and other human
> societies to which we continue to have obligations.[21]

However, it carries on to say that "Grave psychological disturbances, anguish, or grave fear of hardship, suffering, or torture can diminish the responsibility of the one committing suicide."[22] If one takes the position that Míriel's choice can be excused on account of hardship and suffering, another question arises. As a parent, how much do you owe your child? Should Míriel have endured for the sake of her child? Was her choice a moral failing? The fact that Míriel's choice to die led to "disastrous results" would perhaps underscore the fact that yes, it was a moral failing on her part.[23] As Flieger notes, "[t]he death of Míriel has profound consequences that stem directly from the unchecked nature of Fëanor."[24] Motherless, Fëanor was left to embody fully "all the potential for good and evil that characterizes the Noldor."[25]

However, it is important to note that Míriel left the living as she was exhausted after carrying Fëanor. This act *appears* on the surface to be irresponsible. As a mother, she should have been present for the child whom she had brought into the world. However, it is most likely that Míriel was suffering from postpartum depression, something that an Elf can be susceptible to as they are acknowledged to be vulnerable to grief, weariness, and other psychological disorders.[26] Would Míriel have been capable of making a balanced choice and how much of the blame is apportioned to her?

Still, unlike other Elves, Miriel's death was permanent as "from the moment that Finwë and Indis are joined in marriage all future change and choice will be taken from her and she will never again be permitted to take bodily shape."[27] While this was the same fate that awaited her son Fëanor and most of her grandsons as well, hers was not a form of punishment but a consequence of the path she had chosen to take. By welcoming death, Míriel ultimately forfeited the boundaries placed by the symbolic in order to escape from herself. Míriel becomes the phallic mother for she embraced not just a "death," but also the acceptance of not existing within the material world, which is against the natural order of Elves.

Nevertheless, despite her attempt as the mother, Míriel could never have entered the symbolic order. As Luce Irigaray puts forth:

> Female sexuality has always been conceptualized on the basis of masculine parameters [...]
> Her lot is that of "lack," "atrophy" (of the sexual organ), and "penis envy" the penis being
> the only sexual organ of recognized value. Thus she attempts by every means available to
> appropriate that organ for herself.... through her desire for a child-penis, preferably a
> boy[.][28]

However, as the maternal, Míriel was no longer positioned as the Other, as a lack. Her female genitalia, the lack, is no more; she is the womb, which cannot be a lack. It is fertile, and it is *fullness*. Additionally, the female body's function as the maternal is associated with nature. The well-integrated symbolic body, as Kristeva states, must never exhibit its debt to nature. It cannot be defined in context with the penis. It belongs to an entirely different sexual category of its own. As such, it cannot be confined and controlled by the patriarchal rule that belongs to the phallocentric order. It is out of reach.

This situation is resolved by making her the subject's Other. Míriel was cast as the abject, and in the case of Fëanor, transformed into a fetish. The fetish, Barbara Creed states, is the by-product of the monstrous-feminine, whose face in the case of Míriel is the phallic mother.[29] The phallic mother is situated as the uncontrollable, untameable archaic mother of the pre-Oedipal dyadic. Míriel who cast away her life for death defied the code of nature, making it "a type of moral fall among the elves."[30] Her defiance became a threat. To contain her, she was set as the subject's Other and reinstated into the Oedipal scene. Her disinterest in the world of the living coupled with her easy acceptance of the loss of her physical body still puts her in the passive feminine gender construct. Finwe, meanwhile, protests, argues, and finally moves on to remarry and have more children. Creed applies Sigmund Freud's theory of the fear of castration in which he states that the male child has two ways in which to face the Oedipus complex.[31] He could either disavow it or accept the threat of castration and thereby end the threat. To accept the latter choice would mean for the male child to mitigate his horror of castration into a fetish object. The fetish would translate as the substitute for what was given up. Thus, the Silmarils became Fëanor's fetish.[32]

The creation of the Silmarils was a "long and secret labour" which required all of Fëanor's mental and physical skill, and "the heart of Fëanor was fast bound to these things that he himself had made."[33] Fëanor's connection to his Silmarils mirrored the relationship between him and his mother. Christine Chism points out that "[t]his transformation of artwork into heartwork dooms Fëanor."[34] The Silmarils were to him like his children and required all that he could give to create them much like how Míriel spent herself in carrying her son. However, Míriel's absence in her son's childhood caused him to suffer from separation anxiety over his jewels. This fear stemmed from his experience of a mother who left and never returned. Fëanor's horror of castration and the loss of the maternal were projected into his obsessive love for the Silmarils.

Fëanor's defining moment came when Melkor and the monstrous spider, Ungoliant, destroyed the Two Trees of Valinor. Despite the destruction, Yavanna remained hopeful. Both she and Manwë asked Fëanor to grant a little of the Light captured in the Silmarils to salvage what was left of the Trees. Fëanor, after a pause, answered:

> For the less even as for the greater there is some deed that he may accomplish but once
> only; and in that deed his heart shall rest. It may be that I can unlock my jewels, but never
> again shall I make their like; if I must break them, I shall break my heart, and I shall be
> slain; first of all the Eldar in Aman.[35]

Standing in front of the awaiting Valar, the words of Melkor regarding the safety of his Silmarils returned to haunt him. Fëanor began to feel as though he was "beset in a ring of enemies."[36] Much like the One Ring, the allure of the Silmarils seems to now "cripple one's higher nature and alters the perception of the Other in a way that prohibits union and camaraderie."[37] Fëanor no longer perceived the Valar as allies and advisors but viewed them as the Other, dangerous, and untrustworthy to him. The death of his father at the hands of Morgoth was the final straw for Fëanor. He swore a terrible oath with his sons vowing to hunt down with "vengeance and hatred" anyone "whoso should take or keep a Silmaril from their possession."[38] Unlike Miriel, Fëanor could not disavow his ties to his creation. Because of his choice, the Silmarils become something of a cursed object. Jane Chance notes that Melkor too "burns with the desire to possess them; the greed of both leads to alienation from others, division among family and nation, and much destruction."[39] The Dwarves as well succumbed to the lure of the Jewels that culminated in the death of Thingol. This tragic scene does overshadow the point Tolkien makes about Art: that the Dwarves did assent to the project and did create a necklace that held *together* "the greatest works of Elves and Dwarves."[40] What could have been a chance of unity and celebration between two antagonistic races became instead an environment of greediness, othering, and abjection.[41] Chance asserts Tolkien's point that creation should not be for selfish reasons but to advance "understanding and promote healing, for the beauty created by the artist reflects only the beauty of the larger creation and not the greatness of its creator."[42] Not until Fëanor's grandson, Celebrimbor, together with the Dwarf Narvi crafted the Doors of Durin did Middle-earth see a creation of union between the two races.

For Kristeva, the abject is closely connected to art as it is seen as a method that enables the abject to be purified. Art and literature, Kristeva says, is where one can safely explore the abject, "repulsive gift of the Other" by sublimating it and therefore confronting the archaic space.[43] By transcending the abject through art, one is able to prevent the fall away from the various linguistic binary structures of the Self/Other. Art allows for a legitimate catharsis into both the abject and the sublime as one has immersed one's self in the aesthetic experience with the Other ensuring a repugnance to keep the Self from collapsing. Fëanor's fetishized Silmarils with their living sacred Light, manifest as his attempt to purify the abject in him, and thus, complete himself. When Melkor stole the Silmarils, Fëanor was shattered and thrown once again into the limbo he had tried to escape. The incident became the catalyst that led Fëanor to exclude his kin, treating them as the abject that threatened the unity of his identity.

Fëanor's abjection of his kin was an attempt to cast himself as an autonomous subject able to survive in the symbolic through a secured boundary. His kin now existed as the abject with "only one quality of the object—that of being opposed to *I*."[44] This state of abjection, Kristeva concludes, is a "kind of *narcissistic crisis*."[45] Fëanor's attempts were violent as the process usually undertaken by the child to enter the symbolic had been reversed and he had been thrown into it, as yet unready. As a deject, the one who questions the abject, Fëanor can be likened to a stray. He searched for the "*Where* am I?" rather than the "*Who* am I?" and lost his bearing.[46] He became the knife that attempted to cut away the abject. He tainted himself in his need to detach himself. In his obsession to retrieve his Silmarils, Fëanor started the first Kinslaying. He had to remove the abject as it threatened the boundaries of his Self. It was how he coped with his loss. The further he ran, the closer to safety and stability he got. The rejection of Míriel required Fëanor to continuously remind himself that he was not a part of her or that he needed her.

By the violent act of Kinslaying, he was able to survive in the symbolic without Míriel's guidance in the semiotic. As the Noldor were typecast as proud and dominating in *The Silmarillion*, it would have irked the pride of Fëanor when the Teleri refused his demands to aid him in his quest to leave Valinor and overthrow Morgoth. In his anger, Fëanor brandished his sword and killed his fellow Elves. So great was his madness that after appropriating the Teleri ships by force, Fëanor solidified his abject reaction toward his kin by proceeding to burn the ships, thus leaving the rest of *his* kin and company to search for another way to Middle-earth. These acts confirm the statement made by Kristeva who says that abjection:

> ...while releasing a hold, it does not radically cut off the subject from what threatens it –
> on the contrary, abjection acknowledges it to be in perpetual danger. But also because
> abjection itself is a composite of judgement and affect, of condemnation and yearning, of
> signs and drives.[47]

The actions or rituals taken to dispel the abject are violent and urgent as the subject attempts to redraw the border between itself and what threatens it. The blood spilt further secures the abjection of which threatens the border of the body. Unlike that of dismemberment, where the body part is acknowledged as absent yet repulsed for not belonging, the confrontation of blood or excrement is not as horrifying because such excretion happens more often. It elicits a more detached feeling and is therefore all the easier to draw from others.

Tolkien wrote the Kinslaying as a dark and bitter experience, where many on both sides were slain but, "... at last the Teleri were overcome, and a great part of their mariners ... were wickedly slain. For the Noldor were become fierce and desperate."[48] However, the abject can never be fully expelled. It will forever linger, threatening the stability of the constructed identity and social order. It is thus ironic that, ultimately, the abject is needed to "uphold the "I" within the Other."[49] In this manner, the threat followed the Kinslayers when Mandos laid a doom on the Noldor that all of their desires would slip through their hands and all that they touched would turn to evil.

Upon reaching Middle-earth, Fëanor almost immediately engaged in battle with Morgoth. The loss suffered by Fëanor over the Silmarils was connected to the loss of the maternal. For a successful entry into the symbolic, the child must deny the desire for the maternal. This was no longer a possibility for Fëanor as he had fetishized the Silmarils in order to cleanse the abject in him and complete himself. But, as Toril Moi points out, "... there can be no final satisfaction of our desire since there is no final signifier or object that can *be* that which has been lost forever."[50] Thus, for Fëanor, the issue would not have been resolved even if he did manage to reclaim his jewels, evoking the fact that the Music of Ilúvatar governed the lives of the Elves. Knowing this left Tolkien only one solution. Death. Moi elucidates:

> [i]f we can accept that the end of desire is the logical consequence of satisfaction (if we are
> satisfied, we are in a position where we desire no more) we can see why Freud, in *Beyond*
> *the Pleasure Principle*, posits death as the ultimate object of desire - as Nirvana or the
> recapturing of the lost unity, the final healing of the split subject.[51]

Fëanor found death at the hands of Gothmog, and his soul fled to the safekeeping of Mandos.

Of all the Valar, it was Aulë who empathised with the difficulty predicament faced by Fëanor when asked to break his Silmarils, being in that predicament before.[52] But why was it that when Aulë created living beings expressly against the wishes of Ilúvatar, he only received a rap on the wrist unlike Fëanor? Two pivotal variances differentiated them: possessive pride toward one's creation and humility. When Ilúvatar questioned his purpose, Aulë replied, "I did not desire … lordship. I desire things other than I am, to love and to teach them, so that they too might perceive the beauty of Eä, which thou hast caused to be."[53] Aulë's desire to create—although wrong—was still to glorify the Creator. Although he wept, Aulë freely submitted to destroy his creation. It was this act of repentance and humility that caused Ilúvatar to take pity on him and allow the Dwarves to live. Intimately aware of the Bible, Tolkien would have recalled this similarity with the exhortations of Jesus and John the Baptist as they preached for repentance among the Jews.[54]

Chance remarks that "[i]ntellectual heroism in Tolkien's world is achieved through social involvement, service to others, and the disappearance of self-indulgence."[55] Tolkien further explores this idea in his short story *Leaf by Niggle*. Here, Niggle is ultimately unable to complete his masterpiece without the aid of his neighbor, Parish. When it is finally completed, he cries "It's a gift!"[56] Tolkien carries on to say that "he was using the word quite literally."[57] Niggle and Parish's "collaborative work of art becomes a stopover station with power to refresh and heal."[58]

Although Fëanor created the Silmarils and the *Tengwar* script, Shippey questions his legitimacy to sub-creative desire, as Fëanor was also guilty of inventing weapons.[59] Like his name *Spirit of Fire*, Fëanor was capable of creating both good and evil. Instead of acknowledging his creation as a gift as Aulë and Niggle did, Fëanor saw his creation solely as an instrument to define and determine *his* identity. When that takes place, art and creation, rather than "shedding light, they engender darkness."[60] Despite containing a holy Light, the Silmarils were fetishized by Fëanor to fill a gap in himself. The Silmarils like the Arkenstone and the Rings of Power "become degenerations of art."[61] He guarded the jewels jealously unable to realize that while they were his greatest creations, they remained objects. Moreover, with his "overmastering pride" Fëanor lacked the necessary characteristics of humility and empathy to be forgiven.[62] When the Teleri argued that they could neither give nor sell their white ships as they were "the work of our hearts, whose like we shall not make again" an echo of his argument to the Valar, Fëanor chose to "take them away by force."[63] This contradicts what Jesus preaches, "whatever you want men to do to you, do also to them."[64] While Fëanor's parents did play a part in forming his identity and leading him on his path of madness, it is simplistic to place the blame solely on them. Fëanor's driving need to engage in Othering to safeguard his Self meant that he had no balanced view on himself and the world around him. Thus, while Tolkien may have felt a kinship to his character, he could never fully empathise with Fëanor. Spiraling outward, Fëanor hurt those round him in order to save himself, climatically serving as an example of the abuse of one's creative urges.

Notes

1. J. R. R. Tolkien, *The Silmarillion,* ed. Christopher Tolkien (New York: Houghton Mifflin Company, 1979), VII, 70.
2. Tolkien, *Silmarillion*, VI, 64.
3. Tolkien, "From a Letter by J. R. R. Tolkien," *S*, xv.
4. Tolkien, "From a Letter," xiv.
5. See Verlyn Flieger's essay "The Music and the Task: Fate and Free Will in Middle-earth" for an analysis on the complexity of Elven fate. Flieger, *Green Suns and Faërie* (Kent, OH: The Kent State University Press, 2012), 29–31.
6. See Tom Shippey's essay "Saruman and Denethor: Technologist and Reactionary" for a discussion on Saruman's creative desires. Shippey, *J. R. R. Tolkien: Author of the Century* (New York: Houghton Mifflin, 2000), 169–174.
7. Shippey, "Saruman and Denethor," 241.
8. Vomiting, nausea and violent sobs are examples of visceral abjection towards repulsive things such as faeces. Julia Kristeva, "Approaching Abjection" in *Powers of Horror—An Essay on Abjection,* trans. Leon S. Roudiez (New York: Columbia University Press, 1982), 2–4.
9. Tolkien, *Silmarillion*, VI, 63.
10. Tolkien, *Silmarillion*, VI, 64.
11. Tolkien, *Silmarillion*, VI, 64.

12. J. R. R. Tolkien, "The Shibboleth of Fëanor," *The History of Middle-earth: The Peoples of Middle-earth*, ed. Christopher Tolkien, Vol. 12 (London: HarperCollins *Publishers*, 1996), 335.
13. Anne Petty, *Tolkien in the Land of Heroes* (Michigan, MI: Goldspring Press, 2003), 78.
14. Tolkien, *Silmarillion*, VI, 65.
15. Kristeva, *Powers of Horror,* 13.
16. Kristeva, *Powers of Horror,* 72.
17. Sylvie Gambaudo, "The Maternal," *Kristeva, Psychoanalysis and Culture: Subjectivity in Crisis* (Hampshire, HPH: Ashgate Publishing Limited, 2007), 123.
18. Tolkien, *Silmarillion*, VI, 64.
19. J. R. R. Tolkien, "Letter 212," *Letters of J. R. R. Tolkien*, ed. Humphrey Carpenter (London: George Allen & Unwin, 1981), 286.
20. Kristeva, *Powers of Horror*, 4.
21. *Catechism of the Catholic Church,* "Chapter 2: Article 5: The Fifth Commandment: Suicide" par. 2281, http://www.vatican.va/archive/ccc_css/archive/catechism/p3s2c2a5.htm.
22. "Suicide," par. 2282.
23. J. R. R. Tolkien, "Letter 212," *The Letters of J. R. R. Tolkien*, ed. Humphrey Carpenter (New York: Houghton Mifflin), 286.
24. Verlyn Flieger, "Light and Heat," *Splintered Light: Logos and Language in Tolkien's World* (Kent: The Kent State University Press, 2000), 102.
25. Flieger, "Light and Heat," 102.
26. Tolkien, *Silmarillion*, I, 36.
27. Tolkien, "The Shibboleth," 335.
28. Luce Irigaray, "This Sex Which is Not One," *Feminisms, Revised Edition: An Anthology of Literary Theory and Criticism,* ed. Robyn R. Warhol and Diane Price Herndl (New Jersey: Rutgers, The State University, 1997), 363.
29. Barbara Creed, *The Monstrous-Feminine: Film, Feminism, Psychoanalysis* (New York: Routledge, 1993), 20–21.
30. Petty, *Tolkien in the Land of Heroes*, 72.
31. Barbara Creed, "Horror and the Monstrous-Feminine: An Imaginary Abjection," *Screen* 27, no. 1 (1986), 66, doi:10.1093/screen/27.1.44.
32. Creed notes that according to Freud "[t]he fetish object may be a penis-symbol, but not necessarily," *The Monstrous-Feminine,* 116.
33. Tolkien, *Silmarillion*, VII, 69.
34. Christine Chism, "Middle-earth, The Middle Ages, and the Aryan nation," *Tolkien the Medievalist,* ed. Jane Chance (New York: Routledge, 2002), 81.

35. Tolkien, *Silmarillion*, IX, 83.
36. Tolkien, *Silmarillion*, IX, 89.
37. Jane Chance, "The Political Hobbit," *Lord of the Rings: The Mythology of Power* (Kentucky, KY: The University Press of Kentucky, 2001), 48.
38. Tolkien, *Silmarillion*, IX, 89.
39. Jane Chance, "The Creator of the Silmarils," *Tolkien's Art: A Mythology for England* (Kentucky, KY: The University Press of Kentucky, 2001), 193.
40. Tolkien, *Silmarillion*, XXII, 279.
41. See Tolkien, "Of the Ruin of Doriath," *The Silmarillion*, 279.
42. Chance, "The Creator," 193.
43. Kristeva, *Powers of Horror*, 9.
44. Kristeva, *Powers of Horror*, 1.
45. Kristeva, *Powers of Horror*, 14.
46. Kristeva, *Powers of Horror*, 8.
47. Kristeva, *Powers of Horror*, 9–10.
48. Tolkien, *Silmarillion*, IX, 93.
49. Kristeva, *Powers of Horror*, 15.
50. Toril Moi, *Sexual/Textual Politics: Feminist Literary Theory* (London: Routledge, 1985), 101, original italics.
51. Moi, 101.
52. Tolkien, *Silmarillion*, IX, 92.
53. Tolkien, *Silmarillion*, II, 37.
54. Matt. 4.3 and Matt. 4.23 (New King James Version).
55. Chance, *The Mythology of Power,* 23.
56. J. R. R. Tolkien, *Leaf by Niggle,* (London, LDN: HarperCollins *Publishers* 2001), 110.
57. Tolkien, *TL,* 110.
58. J. Samuel Hammond and Marie K. Hammond, "Creation and Sub-creation in *Leaf by Niggle,*" *Inklings Forever,* Vol. VII, Taylor University, (2010) 9–10. https://library.taylor.edu/dotAsset/afcf88aa-52b7-4dda-8e6b-d5efd2e6b1f6.pdf.
59. Shippey, 240.
60. Flieger, "Light and Heat," 141.
61. Chism, 83.
62. Elizabeth Solopova, *Languages, Myths and History: An Introduction to the Linguistic and Literary Background of J.R.R. Tolkien's Fiction* (New York, NY: North Landing Books, 2009), 44.
63. Tolkien, *Silmarillion*, IX, 93.
64. Matt. 7.12.

Bibliography

Catholic Church. *Catechism of the Catholic Church*. Vatican: LibreriaEditriceVaticana, 2003. http://www.vatican.va/archive/ENG0015/_INDEX.HTM.

Chance, Jane. *Lord of the Rings: The Mythology of Power*. Kentucky, KY: The University Press of Kentucky, 2001.

———. *Tolkien's Art: A Mythology for England*. Kentucky, KY: The University Press of Kentucky, 2001.

Chism, Christine. "Middle-earth, the Middle Ages, and the Aryan nation." In *Tolkien the Medievalist*, edited by Jane Chance, 63–92. New York: Routledge, 2002.

Creed, Barbara. "Horror and the Monstrous-Feminine: An Imaginary Abjection" *Screen* 27, no. 1 (1986): 44–71. doi:10.1093/screen/27.1.44.

———. *The Monstrous-Feminine: Film, Feminism, Psychoanalysis*. New York, NY: Routledge, 1993.

Flieger, Verlyn. *Green Suns and Faërie*. Kent, OH: The Kent State University Press, 2012.

———. *Splintered Light: Logos and Language in Tolkien's World*. Kent, OH: The Kent State University Press, 2002.

Gambaudo, Sylvie. 'The Maternal.' *Kristeva, Psychoanalysis and Culture: Subjectivity in Crisis*. Hampshire, HPH: Ashgate Publishing Limited, 2007.

Hammond, J. Samuel and Marie K. Hammond. "Creation and Sub-creation in *Leaf by Niggle*." *Inklings Forever*, Volume VII. Indiana: Taylor University, 2010. https://library.taylor.edu/dotAsset/afcf88aa-52b7-4dda-8e6b-d5efd2e6b1f6.pdf.

Irigaray, Luce. "This Sex Which is Not One." In *Feminisms, Revised Edition: An Anthology of Literary Theory and Criticism*, edited by Robyn R. Warhol and Diane Price Herndl, 363–369. New Jersey: Rutgers, The State University, 1997.

Kristeva, Julia. *Powers of Horror—An Essay on Abjection*. Translated by Leon S. Roudiez. New York, NY: Columbia University Press, 1982.

Moi, Toril. *Sexual/Textual Politics: Feminist Literary Theory*. London, LDN: Routledge, 1985.

Petty, Anne C. *Tolkien in the Land of Heroes*. Michigan, MI: Goldspring Press, 2003.

Shippey, Tom. *J. R. R. Tolkien: Author of the Century*. New York, NY: Houghton Mifflin, 2000.

Solopova, Elizabeth. *Languages, Myths and History: An Introduction to the Linguistic and Literary Background of J.R.R. Tolkien's Fiction*. New York, NY: North Landing Books, 2009.

Tolkien, J.R.R. *The History of Middle-earth: The Peoples of Middle-earth*. Edited by Christopher Tolkien. Vol. 12. London: HarperCollin, 1996.

———. *The Hobbit*. London, LDN: HarperCollins, 1937.
———. *The Silmarillion*. Edited by Christopher Tolkien. New York: Houghton Mifflin Company, 1979.
———. *Letters of J.R.R. Tolkien*. Edited by Humprey Carpenter. London: George Allen & Unwin, 1981.
———. *Tree and Leaf*. London, LDN: HarperCollins, 2001.

CHAPTER 12

The Other as *Kolbítr*: Tolkien's Faramir and Éowyn as Alfred and Æthelflæd

John Holmes

When J. R. R. Tolkien forged his adult identity at King Edward's School and then at Oxford, a number of factors conspired to flag him as alien. For one thing, he was not native born but "colonial," born in Africa. For another, even his name was foreign; the English "Suffield" buried (by his mother's marriage) under the German-sounding "Tolkien." He was, moreover, a Roman Catholic at Anglican schools. He was first fatherless, then motherless. Even in the academic world he loved, his tastes condemned him. The academy, which privileged classical languages, tried at first to accommodate him there, only to see him drift into Germanic philology. Yet, it was there in the otherness of the North that Tolkien first made a name for himself—and, in Icelandic saga literature, *found* a name for himself. The name of ***kolbítr***.

In the heroic world of the Icelandic saga, as in many heroic traditions, there was a way for even the outsider, the nerd, to become a hero. In 1894, the great Icelandic scholar Finnur Jónsson had identified a character type who was stigmatized by the heroic culture of the North as being everything the archetypal saga hero was not. The saga demanded a

J. Holmes (✉)
University of Steubenville, Steubenville, OH, USA

C. Vaccaro and Y. Kisor (eds.), *Tolkien and Alterity*, The New Middle Ages, DOI 10.1007/978-3-319-61018-4_12

hero who was crafty, daring, active, and flashy, standing up to the harsh, frozen, Northern world. The antitype of that hero was dull, domestic, and inactive. Because this negative type merely lays by the fire instead of engaging the world, he was branded *kolbítr*, "coal-biter," or sometimes *eldsætr*, "fireside-sitter." His domestic inaction marked him as not truly masculine; Jónsson asserted that the coals were not even those of the hearth where hunters and warriors might warm themselves after a hard day's bloodletting and spitting, but rather "in der Küche."[1]

It is easy to spot the *kolbítr* qualities of Tolkien's major heroes, Bilbo in *The Hobbit* and Frodo in *The Lord of the Rings*. The whole race of hobbits, indeed *other* in the Age of Men, are overlooked by the hero-cult of the Third Age of Middle-earth, despite Gandalf's insistence that there is something to value in them. But some of the lesser characters reveal their effectiveness as characters when studied as *kolbítr*, and this chapter will focus on two of them. The dynamic of the *kolbítr* is the tension between their unprepossessing start—no one expects any good to come of them—and that shining moment when the biter of the coals gets a chance to, as Faramir put it, "show his quality."[2]

From the perspective of folklore studies—a discipline which did not hold much interest for Tolkien—the *kolbítr* is merely a Germanic version of a supposedly universal motif known in the Aarne-Thompson system of categorizing tales as "The Successful Youngest Child," variously appearing as the "Victorious youngest son" (type L10), "Victorious youngest daughter" (type L50), "Unpromising hero or heroine" (type L100), or the Native American version, "Dirty boy as hero" (type L112.4).[3] This chapter will not pursue such generalizing analysis, however, because Tolkien's consistent principle of storytelling is that in the story, the angel, not the devil, was in the details. "It is precisely the colouring, the atmosphere, the unclassifiable individual details of a story," Tolkien argued in *On Fairy Stories*, "and above all the general purport that informs with life the dissected bones of the plot, that really count."[4] The structuralist approach of Aarne and Thompson made the reading of tales more like sociology than literature. My purpose in connecting two Tolkien characters with two historical figures is not to say that their histories are the "same story" (the folklore approach that Tolkien rejected), but that the *kolbítr* mytheme gives an intelligible structure to the details of the characters' lives that illuminate the pathos of their otherness.

Two characters who fit the *kolbítr* paradigm in Tolkien's *The Lord of the Rings* are Faramir and Éowyn. These two are not coal-biters in their *choice* of a life by the fire, since Faramir is a Captain of Gondor, who by rights should be a heroic type, and Éowyn chafes at the domestic inaction the *kolbítr* is supposed to prefer. Éowyn is, as it were, an involuntary *kolbítr*.

What places Éowyn in the circle of the *kolbítr*, however, is the secret hidden under her helmet: a heroic nature unguessed by the male heroic cult that surrounds her. There is a fairy-story aspect to the transformation of *kolbítr* to hero that is not at all compromised by the fact that the saga genre in which the word and concept arise purports to be true history. In *On Fairy Stories*, Tolkien asserted that "History often resembles 'Myth,' because they are both ultimately of the same stuff."[5] Both Éowyn and Faramir, in their nature as *kolbítr*, have historical analogues in the West Saxon royal family of the ninth and tenth centuries: Alfred, the royal son voted least likely to become king, and his daughter Æthelflæd, who by the nature of West Saxon gender roles seemed destined to a life of passivity, but who rose to become *hlafdige mierce*, "The Lady of the Mark," leading a decisive campaign against Viking invaders that made the survival of English culture possible.

Jane Chance has argued that one of Tolkien's great contributions to epic-romance was subversive, almost reversing its polarity. "Epic battles do rage in the background," she observes of *The Lord of the Rings*, "but Tolkien seems more interested in those who come to battle, if at all, in ways and forms and for reasons that differ from those in the conventional epic-romance."[6] Yet, the traditional Germanic heroic tradition already had a subversive hero (or anti-hero) in the character of the coal-biter. It is tempting to think that the unlikely hero motif bound in the coal-biter is the anomaly in the Germanic tradition, and that the norm is the larger-than-life strong-as-thirty-men behemoth like Beowulf. Yet Jónsson observed that even Beowulf may have eaten his share of coals in his youth. Consider the following six and a half lines from *Beowulf*:

Hean wæs lange,
swa hyne Geata bearn godne ne tealdon,
ne hyne on medobence micles wyrðne
drihten Wedera gedon wolde;
swyðe wendon þæt he sleac wære,
æðeling unfrom Edwenden cwom
tireadigum men torna gehwylces. (218–389)[7]

> Tolkien's translation: "Long was he contemned, for the sons of the Geats did not account him worthy, nor would the king of the windloving folk accord him much honour upon the seats where men drank mead. They much misdoubted that he was of sluggish mood, without eager spirit though of noble birth. A change and end of all his heart's griefs had come for him, a man now blessed with glory."[8]

The moment that the *Beowulf* poet describes here is every nerd's favorite daydream: The moment of that resplendent deed, which redeems his or her image in the popular imagination, transmutes the coal in the coal-biter's mouth to the finest truffle. The passage represents the thoughts of the Geatish people as they watch Beowulf hand a precious neck-piece to their Queen Hygd. The torque has a splendid and half-mythic history, but what it represents at this moment is the mark of great deeds: It had been the gift of Queen Wealhtheow of the Danes in gratitude for legendary valor—and what is flashing through the minds of the Geats as they watch is, according to this passage, in essence: "This is the lay-by-the-fire we thought would never amount to anything!" It is that moment of vindicating their otherness that Tolkien celebrates in both Faramir and Éowyn, and their reflexes in two generations of West Saxon royalty, Alfred the Great and his daughter Æthelflæd.

Faramir/Alfred

Perhaps the most striking similarity between Faramir and Alfred, the only English monarch ever to be styled "The Great," is that neither one seems to belong in this discussion of otherness and exclusion. Both enjoyed the highest circumstances of birth, in being sons of the highest-placed person in their respective worlds. Faramir's father, Denethor II, was the ruler of Gondor. True, his title was "Steward," a caretaker rather than king, but after twenty-four generations, the distinction may have seemed insignificant, as "the Stewards exercised all the power of the kings."[9] This counter-argument against considering Farmir a coal-biter could challenge the portrait of Tolkien himself that opened this chapter. Even at King Edward's School, he achieved status in a number of areas: house captain of the rugby team, a corporal in the cadet corps, a sub-librarian, a prefect, and secretary of the debating society.[10] Any consideration of Tolkien as an outsider, then, calls for qualification, and any relegation of Faramir to the same peripheral status cannot be a matter of caste. Tolkien's assessment of Faramir's reputation in Appendix A to *The Lord of the Rings* reads like classic ***kolbítr***: "He was gentle in bearing, and a lover of lore and of music, and therefore by many in those days his courage was judged less than his brother's."[11]

That the ***kolbítr*** may have realms in which his or her otherness is attenuated does not obviate the experience of alienation. As Benjamin Saxton recently observed, using the prosaic lens of Mikhail Bakhtin to view Tolkien's fiction, personal identity is a matrix with sometimes contradictory features. Even the central hero, Saxton observes, Frodo Baggins, has features that give him status, and others that deny it. "As an enigmatic hobbit," Saxton writes, "Frodo is both aristocrat (a Fallohide) and 'queer folk' (a Brandybuck), insider and outsider, hero and failure, master (of Gollum) and slave (to the Ring)."[12]

Faramir's ambivalent role as ***kolbítr*** is just as multifarious. Faramir enjoyed status, yes, but it was in contrast with his brother—in his brother's shadow, one might say—that Faramir's demotion was effected in the minds of Gondorians. He was no Boromir. Since the Stewardship "became hereditary as a kingship,"[13] the law of primogeniture (the eldest son inheriting the title and its perquisites) officially made Faramir less important than Boromir. Still, that dimming of the second son's light was exacerbated by his father's clear preference for Boromir, and the popular perception of Faramir as a man of harp and pen rather than sword and spear. The motif of the second son languishing in his brother's shadow is a long-standing mythic topos, and Homer's depiction of Hector the warrior belittling his brother Paris for being a pretty-boy (*eidos ariste*), a lover (*gynaimanes,* "woman-crazy") not a fighter, demonstrates that the theme is not limited to Northern saga.[14] But considering Faramir in the category of coal-biter will be useful when we turn to his historical analogue, Alfred.

If Faramir suffered from Younger Brother Syndrome, Alfred's case was four times as virulent. After all, in the dangerous times of ninth-century Wessex, when Vikings can carry off those sons that disease may spare, the death of a primogenitor is not that uncommon, promoting a second son to first place. But Alfred was not just a second son. Nor was he a third son. Nor even a fourth. Alfred was the fifth son of King Æthelwulf of Wessex, the sixth child (we'll turn to Alfred's sister in a moment), and with that distant place in line, no one—least of all his father—expected him to be king.

The names Æthelwulf chose for his sons betray his lack of expectations for his fifth son. When Alfred's grandfather King Ecgberht named his eldest son "Æthelwulf," the name-prefix "Æthel" simply meant what the Old English adjective meant: "noble." But in the next generation, Æthelwulf seemed determined to make it stand for "noble in direct line of succession," and his sons became known as *aethelings*—"princes," a title to which collateral lines were no longer welcome.[15] Æthelwulf conferred the loaded prefix on five children before Alfred was born. In light of the gender exclusion overcome by Æthelflæd, which is the subject of the next section of this chapter, it is worth noting that Æthelwolf does not withhold the benediction of the name from his only known daughter, despite the fact that her gender and her minority (she had three brothers ahead of her) made her rule unlikely. Æthelwulf named his children, in order: Æthelstan ("noble-stone"), then Æthelbald ("noble-bold"), then Æthelbert ("noble-bright"), and then Æthelswith ("noble-strong," Alfred's only sister). Then the fifth and final *ætheling*, Æthelred ("nobly-advised").

But no "Æthel" for the sixth child. What would be the point? Surely by the time all four older brothers died, at least one would have a son old enough to take the throne. The logic of the names actually played out. Alfred's oldest brother, Æthelstan, died before he could claim the West Saxon throne, but all three of his other brothers did reign: Æthelbald from 858 to 860, Æthelbert from 860 to 866, and Æthelred from 866 to 871. The death of three brothers in battle with the "Danes" could not have been anticipated. Alfred was not *supposed* to become king.

The primogenitor of the West Saxons, Æthelstan, was quite unlike Tolkien's Boromir in one important respect: He did not eclipse Alfred in his father's affection, as Boromir did Faramir. For one thing, Æthelstan and Alfred were too far apart in age for them to be rivals. In *The Lord of the Rings*, Boromir is five years older than Faramir. In West Saxon history, we do not know what year Æthelstan was born, but he was already ruling Kent as his father's *undercyning* ten years before Alfred was born. So as a child of Æthelwulf's old age, Alfred is unlikely to have been as scorned by his father, as Faramir was, or as subject to deprecating comparison to a brother several decades older. At least one modern historian, in fact, argued that the reason Æthelwulf sent four-year-old Alfred to Rome in 853 for a papal blessing was simply "that Alfred was especially dear to his father."[16]

Thus, Alfred does not quite fulfill all of the more obvious criteria for *kolbítr* in terms of the scorn or implication of effeminacy excluding him from the male world of combat, the world in which he after all won his fame when his number finally came up. The code words and images for such gender-marking, such as the lyre (*kitharis*) and curly hair (*komē*) that Hector clearly intends as a slight on his brother Paris' manhood,[17] and its analogue in Faramir as "lover of lore and music" for which the Gondorians judged "his courage … less than his brother's"[18] may not have been as readily evident in Alfred, but Tolkien's inclusion of "lore" as a co-indicator with music of the girlish leisure implied by coal-eating may give us another parallel between Alfred and Faramir.

Like Faramir, Alfred loved scholarship, an affinity that requires a leisure not always compatible with a warrior's life, and so limited in Alfred's world to the clergy—or the infirm. References to Alfred's sickly childhood provide an additional barrier to the male warrior "norm" that links him to the *kolbítr*.[19] At any rate, the love of lore that made Alfred a patron of (and a dabbler in) scholarship during his reign, is reflected in a story his contemporary biographer Asser records. Alfred's mother Osburh (or perhaps his step-mother Judith, as J.A. Giles argues) offered "a Saxon book of poetry" to whichever of her sons could first learn the verse by heart. Alfred, of course, "spoke before all his brothers, who, though his seniors in age, were not so in grace," and won the prize.[20]

Even if we do not grant Alfred the status of an outsider, his life story still resembles the mytheme of the coal-biter in its trajectory from low expectations to unexpected high achievement, because there turns out to be more in Alfred than the narrower warrior culture can guess, as Gandalf in both of Tolkien's major novels continually observes about hobbits. The plot mechanism of that shift could easily be considered a species of what Tolkien called *eucatastrophe*, the unlooked-for happy twist that brings victory out of seemingly inevitable defeat.[21]

Readers of Tolkien's essay have long understood how essential the concept of *eucatastrophe* is to Tolkien's fiction, and Christian criticism has recognized its resemblance to the theological concept of grace, the unmerited supernatural help that lifts the faithful out of otherwise inevitable defeat. But if the *kolbítr* story is a species of fairy story, then eucatastrophe is unquestionably integral to its plot. The eucatastrophe of every coal-biter tale is the moment when the supposed ne'er-do-well surprises everybody—except, perhaps the reader. The reader's suspicion that there is more to the un-hero *kolbítr* than his culture suspects is one consideration that might make an assertion of eucatastrophe in such a tale suspect. Yet, I would argue for it nonetheless. The fact that readers instinctively know that the lie-by-the-fire who takes her very name from the coals, Cinderella, will overcome all obstacles, does not make the fairy tale's eucatastrophe any less wondrous to those within the story. Or to the reader who enjoys "literary belief," that surrendering to the story for which Tolkien found Coleridge's "willing suspension of disbelief" too weak a formula.[22]

The eucatastrophe is precisely what *kolbítr* stories are all about. Alfred's story has eucatastrophe in spades, and the fact that his story is actually historically true does not diminish its status as a fairy story element, as Tolkien observes in *On Fairy Stories.*

Considered in light of the eucatastrophe, I would say that even a heroic figure as manifestly larger-than-life as Aragorn in *The Lord of the Rings* has claim to *kolbítr* status, considering his low reputation among "decent" folk in the Shire. Jane Chance says as much in her essay on "Tolkien and the Other," calling Aragorn "a dirty Ranger who also emerges as the long-concealed King of Gondor."[23] That wording could strike the historian of the Alfredian era as one more evocation of the eucatastrophe implicit in the coal-biter story—and one more Alfredian parallel to *The Lord of the Rings.* For Alfred, too, had his period of exile as a king in hiding. In the first week of May, 878, Alfred emerged from a winter's hiding in the marshes of Somerset, and the people rallied to him—suggesting that he had maintained a popular loyalty even while living the life of a gangrel Ranger while the Viking hosts seemed to have control of much of the kingdom.[24]

Æthelflæd/Éowyn

If connecting Alfred as historical *kolbítr* analogue to Tolkien's Faramir is interesting, counting his daughter Æthelflæd as an Éowyn-figure might actually be useful. For while there may indeed be sources for Éowyn's character in Norse and Old English literature, there are also historical precedents—or at least one. Leslie A. Donovan describes Éowyn as a valkyrie figure, and indeed, this literary type, found all through Norse and Old English literature, was important enough to Tolkien for him to retell one or two of the most celebrated examples of the type, Brynhild and Gudrún in *The Legend of Sigurd and Gudrún*, and the type would have informed his creation of Théoden's admirable niece. But so, too, would his knowledge of historical exemplars of the "valkyrie reflex," including two or three members of Alfred's family: his older sister Æthelswith, his step-mother Judith Martel and his daughter Æthelflæd.

The historical situation of Tolkien's Rohan, home of Éowyn, has many similarities to tenth-century Mercia's, though since *The Lord of the Rings* is neither history nor allegory, there are also differences. Gondor and Rohan in Tolkien's legendarium have a relationship similar to Wessex and Mercia (though in another context, a better analogy would be Gondor as Rome and Rohan as all the Germanic kingdoms, especially the Goths, after the fall of the Roman Empire).

The King of Rohan during the War of the Ring was Théoden, son of Thengel. King Thengel's Queen Morwen was Gondorian, and her epithet in Rohan, "Steelsheen," may tell us something about her granddaughter Éowyn, for Tolkien tells us that Éowyn inherited her "grace and pride" from her grandmother Morwen.[25] It is possible that the epithet "Steelsheen" refers merely to Morwen's beauty, for Tolkien the philologist and Anglo-Saxonist consistently associated the English word "sheen" more with the context of "beauty," the Old English meaning, than "light," the modern English meaning. Indeed, the modern German cognate, *schön*, means simply "beautiful," with scarcely a trace in the modern German mind of any sense of "shiny." In his early years as an instructor of Old English at the University of Leeds (1920–1925), Tolkien had written a poem in Old English under the title of "*Ides Ælfscýne*," or "Elf-fair Lady." It told of the shining beauty of an elf-maiden that captivates the speaker of the poem.[26] Yet, the shining beauty of Morwen is specifically the sheen of *steel*—not of jewels or gold or silver, as we might expect of a feminine image in a masculine warrior culture. Steel is a hard metal, used for armor and blades, not for adornment. When the Russian revolutionary Iosif Vissarionovich Dzhugashivili wanted to remake himself in a tough-guy image, he renamed himself *Stalin*, "steel," forged in fire and testosterone. Superman was the Man of Steel. Yet here was a woman of steel, praised as such by the Rohirrim who welcomed her as their queen, as did, presumably, Tolkien her creator.

Since the first publication of *The Lord of the Rings*, critics have asserted that its female characters are few, idealized, and even antifeminist[27] The first charge is purely a matter of statistics, and is undeniable. Of the more than 500 names listed in the character index in *Lord of the Rings*, only 19 are female, and of those nine are only referred to once;

several more (Elbereth, and the numerous "Entwives") are mentioned by other characters but never appear in the narrative.

But the other two charges are subjective and difficult to categorize. Is Éowyn "idealized"? Perhaps. But whose is the ideal? Her heroism is not restricted to the home, the feminine sphere of the supposedly "primitive" Germanic culture, but extends to the male world of the battlefield. She is four times identified as "shieldmaiden," Tolkien's translation of the Old Norse *skjaldmeyjar*, a common epithet for valkyries in Norse poetry.[28] It is she, disguised as the warrior Dernhelm (Old English, "secret helmet"; her helm disguises not only her identity, but also her gender), who delivers the death blow to the Lord of the Nazgûl, the giant zombie-like "Ring-wraith." Certainly, Tolkien does not deny heroic action to at least one woman.

No doubt Tolkien's image of female heroism owes a great deal to the figure of his mother. We do not need Freud to tell us how natural that is. And we know from Tolkien's later family letters that he saw his mother in grand heroic terms, battling family and local prejudice to keep her sons Catholic in Protestant England. "My own dear mother," he wrote in his undergraduate years, nearly a decade after her premature death, "was a martyr indeed … who killed herself with labour and trouble to ensure us keeping the faith"[29] Her death, Tolkien told his son Michael, was "hastened by persecution of her faith" (Letter 54).[30] Humphrey Carpenter has argued convincingly that Tolkien had his own parents in mind when he represented Bilbo Baggins, the hero of *The Hobbit* as receiving his adventurous side from his mother's side of the family—described in the novel in details that match Mabel Tolkien's Suffield relations.[31]

Continuing Éowyn's family history: The reason that her grandfather Thengel was in a position to marry a princess of Gondor was that he left Rohan "when he came to manhood" and lived in Gondor. The foreign influence was resented when he returned (with a wife seventeen years younger than he), as "the speech of Gondor was used in his house, and not all men thought that good."[32] It may not be significant to the historical parallel, but Æthelflæd's own grandfather, King Æthelwulf, also left his homeland in 855 (for Rome, which, as stated above, sometimes acts as an analogue for Gondor), stayed for more than a year, and returned with a much younger wife (by at least 35 years, double the difference between Thengel and Morwen).

This young wife, moreover, became iconic in the late ninth century as a strong female leader. She caused a stir in some West Saxon circles when her marriage to Æthelwulf (in France) included anointing and coronation—privileges reserved in the past for kings. In Wessex, she was proclaimed "Queen," even though she was not of West Saxon *ætheling* blood. Her blood, however, could not be questioned by the standards of the Carolingian empire: She was the daughter of Charles Martel, Charlemagne's grandson. She must also have raised some West Saxon eyebrows when, at Æthelwulf's death in 858, she married her stepson Æthelbald, who had contested his father's throne on his return from Rome. Alfred's biographer Asser attributes the rancor against Judith to Saxon memories of the "wicked queen" Eadburh[33]; following that thread would entail quite another essay, but Tom Shippey has already written it in a study of the "Modthryth" reference in *Beowulf*.[34]

On top of the stir over her coronation, Judith Martel was named for one of the rare valkyrie-figures of the Old Testament, Judith, the valiant Israelite woman who slew the Assyrian general Holofernes. An Old English heroic poem about the Biblical Judith, preserved in the same manuscript as *Beowulf*, appeared shortly after this time, prompting Old English scholars of Tolkien's generation to speculate an intentional connection on the part of the poet with the West Saxon Queen Judith. Such connections are now in doubt, but Tolkien knew the poem well, and it was the source of the Old English phrase *Ides Ælfscine*, which he used as the title of an early poem. The Judith of the Old English poem was "wise in thought" (*glaw on geðonce*) and "fair as an elf" (*ælfscnu*).[35]

Queen Morwen bore five children to King Thengel, four daughters and one son. Of these, Tolkien only gives us the names of two who figure in the story: Théoden (Old English, "the people or nation," later "king"), the only son, and Théodwyn ("friend of the nation"), his youngest sister. Théoden is King of Rohan at the time of the novel. Before his first appearance in the narrative, his only son Théodred ("advised by the nation") has died in battle. Despite the fact that Théodred had no younger brother to languish in his shadow, there is a clear parallel to the throne of Gondor (and Wessex) in the question of succession. For just as Denethor (nearly an anagram of *Théoden*) did not appreciate the leadership abilities of his younger son Faramir, Théoden, under the baleful influence of the evil counselor Gríma, ignored the claims of his nephew Éomer. Thus, while our main interest here is the exclusion of Éowyn, her brother Éomer was out of favor as well.

Éomer and his sister Éowyn were the only children of the King's sister Théodwyn. In their childhood (some seventeen years before the main events of the novel), Éowyn and Éomer were orphaned, and King Théoden raised them in his household. Not only does this circumstance make Éomer an adopted son of the King, and so more clearly parallel to Faramir/Alfred, but even without the adoption, the relationship between a man and the son of his sister (Old English *swēostorsunu*) is the most intimate male relationship in Germanic culture, closer even than father and son. Tolkien clearly suggests that the closeness of this kinship applies in Middle-earth as well; Théoden thrice names Éomer by the title "sister–son," and twice acknowledges Éowyn as "sister–daughter." Similarly, in *The Hobbit*, Tolkien deems the sister-son kinship sufficient reason for two dwarves to give their utmost to Thorin: "Fili and Kili had fallen defending him with shield and body, for he was their mother's elder brother."[36]

If Éomer is next in line to the throne of Rohan, then, where does that leave his sister Éowyn? As mentioned above, she refers to herself four times as "shieldmaiden," but she is first introduced as "Lady of Rohan." The title "Lady" is ambiguous, both in Tolkien's novel and in British history, but the context of that shifting word is crucial to the career of Alfred's daughter Æthelflæd. The kingship of Mercia in Alfred's time was downgraded to a vassalage of the West Saxon king. In recognition of the reduced status, Æthelræd of Mercia did not claim the title "king" when he swore fealty to Alfred, but rather called himself "Eoldorman" and "Lord" of Mercia. Alfred rewarded this noble condescension, and at the same time, consolidated his power in Mercia, by marrying his daughter Æthelflæd to the Lord of Mercia.

In doing so, Alfred may have been merely following the Germanic practice of limiting women to *freothuwebbe*, "peace weaver," using his daughter as a political pawn. Or it is just possible that he was on the contrary elevating the status of the queen back to its pre-Eadburh level, as his father had with his second wife Judith, and with Alfred's older sister Æthelswith. In 853, Æthelwulf married his daughter to King Burgred of Mercia, which entailed Burgred swearing fealty to Æthelwulf, subordinating Mercia to Wessex, as Æthelwulf had already done with Kent, Sussex, and Surrey. Æthelwulf could not have been unaware of the "Saxon" murmuring against crowning queens, and even if his motives were more the consolidation of his own power than any respect for women, the real, however unintended, consequence of these political marriages must have been a gain for West Saxon queens.

It is at this point in her life—taking the throne of Mercia—that Æthelflæd's story begins to resemble Éowyn's. The heroic culture of Rohan seems to have a role for a warrior woman—Éowyn calls herself "shieldmaiden" as if it entitles her to ride with Théoden's army—"Am I not of the House of Eorl, a shieldmaiden and not a dry-nurse?" and "I am of the House of Eorl and not a serving-woman."[37] The dry-nurse and serving-woman categories would have marked her as *kolbítr*. Yet there is clear evidence that the Amazon or Valkyrie figure was as anomalous, as counter to gender roles in Rohan as in other cultures. Nothing demonstrates the anomaly of Éowyn's warrior status so much as the scene of her elevation to the title of "Lady of Rohan"—using *lady* in a newer, larger sense—in a key scene before the climactic battle in which she (Judith-like) defeats the supernaturally powerful Lord of the Nazgûl.

The scene is in Chapter II of Book V of *The Return of the King,* "The Passing of the Grey Company." The riding out into battle—with little chance of success—of Théoden and his heir Éomer leaves a succession crisis in Rohan. If both King and heir are riding to probable death, who will be left behind as viceroy, to rule in the King's name? Tolkien delights in stymieing the court of Rohan with this question. To the whole body of his retainers, Théoden states the problem clearly: "But to some one I must now entrust my people that I leave behind, to rule them in my place. Which of you will stay?"[38] It clearly is a dilemma for male honor among the Rohirrim: duty and desire call for action, taking the battlefield to protect the homeland. No one wants to stay behind like a woman in this Spartan culture; yet, clearly someone must make the greater sacrifice and do just that. And not for a Rider of Rohan is the bitter consolation Milton gave himself (in his 19th sonnet) for making a similar choice when serving the Puritan cause from a secretary's desk during the English Civil War: "They also serve who only stand and wait."

At this point in the narrative, Tolkien tightens the halter even more. Théoden's most trusted advisor, his doorward Háma, reminds the king that the choice of viceroy must be restricted to the House of Eorl—that is, Théoden's own family. This is similar to the historical insistence on an *ætheling* king in Æthelwulf's Wessex, if we accept as definition of this shifting word "son of the king." Tolkien has given us a similarly shifting noble name in the "House of Eorl." In Tolkien's invented history, Eorl was the name of the first King of Rohan, from whom all subsequent kings descended. Eorl, of course, is the earliest Old English spelling of the modern title *Earl*: In choosing the name, Tolkien knew that his readers would hear in it connotations of nobility. Yet, the word is one of those touchstones in Tolkien's profession of teaching Old English.

As Tolkien observed in his 1940 essay "On Translating Beowulf," poetry will often use certain words in an older sense than prose of the same era. *Eorl* is one of those words. In poetry, it tends to have the older, more generic meaning (contracted from its earliest Old English form *ealdorman*, "elder," though as Tolkien warns in the essay, "an *ealdor* is not an 'alderman,' but a 'prince'"; etymology is not semantics). In prose, including the chronicles of Alfred's era, *eorl* tends to mean "nobleman." Tolkien, again in the translation essay, includes it with *ætheling* as "words implying noble birth."[39] The later meaning is perhaps influenced by the Danish cognate *jarl*, wielded by the leaders of the Vikings faced by the West Saxon *eorlas*. Tolkien has handed us a loaded word, but the narrative point is that we are predisposed to think of the House of Eorl as the only legitimate source of a viceroy, which is precisely the way the Riders of Rohan feel—and in case we missed it, Tolkien has just had Háma spell it out.

But the House of Eorl is virtually empty. Théodred has just died in battle, and as Théoden protests, "Éomer I cannot spare … and he is the last of that House." But of course Théoden is wrong about that: The House of Eorl still has one noble offspring, as Háma is quick to remind his lord: "There is Éowyn, daughter of Éomund … she is fearless and high-hearted. All love her. Let her be as lord to the Eorlingas, while we are gone."[40] Háma's phrase "let her be *as lord*" is curious, and as carefully chosen as each of the half-million words in *Lord of the Rings*. But the reasons for his choice do not, I think, include gender implications. One might well think so, for why didn't Háma say "let her be lady"? Well, a good rule of thumb for interpreting Tolkien the philologist is to begin on the level of the word, and to approach each word historically. And in Æthelflæd's generation, the word *lord* (Old English *hlaford*) was even more politically charged than *eorl*.

We have seen that the formerly independent kingdoms of Essex, Sussex, East Anglia, and Kent had been in a practical sense absorbed into Wessex, a subordination Æethelwulf had maintained by naming his sons "sub-kings" (Old English *undercyning*) of these former kingdoms. When Æthelred of Mercia swore fealty to Alfred, he avoided even the implication of "first among equals" in the title *undercyning*, and asked the *witenagemot*—the body of noblemen who preside over succession issues—to recognize him not as *Myrcan cyning* or *Myrcan undercyning*, but *Myrcan hlaford*—Lord of Mercia. Once again, Tolkien was faced with a word like *eorl*, which he knew most of his readers would apprehend without his historical, philological sensitivities. The original connotations of the word *lord* were quite homely: The *hlaford* was the *hlaf weard*, the "loaf ward," the man of the house who guarded the bread within it. The woman of the house was the *hlafdige*, the kneader of the dough inside the house.

Tolkien is not dealing with this earliest meaning of the word: Háma uses *lord* in Æthelred's ninth-century sense of a national leader. Tolkien knows, however, that the word, after shooting up the scale from "bread guard" to "national leader," dropped halfway down again in the lexicons of his twentieth-century readers. In Anglo-Saxon times, the lord ruled his retainers; in modern times, the lord *was* one of those retainers in service (ostensibly, in theory) of the monarch. Whenever Tolkien uses a word in its older sense, he carefully prepares his readers to "hear" it differently by controlling either syntax or context or both. In the case of the word "lord" in this scene, Tolkien prepares us first of all by making it clear that Théoden is *king*. The King of Rohan had been referred to since his introduction, and again in his final ride to battle, as "Théoden King" (an etymological redundancy). But in between, in the elevation of Lady Éowyn, Tolkien takes pains to have the dwarf Gimli address Théoden as "Lord of the Mark"[41] The title has very specific historical cues: As noted above, rulers in Mercia before Æthelred—including Alfred's brother-in-law Burgred—were hailed as king; after Æthelred, they were *Myrcan hlaford*. *Anglo-Saxon Chronicle* C under the year 886, C and D under 893 and 911, all refer to Æthelred as *eoldorman*. D and E call him *hlaford* under the year 910, and the *Mercian Register*, as one might expect, does the same under 919.[42]

It is in this precise historical context, then, that Tolkien gives us the scene of Éowyn's elevation to the throne. If Théoden's blind spot concerning his niece's place in the House of Eorl makes a point about gender roles in Rohan, it does not seem to mean that gender anomalies are not tolerated in the Mark. Éowyn's swearing-in is presented with as much pomp and dignity as the press of immanent battle will allow. Tolkien tends to present such ceremonies as tableaux, and so this is: Éowyn is presented iconically in terms traditionally masculine, with all of the metal imagery inherited from her grandmother "Steelsheen": "the sword was set upright before her, and her hands were laid upon the hilt." The difference between this and two other sword-oath scenes later in the novel is striking. When Pippin is sworn in as a thane to Denethor, and Merry to Théoden a chapter later, the sword is horizontal, on each king's lap, as a symbol of subservience to the king.[43] When Éowyn takes the oath, the sword is "set upright," as a sign that she serves only her people, as their leader (if only to relinquish that leadership should the king return). Nor is the sword the only steel about her. "She was clad now in mail and shone like silver in the sun."[44] Steelsheen indeed. Now the title under which we first met Éowyn, "Lady of the Mark," has a larger context. "Lady" now is the equivalent of "Lord" in Æthelred's sense.

As carefully as Tolkien has imagined the sociological setting of a male cavalry culture delightfully surprised into accepting a female leader, his imagination may be as historically cogent as it is creative here. The conversation between Háma and Théoden in this brief scene is likely very close to what the *witenagemot's* deliberations must have been in Mercia in 911, the year of Lord Æthelred's death. Æthelred had no heir: His only daughter, Ælfwyn, was scarcely thirteen. Worse, the Danes whom Alfred's wars had confined to Northumbria were making raids into Mercia, which meant that whoever the *witenagemot* chose would have to be a proven military leader. There were no "figurehead" monarchs in the tenth century: The hand that grasped the (upright) sword in accepting the throne had to be able to lead armies, not just order them.

The Mercian *witenagemot* of 911 chose Æthelflæd, under the title of *Myrcna hlæfdige*—the very title, allowing for translation and more than a millennium, taken by Éowyn "Lady of the Mark."[45] In truth, there was probably a great deal less hesitation and surprise in Mercia than in Théoden's Rohan, for the *Mercian Record* suggests that Æthelflæd had been the de facto ruler of Mercia—both politically and militarily—for some years, perhaps, as the Irish chronicle known as "The Three Fragments" suggests, because of Ealdorman/Lord/Underking Æthelred's failing health.[46] As early as 902, Æthelflæd's name, and not her husband's, appears on a military safe passage and land grant. In 905, when the very people to whom she had granted passage attacked the Mercian town of Chester, she responded defensively by fortifying Chester in 907, and offensively by leading the Mercian flank of a joint attack with Wessex (where her brother Edward was now king) on East

Anglian Danes. The *witan* could not have asked for a fuller military resumé.

The heroism of all four of the figures we have examined in this chapter arose out of the straits of alterity. All were prized by the majority culture, to be sure—Alfred and Æethelflæd each called a king Father; Faramir's sire was not styled "king," but ruled in a line that had reigned for generations; Éowyn's king was her uncle. Yet, each was stigmatized as hopelessly different. Each of the four generates a narrative, two fictional, two historical, powered by the tension between an implicit heroic norm and a scorned deviation from that norm. Alfred was the king's beloved son, but in line behind three older brothers; like the *kolbítr*, he preferred song to sword. Faramir, too, found himself in lineal minority, though only one brother stood before him; like Alfred, he was said to be a "lover of lore and music."[47] Both Æthelflæd and Éowyn enjoyed the highest possible rank in blood, daughters of kings—but found the female-marking force of the *kolbítr* identity excluding them from the male-marked role of warrior. In all four stories, a eucatastrophic moment startled each character's society into recognizing a hidden heroism. The *kolbítr* mytheme, as a species of eucatastrophe, lifted all four characters in their respective plots to achievements not merely on a par with the heroes who misjudged them, but far above them. Such greatness, after all, is the destiny of the *kolbítr*.

Notes

1. Finnur Jónsson, ed. *Egils Saga Skallagrímssonar* (Halle: Max Niemeyer Verlag, 1894), 76 n. 1.
2. J.R.R. Tolkien. *The Two Towers*, 2nd ed. (Boston: Houghton Mifflin, 1987), IV, v, 289.
3. Stith Thompson. *The Folktale*. New York: Holt, Rinehart and Winston, Inc., 1946, 125–130.
4. J.R.R. Tolkien. *On Fairy Stories*. eds. Verlyn Flieger and Douglas A. Anderson (London: HarperCollins 2008), 21–22.
5. Ibid., 31.
6. Jane Chance, "Tolkien and the Other: Race and Gender in Middle-earth," in *Tolkien's Modern Middle Ages*, eds. Jane Chance and Alfred K. Siewers (New York: Palgrave Macmillan, 2005), 172. See also Chance, Chap. 8 "The Failure of Masculinity: *The Homecoming of Beorhtnoth* (1920), *Sir Gawain* (1925), *The Lord of the Rings*, Books 3–6,

(1943-1948)," in *Tolkien, Self, and Other: "This Queer Creature"* (New York: Palgrave, 2016).

7. Fr. Klaeber, *Beowulf and the Fight at Finnsburg*, 3rd ed. (Boston: D.C. Heath and Company, 1950), 82.
8. J.R.R. Tolkien, *Beowulf: An Edition, A Translation and Commentary, Together with Sellic Spell* (New York: Houghton Mifflin Harcourt, 2014), 76–77.
9. J.R.R. Tolkien, *The Return of the King*, 2nd ed. (Boston: Houghton Mifflin, 1987), Appendix A, "The Stewards," 333.
10. Christina Scull and Wayne G. Hammond, *The J.R.R. Tolkien Companion and Guide: Chronology* (New York: Houghton Mifflin, 2006), 20.
11. Tolkien, *The Return of the King*, Appendix A, "The Stewards," 337.
12. Benjamin Saxton, "Tolkien and Bakhtin on Authorship, Literary Freedom, and Alterity." *Tolkien Studies* 10 (2013): 175.
13. Tolkien, *The Return of the King*, Appendix A, "The Stewards," 333.
14. Homer, *Iliad Books 1–12*, edited and translated by A.T. Murray, revised by William F. Wyatt (Cambridge, MA: Harvard University Press, 1999), 3.39–57.
15. Felix Lieberman, *Die Gesetze der Angelsachsen* (Halle: M. Niemeyer, 1903), Vol. I, 665; David N. Dumville, "The Ætheling: A Study in Anglo-Saxon Constitutional History," *Anglo-Saxon England* 8 (1979): 1–9.
16. Eleanor Shipley Duckett, *Alfred the Great* (Chicago: University of Chicago Press, 1956), 24.
17. Homer, *Iliad*, 3. 54–55.
18. Tolkien, *The Return of the King*, Appendix A, 333.
19. David M. Craig, "'Queer Lodgings': Gender and Sexuality in *The Lord of the Rings*," *Mallorn* 35 (1997): 303–305.
20. Asser, *The Life of Alfred*, in *Old English Chronicles*, ed. J.A. Giles (London: George Bell and Sons, 1906), 51.
21. Tolkien, *On Fairy Stories*, 75.
22. Tolkien, *On Fairy Stories*, 52.
23. Chance, "Tolkien and the Other," 172.
24. Ryan Lavelle, *Alfred's Wars: Sources and Interpretations of Anglo-Saxon Warfare in the Viking Age* (Woodbridge, Suffolk: Boydell Press, 2010), 187–191.
25. Tolkien, *The Return of the King*, Appendix A, 351.
26. J.R.R. Tolkien, "Ides Ælfscine," in *Songs for the Philologists*, by J.R.R. Tolkien and E.V. Gordon (London: University College, 1936), 10–11.
27. Leslie Donovan, "The Valkyrie Reflex in *The Lord of the Rings*," in *Tolkien the Medievalist*, eds. Jane Chance (London and New York: Routledge, 2003), 130 n. 1; David M. Craig, "Queer Lodgings," 11; William Green,

"'Where's Mama?' The Construction of the Feminine in *The Hobbit*," *The Lion & the Unicorn* 22 (1998): 188–195.

28. Donovan, "Valkyrie Reflex," 121.
29. Humphrey Carpenter, *J.R.R. Tolkien: A Biography* (Boston: Houghton Mifflin, 1987), 39.
30. J.R.R. Tolkien, *Letters of J.R.R. Tolkien*, ed. Humphrey Carpenter with the assistance of Christopher Tolkien (Boston: Houghton Mifflin, 1977), 39.
31. Carpenter, *Tolkien*, 179.
32. Tolkien, *The Return of the King*, Appendix A, 350.
33. Asser, *Life of Alfred*, 47.
34. Tom Shippey, "Wicked Queens and Cousin Strategies in *Beowulf* and Elsewhere," *Heroic Age* 5 (Summer 2001), accessed 3 July 2014, http://www.mun.ca/mst/heroicage/issues/5/Shippey1.html.
35. B.J. Timmer, *Judith* (London: Methuen, 1966), 18.
36. J.R.R. Tolkien, *The Hobbit* (Boston: Houghton Mifflin, 1997), 18, 261.
37. Tolkien, *The Return of the King*, V, ii, 57.
38. Tolkien, *The Two Towers*, III, vi, 127–128.
39. J.R.R. Tolkien, "On Translating Beowulf," in *The Monsters & the Critics and Other Essays*, ed. Christopher Tolkien (London: HarperCollins, 1997), 56–57.
40. Tolkien, *The Two Towers*, III, vi, 128.
41. Tolkien, *The Two Towers*, III, vi, 127.
42. Michael J. Swanton, *The Anglo-Saxon Chronicle* (New York: Routledge, 1998), 80, 86, 95 n. 14, 96.
43. Tolkien, *The Return of the King*, V, i, 28; V, ii, 50.
44. Tolkien, *The Two Towers*, III, vi, 128.
45. Swanton, *Anglo-Saxon Chronicle*, 134 n. 1.
46. John O'Donovan, ed. *Annals of Ireland: Three Fragments* (Dublin: Printed at the University Press for the Irish Archaeological and Celtic Society, 1860), 227.
47. Tolkien, *The Return of the King*, "Steward," Appendix A, 337.

Bibliography

Asser. *The Life of Alfred*. In *Old English Chronicles*, ed. J.A. Giles, 43–86. London: George Bell and Sons, 1906.

Chance, Jane. "Tolkien and the Other: Race and Gender in Middle-earth." In *Tolkien's Modern Middle Ages*, edited by Jane Chance and Alfred K. Siewers, 171–186. New York: Palgrave Macmillan, 2005.

Craig, David M. "'Queer Lodgings': Gender and Sexuality in *The Lord of the Rings*." *Mallorn* 35 (1997): 11–18.

Donovan, Leslie A. "The Valkyrie Reflex in J.R.R. Tolkien's *The Lord of the Rings*: Galadriel, Shelob, Éowyn, and Arwen." In *Tolkien the Medievalist*, edited by Jane Chance, 106–132. London: Routledge, 2003.
Duckett, Eleanor Shipley. *Alfred the Great*. Chicago: University of Chicago Press, 1956.
Dumville, David N. "The Ætheling: A Study in Anglo-Saxon Constitutional History." *Anglo-Saxon England* 8 (1979): 1–33.
Green, William. "'Where's Mama?' The Construction of the Feminine in *The Hobbit*." *The Lion & the Unicorn* 22 (1998): 188–195.
Homer. *Iliad Books 1–12*. Edited and translated by A.T. Murray, revised by William F. Wyatt. Cambridge, MA: Harvard University Press, 1999.
Jónsson, Finnur, ed. *Egils Saga Skallagrímssonar*. Halle: Max Niemeyer Verlag, 1894.
Lavelle, Ryan. *Alfred's Wars: Sources and Interpretations of Anglo-Saxon Warfare in the Viking Age*. Woodbridge, Suffolk: Boydell Press, 2010.
Liebermann, Felix. *Die Gesetze der Angelsachsen*. Vol. I. Halle: M. Niemeyer, 1903.
O'Donovan, John, ed. *Annals of Ireland: Three Fragments*. Dublin: Printed at the University Press for the Irish Archaeological and Celtic Society, 1860.
Pálsson, Hermann, and Paul Edwards, ed. and trans. *Egil's Saga*. Hammondsworth: Penguin Classics, 1976.
Saxton, Benjamin. "Tolkien and Bakhtin on Authorship, Literary Freedom, and Alterity." *Tolkien Studies* 10 (2013): 167–183.
Scull, Christina, and Wayne G. Hammond. *The J.R.R. Tolkien Companion and Guide: Chronology*. New York: Houghton Mifflin, 2006.
Shippey, Tom. "Wicked Queens and Cousin Strategies in *Beowulf* and Elsewhere." *Heroic Age* 5 (Summer 2001). Accessed 3 July 2014. http://www.mun.ca/mst/heroicage/issues/5/Shippey1.html.
Thompson, Stith. *The Folktale*. New York: Holt, Rinehart and Winston, Inc., 1946.
Timmer, B.J. *Judith*. London: Methuen, 1966.
Tolkien, J.R.R. *Beowulf: An Edition, A Translation and Commentary, Together with Sellic Spell*. New York: Houghton Mifflin Harcourt, 2014.
———. *The Hobbit*. Boston: Houghton Mifflin, 1996.
———. *Letters of J.R.R. Tolkien*, ed. Humphrey Carpenter with the assistance of Christopher Tolkien. Boston: Houghton Mifflin, 1977.
———. *On Fairy Stories*. Ed. Verlyn Flieger and Douglas A. Anderson. London: HarperCollins, 2008.
———. "On Translating Beowulf," in *The Monsters & the Critics and Other Essays*, edited by Christopher Tolkien. London: HarperCollins, 1997.
———. *The Return of the King*. 2nd ed. Boston: Houghton Mifflin, 1987.
———. *The Two Towers*. 2nd ed. Boston: Houghton Mifflin, 1987.

——— and E.V. Gordon, *Songs for the Philologists*. London: University College, 1936.

Whitelock, Dorothy, trans. and ed., *The Anglo-Saxon Chronicle, Rev. Ed*. New Brunswick: Rutgers University Press, 1961.

Index

C. Vaccaro and Y. Kisor (eds.), *Tolkien and Alterity*, The New Middle Ages, DOI10.1007/978-3-319-61018-4

Printed in the USA
CPSIA information can be obtained
at www.ICGtesting.com
CBHW070013140824
13171CB00004B/92